LOW LIFE IN THE HIGH DESERT

David Hirst was an Australian journalist, documentary filmmaker, and author of *Heroin in Australia*. A great love of the American West took him to California and ultimately to a life in the Eastern Mojave Desert. Upon returning to Australia, his prescient and revolutionary finance column, "Planet Wall Street", was widely read in *The Age* newspaper. David died in 2013.

David Hirst

LOW LIFE IN THE HIGH DESERT

— a California memoir —

SCRIBE
Melbourne • London

Scribe Publications
18–20 Edward St, Brunswick, Victoria 3056, Australia
3754 Pleasant Ave, Suite 100, Minneapolis, Minnesota 55409 USA

First published by Scribe 2018

Typeset in 13/17pt Fournier MT by the publishers

Printed and bound in the UK by CPI Group (UK) Ltd, Croydon
CR0 4YY

Scribe Publications is committed to the sustainable use of natural
resources and the use of paper products made responsibly from
those resources.

9781947534315 (US edition)
9781925713282 (Australian edition)
9781925693263 (e-book)

A CiP entry for this title is available from the National Library
of Australia

scribepublications.com
scribepublications.com.au

For my brothers, Peter and George

FOREWORD

by Valerie Morton

Recently I picked up a large box that had been mailed to me from California. Inside was something precious: a dearly departed friend's hat. It was Buzz Gamble's dress Stetson, the one we had filmed him wearing at his son's wedding. Buzz had spent most of his life in the US's worst prisons, including the notorious Huntsville, home of Old Smokey, but when he opened his mouth and sang the blues, this west Texan could heal the most crushed heart.

The first time we heard Buzz sing was in Pappy and Harriet's Pioneertown Palace, a rough saloon in California's Eastern Mojave Desert. Most people were intimidated on first encountering Buzz — his scars, faded old prison tatts, and a voice that sounded like he'd been gargling rocks. David bought him a Kessler, and they disappeared into the beer garden where the other wild men of the desert were gathering to check out the shooting stars and discuss important matters of state.

"You are one crazy motherfuckin' Australian," Buzz concluded, as David told the tale of us moving from Sydney to

Los Angeles to the assembled company. "You oughta come and live out here."

It took a while, but we eventually did, moving into a house that clearly only crazy Australians would take on. Hidden away at the end of a canyon, fifteen miles from Pioneertown, population a few hundred, it was the closest we were ever going to get to living in the authentic Wild West — without the hangings.

Since he'd been a kid in the Australian bush, David had been obsessed with the American West. Other than politics and history, the books he read were Westerns, old dime pulp fiction, with titles like *Blacksnake Trail* and *Write His Name in Gunsmoke*. We had hundreds of them. So as the clock ticked over into the new millennium, we stepped back into the 1800s, to a landscape not only straight out of a Western, but where the Westerns had been filmed, before Gene Autry and the Cisco Kid rode off into the sunset.

For six years, from 2000 to 2006, we made our home amidst the neighboring tough men and tougher women, and the ghosts of Gram Parsons and Mojave Indians. High up in Boulder House, overlooking the sweep of the High Desert and its massive rock formations, David began writing about our life in this Twilight Zone. Had he lived to finish the book, he would have had the sad task of recording the many deaths of our friends, including Buzz's. Instead, he went off to join those old cowboys, wherever they went when they walked through the batwings for the last time. I choose to think that somewhere in heaven, or the great corral in the sky, there is a bar where they are all huddled around an avocado-wood fire, telling the old stories and listening to Buzz sing 'Trouble in Mind' one more time.

1

I have absolutely nothing against the smoking of cocaine, and might have done it myself at some stage in my life if I knew how. I do object to the smell it makes. It's a foul smell, and as the process of cutting and reformulating the stuff involves the use of chemicals, not to mention kerosene, it is not something to start the day with. But the old houses of Venice, California, in the years when gentrification was just taking hold, were pressed together. In keeping with the new type on the block, we had the misfortune to have a new, rich, white, and psychotic neighbor who seemed to need crack cocaine with the intensity of those who care for napalm first thing in the mornings.

With my girlfriend, Boo, I had taken a house on one of the pretty little walkways a few blocks from Venice Beach partly to get the air before the rest of Los Angeles, and an acrid opening to the morning before dawn had bothered to break was beginning to unsettle us.

Venice, before its hostile takeover by Hollywood executives and dot-communaires — and later the bankster class — was a delight. The canals were putrid, cholera had been detected in the sand, and the surf was deplorable. Young men paddled around trying to catch a wave the size of a large hand. I was astonished that songs could be written about Southern Californian beaches, and presumed The Beach Boys had plenty of time to record their surfing music because of the absence of surf. Had they lived near an Australian beach, the world would have forever been deprived of their sound.

In Venice, we had some eminent gangs. Extremely active ones. Two Black and one Latino. Crack cocaine could be bought at most stop signs, and the bars were awash with powder.

Our neighbor, the crack smoker, was a deeply troubled soul whom Boo had dubbed 'The Man with No Brain'. Though filthy rich, he was a poor neighbor. His backyard gleamed with classic Firebirds from the sixties. He rarely drove them, but had them washed and polished by long-suffering Latino folk every other day. He had taken to driving a stretch limousine even though he was its only occupant, unless he happened upon some unfortunate young man to bring home to his fortified dwelling in our otherwise quiet lane. He might have been handsome once, but had become bloated as a result, I imagined, of the use of lithium.

John, our neighbor on our other side, did not suffer as badly from the first breath of dawn, but objected to his baby being woken by the putrid air each morning. An extremely muscular black schoolteacher who had married a white schoolteacher, John, like most folks, was deeply protective of his small clan, as I tried to be of mine. But the border war with Brainless, as he was by now widely known, soon escalated to include most of the block, and we all discussed what might be done to rid the air of this pestilence.

The police were not interested, and in those days were known to voice the opinion that people who lived in Venice deserved what they got. The cops lived in indescribably boring places—white enclaves like Simi Valley—and did not have to coexist with a lunatic whose house was separated from theirs by three very short feet. Thirty-six inches. They did not see him screaming at their fence, still clad in his pajamas at six in the afternoon, with a dry white film about his mouth.

John, being a schoolteacher in Los Angeles, knew a lot about how dangerous life can get, and began suggesting that we make a formal approach to the police after Brainless took a sledgehammer to my '67 Red Mustang with white racing stripes. I declined. I had no proof that he had done it, and I was closer to him than John. I knew how crazy he was, and I didn't want to make him any madder. And I doubted the police would move against him. He was white and very rich. The police had found cause to take him into custody in the past, but an indulgent mother in Brentwood always had him bailed out and back home in time for his pre-dawn smoke. Lawyers would handle things thereafter, and he would puff away after these encounters as though enlivened, and without an apparent worry in the world. I had to worry about the safety of Boo and my springer spaniel, Harry.

When he finally built a bomb, and hurled it at the door of the apartment behind John's, almost incinerating the woman who lived there, the police became more concerned. They called a "community meeting", and we gathered in John's living room to discuss the threat from the west.

As I was the closest combatant, I was asked first what should be done.

"You should put him in jail," I told the cops.

The residents who had gathered nodded, and looked expectantly at the three officers sent to calm an increasingly troubled community. But the terrified neighbor who had been firebombed had left in a hurry, and failed to file a complaint. She could not be located.

Jailing Brainless, the senior LAPD officers gathered before us explained, was not possible at this stage. The courts were cluttered, and the wheels of justice were unlikely to move him towards a cell any time soon. In other words, the man had money behind him. I could not prove he had crushed the side of the Mustang, and smoking cocaine at sun-up was not a serious-enough offence to bother the courts, unless one was black and poor, and Brainless was neither. His other offences would be erased with the stroke of his mother's hand across her checkbook. In fact, the city of Los Angeles was making good money from the antics of The Man with No Brain. It was, as they say, a no-brainer.

The officer in charge, aware of his civic responsibilities and the increasingly unruly fury that attended his denial of our civic rights, took an upbeat view of things and cheerfully suggested that I, as his closest neighbor, shoot him.

"*You* shoot him," I replied. "You're the cops."

The senior cop explained the difficulties they faced in shooting a white man with a rich mother, though they didn't say that precisely. However, he pointed out in a kindly fashion that, if Brainless were to be shot, and if I could ensure that his body was on our property by the time he or a colleague arrived, all would go well for me. He would personally testify to the threat posed by this lunatic, and jail would be out of the question.

"I don't have a gun!" I exclaimed.

John, our communal host, sped to his cabinet and uncovered a good deal of weaponry: a shotgun, an automatic rifle, a super-powerful bow with high-tech arrows, and some handguns. He offered me a Colt .45. The cops, with their boyish crewcuts, nodded earnestly, and my neighbors beamed with approval.

Though 99 per cent sure the cops would be as good as their word, I demurred, reminding them that shooting the Man with No Brain was their job, pure and simple. To the chagrin of cops and neighbors, I brushed away John's shooter and returned to our endangered cottage. I didn't want to mess with any bodies. Bodies were what I had come to California to get away from.

2

There had been a lot of murders. First, it was Danny Chubb. Hardly a soul in Sydney knew Danny existed until he ceased to exist, but the manner in which he left life gave him — in passing — some status. Danny left life in unusually public fashion. Shot dead, gunned down if you like, in the street. Right in front of his mom's home. And no attempt to clean up the mess. It was an ill wind, and a harbinger of a tempest of death. A vital convention had been broken — removing and disposing of the body. That should have told us something. Danny Chubb was, like any man who carried such a numbing name, small fry. But as a career criminal, he deserved to have his body catered for by the killer, or killers. Leaving him for the morning newspapers and news crews was, well, new. New for Sydney Town.

His death rated no mention at *The Australian*, a newspaper that concerned itself with politics, the union movement, business, sport, and increasingly, to my despair, fashion. Australia's national daily was above such things as common murder. This mighty organ had employed me for some fifteen years, and I had written for most sections of the paper, excluding fashion.

Wise now, after the event, I might have reflected that, as Danny was a criminal, and the Sydney underworld had a fine tradition of disposing of its victims while sparing the public such grisly sights, something had changed in the town. The criminal fraternity would catch and kill their own, as they were proud to say, and we all felt that included the disposal side of things. Disposal is not such a difficult thing, and a variety of caterers provided the service.

There was The Chicken Man, who would wrap a body in chicken-wire mesh, through which he wound tiny pellets of dynamite. The body would be taken out to Sydney Harbor and tossed overboard, where the pellets would explode with faint puffing sounds. The sounds of these tiny explosions were lost in the wash of the water, but the flesh was extracted from the bone. The Chicken Man did not feed the bodies to the sharks, but to the fishes. He was respected for his skill in calculation. The wire mesh carried the bones through the fathoms to the harbor floor. The Chicken Man's occupation came to an end with the extension to Sydney's International Airport. By the time the concrete pours stopped, the new runways had been laid upon the bones of those who fell from favor in the criminal fraternity. Today, as your 747 touches down at Sydney Airport, it is landing upon, or above, the remains of those who had done that which they should not have done, or had not done that which they should have done. Rumor has it that The Chicken Man himself is encased in the runway's concrete, a mass grave for men who thought they could outsmart the crime bosses.

At *The Australian*, we managed to ignore the next public murder, even though it occurred in a better part of the city. A third slaying followed, a few days after, and then a fourth. Les

Hollings, our editor-in-chief, meandered towards my desk on the day of the appearance of a fifth stiff in our fair streets.

Les was not a clever man, but he was wise. He was thin of frame, a Yorkshireman by birth who had escaped the north of England for a job with a newspaper in Wales, and had ended his career in New South Wales. His time was almost up. The time of the wise was gone, and the clever were taking charge. He wore a long gray cardigan that lesser men mocked. He spoke slowly, at the speed of his thoughts. He was now a very powerful man in Sydney, and a man of influence across the nation. His shoulders had stooped under the weight of his importance.

Les suggested there "might be something going on with all these murders", and perhaps I should take a look. He seemed to credit me with some sort of understanding of the criminal mind. Apart from being charged with inciting a riot in an anti-war, anti-apartheid, and Aboriginal rights "Day of Rage", twenty years before, I had no record. Les suggested that my familiarity with the trade union movement gave me some special insight into criminality.

"You will be talking to the same people," he said.

He didn't really mean that the leadership of the Australian trade union movement was responsible for the carnage, but he suspected, with some reason, that certain members or certain unions might be worth, as my favorite spy inside organized Labor would say, "a chin wag".

The murders, I soon learnt, were only faintly related to the trade union movement. As I began scratching around for an angle, another body fell, literally, by the wayside. Having determined that the local crime bosses were equally unhappy with the carnage, my suspicions were directed, naturally enough, to the police. In those days, it was generally assumed by the crime writers that the Vice Squad ran vice, and that the Drug Squad did likewise with drugs, so there was reason to speculate that the Homicide Squad was responsible for homicide. But the cops appeared as mystified as the robbers. Organized crime was becoming very disorganized.

Unhappily, Les had such confidence in my investigative powers that he had allowed the advertising department at News Ltd to promote my coming exposé on radio and television. This came to me as a shock. I had no idea that they were promo-ing my article, and was surprised to hear someone on the radio informing the nation that I would expose all in the following edition of *The Weekend Australian*. I looked at my paper and checked the day. Wednesday. The weekend paper went to bed Thursday night, and I had only the faintest idea of what was happening. I remain, to this day, as do the judicial authorities, ignorant of what exactly caused these events.

But I had found a crack. I had visited some unsavory pubs for a spot of fishing, and discovered that a man who had tried to pull a gun on me years before in Melbourne had arrived in Sydney. Rumor had it that he was pulling and shooting guns as part of a war in the underworld, and seasoned gangsters were becoming less seasoned by the day. The story was a bit thin, but I drew the bow wide, and produced for the weekend paper a piece plausible enough to cause the Murder Task Force to raid the newspaper in search of my files.

The cops arrived early on the day following my "exposé." I was sound asleep, it being my Sunday off. My colleague Lynch, who most called Lunch, was acting chief of staff. He woke me with a telephone call explaining that "the cops are all over the place". Demanding files.

I assured Lynch that I was not in possession of a single file (I did have notes), and suggested that he tell the cops to leave the building before our lawyers were called into play. They had no warrant, and this was the headquarters of News Ltd, the father company of News Corp, owned by the most powerful man on earth, and in all of human history, Rupert Murdoch. Having heard Lynch tell the cops they should "fuck off and find some criminals", I returned the phone to its bed, and slept.

Monday morning dutifully arrived, and I met Lynch in the foyer. Another body had been found, and there was a distinct possibility that something I had written might have been cause for the tragedy. I was flattered at the thought that my analysis might have been studied by a lot of people who do not, as a rule, buy a respectable paper like *The Australian*. As we rode to the third floor, Lynch told me the cops had turned tail at the very mention of our lawyers—as well they should. We made our way to our desks, and I noticed Les weaving his way past the desks that separated us hacks from our betters.

"David," Les said. He took about five seconds to pronounce my name, but there was a kindly touch to his north English drawl, "You are supposed to investigate murders, not cause them."

Coming from a man who was a stranger to flattery, these words rung rich in my ears, and I beamed as he turned and went his way to attend to the task at hand—bringing out the next day's newspaper.

Lynch and I went to the pub, where we remained till darkness fell and we had to retrieve our coats. The iron law of journalism is "You are only as good as your last story", and if that story led to someone being killed, it was a good story. One could live off the story for a few days. Some did for the rest of their careers.

Then we returned to the office, and I determined that, as I was riding high, I would spring my plan to escape Australia—with the approval and support of my editor-in-chief. After three months apart, I would join my beloved, who had just been commissioned to write a screenplay for Disney in Los Angeles about some uncouth Australians.

I had accumulated some thirty weeks of holidays, but would request unlimited leave to travel to America to help with the project. Like most journalists, I considered myself essential to the working of the paper. Les, my heroic editor-in-chief, seemed to think otherwise. He immediately granted my request with an enthusiasm I felt could have been more restrained. But the word was out that the crime war was close to being settled, and Les was of the opinion that younger journalists should expose themselves to as much of the world as possible. I expect he doubted I would be gone any longer than the leave that was my due.

My self-esteem lifted when I visited the pay office and was handed a grand check. When I returned to the newsroom, Jenny, Les's secretary, gave me a letter of introduction from him to the authorities of the New World.

Although armed with the ringing endorsement of the editor-in-chief of my nation's most influential newspaper, I made my way through customs with some dread. The dread was a vague one, but dread it was. I had been warned by half of Sydney's journalists about the dangers of Los Angeles.

Inevitably, amongst the gifts thrust upon me as I bade goodbye, was a copy of *The Loved One*. But mostly, I was showered in warnings. LA, all agreed, was rather like Africa when discovered by the White Man. A good life and great wealth could be had, but the price was living with dangerous savages—and that was just the film industry. Stan Deadman, a distinguished sub-editor on the *Telegraph*, took a grim view of the place. Stan was taking a grim view of life in general at that stage, so I carefully weighed his words.

Thrown out of his home, he had taken to sleeping on the couches of the Journalists' Club while he contemplated his next move. While making his way from his happy home to the train station a few weeks before, Stan had noticed the local office for the registration of animals and, though running a little late, found time to register his wife as a dog. For the sum of twenty dollars, Mrs. Deadman was duly registered as "a short-haired, long-nosed mongrel bitch". Stan forgot about this lark for a week or so, but the people to whom he had given his twenty dollars did not, and the wheels of the city began turning. Stan's wife was surprised to receive a certificate of registration in the mail accompanied by a name tag to hang around her neck, and Stan was even more surprised to discover that he was no longer the master of his domain.

Having experienced the shortcomings of life on the outside, he pleaded with me to reconsider my own folly and abandon my plan to move to LA. People I hardly knew joined him in urging me to reconsider.

"Hirsty," Stan said, staring through the film of his eyes, "you are mad. Fucking crazy, mate." Bernie Leo, chief sub-editor on the *Telegraph* in those days, a man whose struggle with the demon drink was as ferocious as Stan's, nodded agreement. Kerry, an old hack, issued an earnest warning.

"Don't wear jewelry over there, Hirst. They'll cut off your hand to steal a ring."

This seemed odd advice, as I never wore jewelry, and did not even possess a wristwatch.

"They would be cutting off my hand to spite my arm," I replied.

The gift of *The Loved One* proved a mixed blessing. It was not particularly useful as an introduction to modern LA, but turned out to be a distraction from a nuclear physicist that the fates had implacably placed beside me on the long flight to the New World. I hadn't read the book in years, and set about the task with the enthusiasm of a schoolboy assigned homework.

As we soared above the Tasman Sea, and I began my studies, the nuclear physicist introduced himself, and wondered what occupation I enjoyed.

"I'm a journalist," I replied, instantly regretting it. For not only was the professor at my side a nuclear physicist, but he was of a singular mind, and was devoted to the cause of nuclear energy. The prospect of having a journalist as a companion for the seemingly millions of miles that stretched before us brought a brightness to his eye that journalists learn to be wary of.

I had studiously avoided the subject of nuclear power (except during a brief stint years before when I was acting foreign editor, and things went horribly wrong in a place called Chernobyl), but my companion had not. Indeed, he was a champion of nuclear energy, and by the time the first drinks arrived I knew that this would be a painful trip. My new acquaintance was acquainted with all that is known about atoms and other things that are too small to be detected by the naked eye. I, on the other hand, had never had the slightest interest in things that cannot be seen, except for viruses, and even then only exotic ones like Ebola and foot-and-mouth.

The professor spent an hour or so explaining the dangers of fossil fuel, and the joys of fission or fusion, or both. He reached for his briefcase, and in merciful relief I returned to *The Loved One*, noticing that while we had traveled a distance that an early seafarer might have covered in a full week, I had only reached page five. As the book began on page three, it was not much of a start.

"But if I could just get back to my book," I murmured.

I looked urgently for the drink cart. Some years back, a stewardess on an Air New Zealand flight had confused her medication and become so excitable that she ended up sitting, sans-culottes, on the face of a first-class passenger. This novel gesture of in-flight hospitality led to Air New Zealand henceforth being known as "The airline that *gives* a fuck."

Airplane service has deteriorated since then, in my opinion, but in those not-so-far-off years, the mere wave of the hand would procure a glass, even a bottle, of something from Hawkes Creek — a decent Chardonnay — or a bold red from the Hunter Valley. Or perhaps one of the fine white wines from the north of Tasmania. The sky was the limit. I managed to obtain a drink, but all the wines of Australia, and all the beer in Mexico, could not have made my companion companionable.

By the time the video screen indicated we were approaching Fiji, I had promised to dedicate my life to the nuclear cause. An hour later, I would have happily handed my mother over to the Nazis just to shut this man up. Though I stared determinedly at the pages of my book, the professor, powered by some inner reactor, ploughed on. He neither slept nor used the toilet. Like the great physicist he no doubt was, he would not be distracted by human demands.

Finally, I excused myself, and took *The Loved One* to the bathroom and read much of the volume. When evidence grew apparent that the plane was waking and that others needed my seat, I returned to my seat. My friend was delighted to see me. He had just located an article that proved that Chernobyl was not the human catastrophe that I knew it to be. But we were about to land at LAX, where my girl awaited me, and nothing could restrain my spirits.

Nothing but some nasty immigration officers, who took one look at me and decided that I should get what they probably call The Treatment. Free of my physicist friend — he had been caught short and forced to repack his papers — I had breezed past the regular officials, and was about to find Boo on the other side of the line when a man in a uniform suggested I come with him. The man had some friends; they also wore uniforms, and it was soon apparent that I was in the company of an elite drug squad customs force determined to rid LA of the scourge of dope by searching the most private parts of my body. I was already glad I wasn't wearing jewelry.

As I was led into the sparse room, where one is dehumanized by strangers who take pleasure in such things, I asked what they thought I might be bringing into LA from Sydney.

"Guns?" I wondered, out loud. "I would hardly be bringing guns into LA," I said, with the best I could muster of a sneer. "Or drugs? I believe there are plenty to go around already."

I was ordered to remove my boots, which I will concede had rather large Cuban heels. As I took them off, I suggested they read my letter of introduction from my editor-in-chief, but Les's influence clearly stopped at the border. They responded by twisting my boot heels one way and another, and I asked whether Max Smart was still popular on local TV.

That must have been deemed an insult, because I was thrust against the wall and ordered to stretch my arms as high and wide as possible and my legs as wide and low as I could. I was thoroughly searched. Nothing was found. I asked for my boots back with an air of anger poisoned by a touch of fear. Instead, the bloodhounds decided on an even fuller search—a search that involved cavities. The cavity they seemed most interested in was the one surrounded by my bottom.

Although I had spent four or five hours in the toilet escaping the nuclear physicist, I had not actually "gone" to the toilet. This extraordinary juxtaposition of internal events had caused me to build up a considerable amount of wind, in and around the posterior. My desire to relieve that wind while in flight had been "swallowed", as Bernie Leo might say, by consideration for my fellow travelers.

My boots were off, my jeans were removed, and I was straddled against the green paint of their little cell. Two of the officers bent behind me while the others kept watch.

One began to remove my underpants, an act of folly no man has succeeded in. After hours of tension and restraint, my back passage began to make ominous sounds, and had smoking been permitted we would all have been subject to a flash of blue methane that might have interested the nuclear physicist. But the only flash was of my interrogators as they fled their positions and allowed me to march past all hurdles, into the home of the brave and the land of the free, and the arms of my beloved Boo.

3

Venice was having its own dirty little war, and bodies were beginning to pile up at a rate that made Sydney look like a pleasant seaside city with an Opera House and a wondrous bridge. I didn't have to write about them, and although the Black–Latino war was being fought within earshot, it was almost in another world. Our problem next door, on the other hand, wouldn't go away. The Man with No Brain's dementia worried the immediate residents far more than gang shootouts in the 'hood, which had nothing to do with them.

The possibility of Boo being caught in the crossfire was of concern to me, as she had ridden through or past bullets while taking her daily exercise. But she would not be deterred, and the last time a respected member of the public had been shot in nearby Santa Monica, the police reaction was so intense the gangs were apparently taking some care not to kill whites, Asian-Americans, or tourists.

But the Man with No Brain had no such compunctions, and the terror finally reached the point where even the Venice division of the LAPD was forced to take action. Following my cowardly failure to "pop" him, Brainless, perhaps sensing the broadening of hatred throughout the entire block, decided to intensify and widen his targets.

We were quite blithe to the incident that was to finally lead us to the lip of the Mojave Desert, until 11.00 one evening, when there was a quiet knock at the back door. I was lighting a joint at the time, and, assuming someone was dropping in on their way home from The Circle Bar, casually opened the door to find the Venice cop, the one who had suggested I take out my neighbor, standing respectfully on the crumbling door step.

He asked if he might come in, and I asked him to wait. I shut the door, extinguished the joint, and returned to the friendly sergeant and ushered him into the kitchen. He entered, and to my surprise brought a few friends with him. The better part of a SWAT team began to pour into a house not designed to accommodate SWAT teams. All were wearing body armor, and carrying automatic rifles or shotguns or both. Their comrades were being assembled outside. The sergeant explained that The Man with No Brain had finally gone a few feet too far. He had in fact, deliberately driven down and over a woman who lived in the adjacent alley, breaking at least one of her legs. A female Caucasian, no less.

I gave them the freedom of the house, and they took up positions in the living room, aiming their weapons out the window, into the darkness and at The Man with No Brain's house, which was so close that their rifle tips almost scraped his asbestos sidings. I pointed out that it was blue asbestos, and was more dangerous than the occupant. Two SWAT members took up positions behind the lemon velvet love seat, which I suggested was unlikely to deter gunfire. The sergeant informed me that a machine-gun post had been established on the roof of an apartment building opposite, and it might be best for Boo and me to join the crowd of evacuated neighbors that was gathering in the alley. Leave it to the experts.

On the scale of overreactions, this was shaping up like another Waco. At this stage, Harry, our black-and-white springer spaniel, awoke, and began snarling and barking at the SWAT members, no doubt confusing them with the detested mailman — due to their uniforms. As the SWAT members cowered before Harry's wrath, I found his lead, and we exited the house. Out in the alley, a sizeable crowd had gathered. Some were evacuated neighbors; others, folks who had wandered out of The Circle Bar and had stumbled into the action. Marijuana was strong in the air, and lines of cocaine were being chopped out on the trunk of an LAPD black-and-white. Beer arrived, and the stakeout party was soon in full swing. Neighbors started taking bets on whether the cops would shoot Brainless. The air was festive; the mood, Woodstock. The remaining SWAT members started to form a phalanx that would have done justice to the Romans. As they marched past us, Harry escaped the lead and flung himself into their midst, utterly disrupting their formation. I retrieved him, and the small army regained its composure.

One of the SWAT ringleaders produced a bullhorn, and demanded that all occupants of the house come out with their hands up — or words to that effect.

The crowd was assuming the mentality of a mob of vigilantes, inciting the police to open fire and loudly reminding them that he was a "druggie". The house was in darkness, and I wondered if The Man with No Brain was actually home. It was impossible to tell. He owned so many cars I could not figure if one was missing. Nothing transpired, so a couple of SWAT members aimed their tear-gas launchers towards the house and, after a few more warnings on the bullhorn, started peppering the place with the gas.

For a moment, silence reigned, but as the first familiar whiffs of tear gas drifted back to our assembly, a young man stumbled out in pajamas with his hands raised. A cop asked me if he was the target, and I assured him he was not.

More tear gas.

Finally, the moment we had all waited for. The Man with No Brain, to the cheers of the now huge crowd, lumbered into the glare of the lights from the circling choppers, dressed in a white bathrobe. It wasn't white for long. Before he could be cuffed, our neighbor lost control of his bowels in a fashion quite different from mine at LAX, and soiled himself severely. The stench, as he was thrown into one of what appeared to be the entire fleet of LAPD police cars, overwhelmed the tear gas, and I felt sorry for the cops who had to accompany him on his ride to the slammer.

Boo, Harry, and I returned to our home, now thick with tear gas. It was to be days before the smell passed, and Boo wondered whether we really wanted to live in Venice forever. So did I.

4

"Good afternoon. This is Bill Lavender."

"Hello, Mr. Lavender. I hear you have a house for sale. Boulder House?"

"I might have. That depends."

"On what?"

"On who's asking."

I lit a cigarette and lay back on the bed, reflecting that this wasn't going to be your straightforward house purchase. The voice sounded as aggressive as his words. Bill explained that he was considering selling and moving to another state. California was really starting to piss him off.

"I'm a redneck gun-nut. I haven't killed anyone in years, but if I want to kill someone that's my goddamn right, and I don't give a red rat's ass what anyone says," Bill bellowed. "It's bad as taxes. Goddamn taxes are getting to be higher than a damn cat's back," he added emphatically.

"Er … I believe you breed dogs out there," I ventured.

"You goddamn better believe it. I'm a horse's ass when it comes to dogs."

"Well," I responded, trying to move the conversation along,

"I'm interested in looking at the place. I've been to the High Desert many times, but I was wondering, where exactly is Boulder House?"

Boulder House was, and remains, located at the very end of Coyote Road, which, as most readers will know, snakes south from Roadrunner Rut and Gamma Gulch. It forks backwards through the High Desert from Pipes Canyon Road—a tributary, if coming from the south, of either Pioneertown Road or Rimrock Road. From the east it diverges from the even better-known thoroughfare of Old Woman Springs Road. For those less intimate with the higher reaches of the Eastern Mojave Desert, it is about a two-and-a-half hour drive east of Los Angeles, a twenty-minute drive from Joshua Tree National Park, and thirty minutes due north, into the mountains, from Palm Springs.

Boo was visiting Australia, and I had talked my mate Ed into taking the trip out of LA to the High Desert, deeming his convertible Le Baron the appropriate machine for the two-hour drive. He had vindicated my decision, and managed to get us from LA to the tiny vale of Pioneertown, the capital city of the sparsely populated land, in an hour and a half. As Ed careened up the rutted incline, I reflected that Chrysler had not produced this car for outback driving.

To call Coyote Road a road is being rude to roads, even dirt roads. We left the blacktop of Pipes Canyon and passed, with great care, through two great granite boulders that brought to mind a vehicular version of the Rocks of Gibraltar. Joshua trees, or Dr Seuss trees, as they are fondly known, contorted this way and that like some rubbery comedian who has just received a powerful electric shock. They waved at their more sober cousins, the giant yuccas, and the granddaddy of the High Desert, the ancient wind-twisted juniper. Roadrunners and quail darted between a botanical garden of cactus, dodging cottontails and jackrabbits. Great jumbles of giant rocks beckoned us forward. Each seemed to have a personality of its own, and many had faces that seemed familiar. I pointed out two members of the Supreme Court huddled together with Bugs Bunny and Kareem Abdul-Jabbar, all laughing their heads off. Not to be outdone, Ed promptly located Darth Vader watching, disapprovingly, from a rocky outcrop nearby.

After a quarter of a mile, the road started to rise, and Ed steered cautiously towards a precipitous incline that was actually a pass through cliffs that towered hundreds of feet above. The cliffs resembled a medieval fortress, but one sculpted by a supernatural hand. If a band of Comanche had appeared upon the top of this buttress, it would almost have been a cliché. Giant trees, pinyon and pine, grew almost as high as nature's great wall, fed no doubt by the run-off from the cliffs. Halfway up the rise a post had been erected long ago and the words DEAD END had been crudely hand-painted in dripping red paint. It left the distinctly chilling appearance of having been written in blood.

A small, apparently deserted cabin stood on a ridge to our left. Its windows were battened down, and it had a grim quality. But I hardly noticed either it or the dark dormant volcano that towered above it, because the road suddenly swerved to the right, down a gully, through tall, black iron gates and into a circular driveway surrounded by adobe buildings that formed a sprawling compound. The adobe was the exact color of the rocks, blending into the land. We pulled up before the main house. It looked huge, and seemed to have been built directly out of the rock — which, we were to discover, it had.

As Ed and I marveled at the wonder of the place, a stocky, well-weathered man came forward to meet us.

Bill Lavender was proud of his erection. Boulder House, fortified from behind by towering boulders, commands a front view of the valley below, stretching to the foothills, and beyond, to the San Bernardino Mountain Range. As it was constructed in the early 1980s when the Soviets were still willing, it might have been built to withstand a decent army. A nuclear attack, which would certainly target the 29 Palms marine base twenty miles away, would be deterred by the granite outcrop behind the fort.

As if to complete the picture, Bill seemed to be the product of crossing George C. Scott with a pit bull. His white hair was cut to the crop; his jaw was eternally thrust forward, as if demanding just one more punch. He was well muscled for a man of seventy-three, and the muscles were not of the kind earned in a gym. The word 'feisty' might have been invented for Bill. I was glad Ed was with me. Ed is a big, comforting sort of man with a background in the more shadowy aspects of the military. Even so, he's the sort of man people instantly trust, and Bill was clearly a suspicious type.

Bill's apparently hostile presence was not leavened by the activities of four extremely large Rottweilers. The largest of the Rots, Chopper, Bill's main non-female companion, was more than capable of scaring the unwary. In the background, his friends hurled themselves on the steel fences that constituted their elaborate runs, adding something of an air of menace to our arrival. I noticed the personalized license plate on one of Bill's cars, "DOMOTD", and figured it was an anagram for some military order. But Bill informed me sharply the letters stood for Dirty Old Man Of The Desert.

Bill didn't show us the house. He introduced us to it. It took some time. The front door opened into a small study that, in turn, opened into a large expanse of red Mexican terracotta tile. The walls were blackwood, and the area bereft of windows. It was just possible to see stairs reaching up into the darkness above. Darkness was the order of the day. It was so dark that I wondered if we shouldn't be joined by ropes in case Ed got lost. We felt our way into what one might describe as a den.

Dens are something of an American phenomenon, and are rare in Australia. They are a place where men, back in the days when we endured a separation of the species, could don gowns and slippers, and study *Playboy*. But this was a den in the biblical sense. The sort of one that Daniel might inhabit.

Bill had forsaken lions — not that the property was devoid of them — for dogs. Light from a window revealed that a good part of the den's walls were of raw granite.

We had heard that Boulder House was built into the boulders, but I hadn't quite understood that the boulders were an integral part of the house. The den even came equipped with a cave, of sorts. It was actually a dog run that ran out to a courtyard. It seemed like a large run, and in the gloom I wondered whether a human could use it. It occurred to me that the house had been built for the dogs first, and humans a distinct and distant second. If dogs could design and build a house, I expect this is about what they would have come up with.

At the end of the den was another staircase, this one spiral. Dogs have trouble climbing spiral staircases, so obviously they hadn't been involved in this aspect of the construction. If the raw rock walls were a surprise, the first upstairs room was a shock. Its walls and floor were entirely enclosed in the natural granite faces, giving the impression of standing in a large cave—a cave where unseen things lurked. In the center was a huge waterbed, perched atop a four-feet high, enormous flat boulder. Above the bed was a skylight. One could drift off at night staring at the stars.

Bill was fortunate getting the floor cut. Back when the CIA was helping the Mujahideen clear the Ruskies from the Khyber, and the other passes of Afghanistan, when they were our "sons of bitches" and we could help build a Muslim utopia in that fortunate country, they sought the help of the Bechtel Corporation. Machines were brought in to cut caves in the rocky passes where the fighters could flee to safety after shooting their Stinger missiles at the helicopter gunships and SU70s that would fly low past the cliffs on their bombing runs. One such rock-cutter found its way to the nearby 29 Palms marine base, and Bill, not a friend of the communists, and close to some of the senior men at the base, managed to have the device brought to Boulder House. He was rewarded in his fight against international communism by having a floor cut into hard granite, the base for a magnificent rock room. All that was missing was Barney Rubble.

Bill, meantime, was expounding his dislike for the modern state, of which communism had been the most dangerous and extreme manifestation. My suspicion that Bill had built this fort with the view to making a last stand against the commie rats was fortified. That would also explain the artillery and tank shells that were in evidence, and I decided not to mention my brief flirtation with communism in my youth. Instead, I moved the conversation to the woes of the Democratic Party. Bill has an abiding hatred for the social engineers that comprise social-democratic parties.

I had expected that on the question of the greatest of all American social interventionists—the unimpeachable American,

Franklin Delano Roosevelt, the man who saved the world from the Depression, the Japanese, and, according to US folklore, the Germans—we would be united.

It was not to be.

"That son of a bitch brought in the child work laws," Bill hollered as we made our way from the rock room past what appeared to be two bathrooms, towards the library.

Though unfamiliar with some of Roosevelt's policies, I conceded that his attacks on child labor exploitation were part of some legacy—or words to that effect.

"Yeah." Bill turned on me like a snake. "I was eight years old. And I had a job. That damned commie took my job."

The library was blessed with another skylight, presumably to facilitate reading. There was plenty of scope for that. Bill had six thousand books, many first editions, and almost all of the masters were on display: Shakespeare, Milton, Wordsworth, Twain, the Greek classics, the French, as well as popular writers like Tom Clancy and Robert Ludlum. Inevitably, there were hundreds of books on war and military history, and Bill explained he had reviewed military works for the *LA Times*. Wherever he went, he carried a pad with the titles of works he had to acquire to complete his collection, and he thrust it at me, telling me these were the titles he sought.

Not content with a book collection that would honor a public library, Bill had put his hand to collecting movies, accumulating thousands of them. I can pass on movies, but I do like books. However, Bill made it clear that the collection did not come with the house as we exited the library to find ourselves on a large landing.

As we passed a sign on the wall that read "A DULL WOMAN KEEPS A TIDY HOUSE", I figured that Bill's views on female suffrage might be unique, and inquired after his opinion on emancipation. It was not so much voting rights or jury service that he most begrudged. "Shoes," he growled. "They should have never given them shoes." Bill's head jutted forward in indignation.

We took another stairway down into the dark depths of the first floor, and soon found our way into the main bedroom. It was huge: forty feet long, and almost twenty wide, larger than the dwellings that many of the world's inhabitants enjoy. It was dominated by a bed too large to move—nine feet across and as many long, encased in great bolted black Cypress beams that rose ten feet above the floor. While Bill's books might be going with him, this was a bed that was staying in the house. The scale of the bed and Bill's license plate was convincing evidence that Bill was still an active man.

The walls were mostly bare, whitewashed with blackwood trims. The house, inside and out, lent itself to the California look—that is, the style of the elegant masters of California prior to the mass arrival of Europeans. There was, of course, another bathroom (I counted five in all), and the greater bedroom led to one of the courtyards, which housed a Jacuzzi. We negotiated a maze that took us out to the back and into a confusion of courtyards. There were three, four, even five of them—depending on how one defines a courtyard. The whole back of the house was enclosed by rock faces that soared, almost sheer, some seventy feet above. One courtyard was encased in concrete—part of a dog run that was joined, through the tunnel, to the "dog room" or den.

It was cold out there, and we returned inside. Bill figured he'd done his bit by showing us the house, and left the exploration of the property to us. I guess he figured the landscape spoke for itself.

The driveway rolled out past a good-sized swimming pool and accompanying pool house into an acre-sized amphitheater. Here, the flat land was punctuated by spiky yucca, Joshua trees, some pines, junipers, and a dense floor of brush. And cactus. The property was mostly rock, with great seams of rimrock—furrows of granite that looked like man-made brick walls—running in broken streams through the terrain like a stone hedge. About three hundred yards from the front porch, the land fell away into what was once a small swamp. A battered bridge stood over the outline of a creek, but the stream was now dry. Halfway up a short ridge stood the stark skeleton of a large pine that apparently had been struck by lightning. The charred wood had burnished over the years, and much of the tree had turned gold.

"It looks like a hanging tree," Ed remarked.

"It's the ten years ago tree," I decided. Ed gave me an odd look.

"Ten years ago on a cold dark night." I sung a line from the old Band classic.

"There's nothing in that song about a tree," Ed remarked.

"It's not the words, it's the mood," I replied.

Ed stared at the gnarled but golden dead pine, and nodded.

Neither Ed nor I had any idea what seventeen and a half acres, the land that came with Boulder House, actually comprised, and as the rock face plunged and soared all about us, seventeen acres on a map didn't correspond with seventeen acres on foot. Soon Ed was tired, and so was I. The experience, Bill, the house, and the rock-climbing demanded respite, a few cold ones, and a game of pool at a nearby bar—The Palace.

5

As Ed broke the pool balls, I pondered the sense in even contemplating buying Boulder House. I pondered it to the point of losing the game, and sat watching Ed display his skills to the locals. In theory, Boo and I could, through the internet, still have residence in the wilds and write, edit, make documentaries et al. McLuhan had argued, thirty years ago, that "going to work" was a thing of the past. But the way I saw it, pretty much everyone still went to work.

Who were we, two isolated individuals with tenuous careers and a single dog, to try to prove that one could live and work anywhere in the world?

I stared at my Miller Genuine Draft, and contemplated the madness of buying Boulder House. Barely technologically competent, we would have to assemble all the high technology that might help keep the wolf from the door while attending to life in a world where the nearest light at night shone from a house a mile away. We would be able to see the stars in all their glory, but little else. We would be going a long way from the cities of our lives — Sydney, London, Melbourne, and Los Angeles. We would be passing into a world of wells and rodent control, of rattlesnakes, scorpions, and bullets, of solitude, of wild and unruly people we hardly knew. A place where everything was designed, through ten billion years, to poison and to kill. To a land where hardship was king, and death his maidservant. To the end of the road. Of Coyote Road. A right turn in the dirt off Pipes Canyon Road, once called Rattlesnake Canyon Road, out of Pioneertown by eight miles. We would be at a dead end in the middle of nowhere.

I remembered, with a shudder, that Boo had once jumped out of a moving car because one of the occupants was a moth. Someone had told me the moths out in the High Desert were big enough to eat. The Australian Aboriginal feasts on the Bogong moth when it is in season, but I couldn't see Boo doing so. She is a brave girl who has faced perils all over the world, but her fear of moths is all-consuming. I would be taking her into a world where "if it don't bite, or sting or scratch, it don't belong out here", as I heard a local boast. That was before I heard about the bats.

Bill had commented that life was not "all shits and giggles", and life in the High Desert certainly wouldn't be.

Boulder House was forbidding, straight out of Robert Louis Stevenson. The house was huge, but the rooms were maze-like and dark as the future. There were tiny recesses that gave way to tinier ones. In two hours we hadn't fully explored the house, but it was evident that walls would have to be torn out, wiring and plumbing redirected, and more skylights installed, and that a million other tasks unimagined awaited me. Our budget did not run to employing an army of tradesmen. I would have to do most of the dumb, hard work myself.

The threat of fire was not to be dismissed; but, as most of the property was granite, I doubted brush fires would be a great threat. Boulders tend not to burn. As a kid and later as a journalist, I had felt the heat of bushfires roaring two hundred feet high through eucalyptus forests — fires that advanced on fifty-mile fronts, jumping ravines and exploding rather than burning. So I sneered a little at fire warnings. But there was brush all round the house, crawling out of the cracks in the rock, and if it caught, the house would be threatened. The place was mostly wood inside, and if a few sparks reached the interior, the exterior would cease to be.

Water was also a problem. The well didn't produce enough water to shave with. We would have to haul it in, at the mercy of an ancient water truck, whose owner's eyesight was reputedly failing at about the same rate as his truck.

I pondered my abilities. Axes and chainsaws and all manner of tools that I had not used in years, if at all, would be my charge. I wasn't even a handyman; I was a journalist. Boo was even worse equipped, with no knowledge of the challenges I knew would be our daily lives. She had seen rattlesnakes in the canyons of LA, but she hadn't lived in colonies of them. Many species of rattler inhabited the area, including the Mojave Green, a nasty viper with a temper, whose venom attacks both the central nervous system and the heart. If one of us was to be bitten while exploring the property, we might have to hike a tortuous half-mile to get to the car. That would set the blood racing. Then it would be a twenty-minute drive to the third-world medical treatment now available to most rural Americans.

As a kid, I was never happier than hunting the red-bellied black snake and its brown cousin, both of which were deadlier than anything America had to offer, but that was forty years ago. We were in a different land, and I was almost a different person. I had killed a lot of them, and their American cousins had every reason to take revenge. Rattlers were known to winter in numbers, maybe as many as a hundred. If any place on earth existed where they might be found in such multitudes, surely it would be the tumultuous jumble of wildness that surrounded Boulder House. Falling amongst a few score angry rattlers would be curtains.

The lion also loomed large in my thoughts. We were moving into his territory, and cougars had taken women in the mountains west of San Diego in recent years. Those mountains were only a few hours away. Bill Lavender had cheerfully recounted sharing a beer with his son when they spied a lion at the top of a fifty-feet rock face. They viewed it with awe as it prowled, some one hundred yards from the benches in front of Boulder House. Then Bill had noticed his small granddaughter was missing. The two men sprung from their seats and raced towards the rock. The last they saw of the lion was the flicking of its tail as it disappeared into the caves beyond the main outcrop. At the foot of the rock, the child was playing, oblivious to the death that lurked above.

Then there were the packs of wild dogs. Locals had warned me that they represented the greatest danger. Servicemen posted at the marine base would, when it was time to go, drop their dogs off here in the High Desert. Many were taken in, and people commonly had three dogs. One woman was reputed to have seventy. But there were limits to the largesse of the locals, and packs as large as eight would form. They could do a lot of damage before being shot.

"A pack of dogs is more dangerous than a pack of wolves," Tony, who spent the summers in rural Wisconsin and knew something about wolves, told me as I sipped my beer. "They have no fear of man."

A comforting thought.

"And the marines tend to have big dogs that can fight. Shepherds, mastiffs, pit bulls," he added.

Medical facilities hardly rivaled Cedars-Sinai. I had heard horrendous tales, and been warned of the nearest medical center. Many people reported treating themselves. The local animal feedlot was a popular pharmacy, animal antibiotics being cheaper than the human variety, and, as no prescriptions were required, doctor's costs were eliminated. One gentleman treated his arthritis with WD-40. He swore by it. Modern medicine's great advances had not reached Pioneertown — let alone Pipes Canyon.

Most alarmingly, our nearest neighbor, Danny, from the brooding cabin, would be out of jail within a year. He was finishing up a five-year sentence for shooting a local. I wondered quite a bit about Danny. He would not come out of the Californian prison system a better man.

Perhaps it was the utter madness of the scheme that was driving me to it. Boo and I had both lived in country towns as children, and moved across worlds to ever-greater cities. Each move had been judged by friends and loved ones as folly. Each time we had survived, if not conquered. But this was the folly absoluta.

Mostly, I worried about my ability to keep the huge house running. I knew next to nothing about most technical functions that I would need to know to keep us from boiling, freezing, or burning in our beds.

Neither of us had done a scrap of serious physical work in years, and now we were considering taking on the High Desert.

Pretty much alone. Alone in a strange new world, as far from the places we had inhabited as the moon, which, as Ed and I trudged to the Pioneertown Motel, rose with such brightness that the stars were subdued. The moon lit the granite golden. Venus hung on the other side of the night sky. A wind whipped through a pine, the only noise save our shuffling boots in the dirt. Peace, perfect peace, passing understanding.

We sat outside our room and watched the meteors burn. Soon, the moon grew smaller and the stars brighter. They were as bright as they were in the Australian bush when I was a little boy, and the air was as sharp. Before us was the dark butte that separated the little town from Pipes Canyon and Boulder House. Did the future lie on the other side, in silence?

6

"Well, you wanted a place among the boulders, and tomorrow you shall have them," I told Boo as we departed LAX for Venice. I imagined she would require a few days in the city to recover from the long flight from Sydney, but she seemed invigorated by the trip, and demanded that we head for the hills and Boulder House immediately.

An hour and a half later, three weeks into the last year of the millennium, we forked off the 10 freeway and onto the 62. In twenty minutes we made it to the Pioneertown turnoff, to the steep four-mile climb through the jagged outcrops and into another world — the apparently tranquil world we were in the process of beginning to begin to make our home.

We had arranged to meet Bill Lavender at the house the following morning. When we set out on the five-mile drive, Boo was excited and I nervous. Bill was a formidable man, and though into his seventies appeared to be something of a sex maniac. We traveled down Pipes Canyon Road, and I stopped the car to point out the house from a half-mile away. Although I knew I was staring straight at the large dwelling, it was nowhere to be seen. Before us lay a plume of boulders half a mile long and hundreds of feet high. But Boulder House seemed to have disappeared amongst them. "It's up there somewhere," I muttered, hoping that to be the case and wondering if I had finally lost my senses. We drove on.

All the way from LAX and on the phone in Australia, I had told Boo of the wonders of the place, emphasizing the positive—all she wanted to hear. She was behaving like an excited virgin, and I was wondering where the place had gone.

But I kept my fears to myself and turned onto Coyote Road. We traveled a few hundred yards, threading our way through the massive boulders until we came to a place utterly desolate, a place where the land appeared to have been skinned. All life had been removed, and even the soil had been scraped, and we looked out over naked, almost polished granite. I hadn't seen or noticed it on the previous visit, but, as we drove on, we observed a large modern home that looked so antiseptic it might have been a contemporary church. Which is exactly what Boo thought, as our hearts sank.

"I'll bet it's some Christian retreat," she suggested to our collective horror. Those parts of the West not occupied by the armed forces, we have noticed over some years, are settled by Christian groups intent on teaching children the sort of country values that make the Republican Party so exemplary when it comes to family values.

Boo knew, and I knew she knew, that the possibility of me finding peace anywhere near a Christian retreat was as remote as Coyote Road.

After a few more hundred yards, the land returned to its exquisite self, almost as if the desecration had not happened, and our spirits lifted. As did the road.

But Boo's suggestion rang loud. Only Christian fanatics could possibly commit ecocide on such a grand scale, and coexistence with such people was out of the question. The "and when ye have tamed the land, ye shall salt it" type of Christian was capable of producing in me a blind fury that might lead to gunfire.

But that was all soon behind us, and we passed through the towering rock face, away from the land of the dead and into Boulder House.

Bill was a different man. In the face of beauty, he became a charming, kindly, and finally erudite gentleman. He almost bowed as he met Boo, and soon they were in earnest conversation.

I was still shaken by the possibility of Christian neighbors, and remained unusually quiet. Boo must have noticed because she quickly asked Bill what had happened back on Desolation Row.

"That old man ..." Bill returned to his more natural self, and stared towards the desolation that was blocked from sight by the great granite wall. "That old man," he repeated with a growl, "likes to use his bulldozer. He scrapes the land bare. Calls the plants weeds." Bill changed the subject, realizing that such a presence was not a great selling point.

But we were so delighted it wasn't a Christian retreat that we forgot all about the man we would come to know as The Blade Runner.

Bill was hard at it, attempting to charm the pants right off Boo, and I followed the pair through the house. Boo liked it, loved it, even more than I did, so I decided to leave them and to further explore the land. I wandered past the amphitheater, up a ridge and along a natural rampart, high above the yucca-strewn valley floor to my right.

Hard beside me on the left, the boulders gave way to a cliff face that rose, almost sheer, hundreds of feet higher and which, if I could climb it, would take me some seven hundred feet above a valley that was itself more than four thousand feet high. The climb would have challenged Sir Edmund Hillary, and I turned back to see Boo mounting the ridge.

At least, I thought, she's not mounting Bill Lavender. Boo was thoroughly enthralled, and we explored the rocks, finding all manner of vegetation, including at least a dozen different cacti. Caves abounded, and she recounted Bill's story of his son finding an intact Indian pot containing seeds. The sun was conquering the cool, and we returned to Boulder House and Bill, who had perched himself on a bench in the shade, from where he could admire our progress.

By the time we arrived, we had agreed to make an offer. All my night-time doubts had been dispelled by the bright morning light.

And so we did.

Bill seemed skeptical. We were, after all, city folks. But we were also Australian, and although Australia, after Israel, is the most urbanized nation on earth, the popular conception of us as a hardy outback people seemed to have infected Bill, an otherwise sensible man.

What, Bill asked, changing the subject from monetary matters, did we think of the other valley?

"What other valley?" I inquired.

"The one over there, the box canyon," said Bill, waving at a rock outcrop that ran from the side of the house to the amphitheater below. We clambered up the steep hillside that ran behind the house and stared at the sight before us—a breath-taking hidden valley rimmed on one side by towering rocks, and on the other by a rolling landscape of boulders that crested high above us before falling away a thousand feet to the canyon floor.

The valley floor, once a creek bed, was well grassed, and it was apparent that a good number of families of coyote lived in the grass under juniper and pine, in considerable comfort. A more sheltered and secluded place could hardly exist, and as we walked the valley we realized why the road was named after the coyote. In the cliffs above, a ledge provided a very large bird — a golden eagle, Bill informed us later — with a bird's eye view of the Hidden Valley. The face of the cliff was stained by the eagle's droppings, and from that perch it could pick off the hares, cottontails, and squirrels and snakes that were in abundance.

As we departed Coyote Road, we swung past the brooding cabin, and I told Boo about what we soon dubbed "the murderer's cottage". She didn't mind. It just made it all the more interesting.

She wanted to buy Boulder House. There was no other house like it anywhere on earth, and though something even vaguely like it — on seventeen acres — would cost a good $10 million in LA, it was a mere two hours from that metropolis and one-hundredth of the price. Our dog could run free, liberated from the leash laws of LA, where all dogs were judged by the standards of the worst fighting pit-bull. We could even have more dogs, Boo enthused. And a horse, she added. Her friend in Malibu had just spent $250 on one single boulder for her garden that did not even approach the beauty of our rocks, and we must have some millions of them. We could leap from a bed that would have easily accommodated Henry VIII and all his wives in the same instance, into a Jacuzzi. We could farm tequila. All the fears and reality checks of the past were swept aside in a rush to judgment, and soon we were burning rubber to The Palace to toast our decision.

To my relief, Tony was on hand, having arrived from Minnesota a few weeks before. Tony might be the strongest man, pound for pound, between Pioneertown and Nova Scotia. In the summer, he cuts down trees and carries huge boulders around the Great Lakes. In the winter, he tears up cactus and carries huge boulders for anyone in Pioneertown who can deal with his fanatical work ethic. Today he was suffering cheerfully from a dental complaint that had gone unaddressed until his face was horribly distorted. The infection had occurred in Minnesota, where he had been carrying huge boulders for one of the bosses at Harley-Davidson. He had ignored the pain until his employer ordered him to leave the site and seek treatment, and by then it was almost too late. Twelve months later, I would threaten to call the police if he did not stop work at Boulder House after six fourteen-hour days had led me to the brink of hospitalization. But on that winter evening we sat at the bar, and, avoiding the ghastly specter of his face, I could inform him that we were looking seriously at buying a place and employing him.

I stared at his hands, big hairy things that extended from unusually long arms—a product, I would later deduce, of lifting things (usually boulders) that humans should leave where they were.

Tony, who had only worked twelve hours that day, was keen to start immediately when I mentioned Boulder House, but I suggested that he wait till we had actually bought the place. I didn't think Bill would take kindly to him lifting boulders for the sake of proving it possible, but Tony seemed anxious to begin lifting things and flexed his long and winding arms. I stressed that Bill was something of a hermit, that guns were in evidence in every room at Boulder House, that ammunition boxes doubled as garden beds, that tank shells made for door stops, that Bill was "forted up," and that while Tony might be capable of flinging a few of the finest fighting Rottweilers bred in the US from Bill's cliffs, we should bide our time and go through the dreary process of paying Bill hard money for Boulder House before we caused the gravel in his driveway to be unduly disturbed. A light went on somewhere in Tony's brain. He studied his beer, and it was clear he was giving the situation some thought. His hopes for an immediate assault passed as he contemplated the cold, hard fact that there are a lot of people in rural America, particularly in the West, who are to be treated with the utmost of care. We exchanged glances—knowing glances. Tony knew that part of America which gets painted red on election night better than I did—and I was not altogether ignorant of the America not confined to the seaboard.

7

Boo and I had come to know the West in a voyage of discovery that had taken some fifteen years and led to Bill's big iron gates. We had been fortunate in that the mention of Australia has a quite dazzling effect on Americans, especially men.

Many veterans, long retired to the West, experienced the fighting qualities of Australia's troops in World War II, Korea, and Vietnam. The very first time we visited the desert, in 1984, we stopped at a store on a bleak section of Highway 62, about halfway between LA, the Colorado River, and the Arizona state line. An old man, sporting white hair and beard, interrupted me while I was buying supplies and asked whether I was Australian. When I acknowledged I was, he extended his hand, saying, "Son, I just want to shake your hand. Best fighting man in the world."

Deeply embarrassed — my only fighting during the Vietnam War was against police in anti-war demos — I left, and never discovered the circumstances from which he drew this conclusion. His looks suggested World War II, but it was hard to tell. In the desert, people age fast.

In one bar, a local proudly announced to his mates that "these Aussies have fought with us in every war". I agreed that this was largely true, but reminded patrons we had, unfortunately, missed the War of Independence, it precluding white settlement. I added that it was doubtful that many Australians had fought in the Civil War.

But this peculiar affection, steeled by battle, remains, and I will admit to unwittingly adding to the Aussie myth myself.

In our journey through the West, Boo and I found ourselves in the town of Cody, Wyoming. We had intended to stay in Utah, but changed our minds when we sat down for a meal in the late afternoon somewhere north of the Zion Monument. I had asked for a wine list, and from the reaction of the waitress might have asked for the Manifesto of the Communist Party. She curtly informed me there was a store for registered alcoholics some thirteen miles to the north. I curtly asked her what was the fastest way out of Utah, and she suggested I consult a map.

We drove, and found ourselves in Wyoming, where I was gratified to see a sign twinkling through the gloaming and the thin sleet that read "COCTAILS". There is something profoundly settling about that sign in a nation with the most confusing quilt of dry and wet states and counties.

We finally arrived in the town of Cody. Cody was dubbed after one of the men responsible for the buffalo slaughter, Wild Bill Cody. It maintains an excellent museum. Much of Wild Bill's guns and clothes are on display, along with the headdress of Sitting Bull, and Annie Oakley's pistols. We spent an hour or so studying the stuff and gleaning bits of history before I repaired to a bar, and Boo set off to check out the local thrift stores.

Most Western bars are dark. This was as dark as the inside of a dog in a cave. I ordered a beer, and was approached by a few drinkers and asked, inevitably, if I was from Australia. Discovering

I was, they invited me to join them at the gaming tables. (Another advantage of being Australian is that one is most unlikely to be an undercover cop.)

The game involved rolling five dice from a special cup with a leather bottom onto the table. Each player gets three rolls, and must accumulate a six, a five, and a four before the other dice can be counted as a score. The highest score wins the dollar or so that each player must pay to play.

The drinkers were cowboys. Two were rodeo hands who had taken leave from their troop due to injuries. One had a broken leg; the other, some sort of spinal problem. Nothing that could prevent them drinking and gambling. The game was, of course, illegal, having been banned about the time women were given the right to vote. I joined them, and in a few moments had won a hand—the game only requires enough skill to be able to count.

As my eyes adjusted to the dark, I noticed that the boys all had small round circular tins on which I read the word "SNUFF". I hadn't tried snuff in years, and was surprised to find what I considered an English pastime here in the center of the American West.

I asked if I could try a little, and a tin was immediately handed to me. I took a pinch, and before I sniffed it noticed that the grain felt thicker than the fine powder I used to sniff. The kick was that of a horse, and almost blew my head off. Tears streamed down my cheeks as the stuff exploded through my nostrils and seared through whatever comes after them.

In the dark, no one could see the tears, or notice that my head had doubled in size, assuming the proportions of an American tourist. Slowly, the pain receded, and I continued to play. But my heart was no longer in the game, and I sorely needed fresh air. I said my goodbyes, and made my way to the batwings. As I stood recovering, I heard the rodeo hand with the broken leg say, in a reverent tone, "Those Aussies are tough. They snort chewin' tobacco."

I was crying like a baby.

We traveled south from Cody and made our way back to 29 Palms, the service town for the world's largest marine base, and for tourists who wish to explore the wonders of Joshua Tree National Park.

In a bar near the base, over a beer and a pool game, I met an unlikely instrument of intelligence. He was of medium build but well muscled. His hair was shaved close, and I naturally took him for a marine.

"You a grunt?" I inquired, as I selected my shot.

"No, I'm Donovan's son," the young man replied.

I was surprised enough to miss my shot. I had not expected to meet the son of a balladeer of the sixties in a tiny dive out in the baking flats amongst rattlesnakes, scorpions, roadrunners, and cactus, all surviving in the harsh and terrible beauty of twisted, mangled and tortured wilderness. And that was before the marines began using the desert to bomb and blast with their cannons and gunships.

"Well, I'm not really Donovan's son. He just married my mother. I'm really Brian Jones's son," the lad continued.

This, I thought, was getting interesting. I missed another shot.

"Make your mind up, man. You're either Donovan's son, and that's nothing to be ashamed of, or you're the son of the man who built the greatest show on earth."

The young man explained his antecedents. Donovan was touring England at the time when Dylan and Joan Baez were doing the "Don't Look Back" tour. I don't think he had seen the film of the tour, and as Dylan had mocked Donovan mercilessly, I didn't raise the matter. The son explained that Brian's wife was pregnant with him when he drowned.

Brian had been my favorite Rolling Stone until his death, and Mick the usurper. We chatted about Brian, and he seemed happy that someone knew and once adored his biological father. How many people had he met out in this redneck wonderland who were even vaguely familiar with his father's legend or the murky circumstances of his death? They knew about Donovan, who had moved to the High Desert and established a recording studio.

So I probed him about the area, about what I might have missed. You have to be keen to find the wonders of the wild parts of America. The best trick is to find a bar and work its inhabitants. Donovan's son, or Brian's son, was dismissive of the desert, and the desert was later to become dismissive of him after three DUI charges.

Perhaps because I knew something of his real father, the son sat and thought. "You might like Pioneertown," he suggested.

An hour or so later, we took the unmarked road that takes one to the true High Desert. These days, a large sign directs far too many travelers away from the Taco Bells, the KFCs, and the Jack in the Boxes of the desert town of Yucca Valley. But back then, you had to find the place yourself. It's only four miles from the stretch of fast-food joints that line the 62 highway, but the climb is rapid, and the world changes fast.

We passed through a wonderland of jagged granite, which makes up the Sawtooth Mountains — rock piled upon rock, towering hundreds of feet above the winding road. Dramatic pink during the day, delicate mauve as the sun falls. We kept stopping, baffled by the drama of the place. Yucca, pinyon pine,

Joshua trees, and cactus of every make and shape added to the sensational drama of a landscape straight out of every Western you've ever seen. Then the road flattened, and the drive was crowned by a huge freewheeling, sprawling saloon.

Pioneertown is a town of the Western imagination. Built in the 1940s as a replica of the towns of the Old West, it was named after The Sons of the Pioneers, a band once as popular as The Rolling Stones, who were almost as popular as The Beatles, who were more popular than God.

It was founded by one Dick Curtis, a villain in many a Western in the 1940s. Dick had lent a lady in need five dollars, and was repaid with the deed to a parcel of land that he turned into a second lot, a place nestled under the mountains, which looked like everybody's idea of the Wild West. His plan was to create, within a few hours of Hollywood, a working movie set — and Pioneertown was born. Old-style, rough Western houses, barber shops, brothels, and bathhouses were built along a dusty lane named Mane Street.

The town's prominent early citizens included Roy Rogers and Gene Autry. Westerns were then so popular that building a town, where actors and crew could stay, created economies of such scale that a single episode of *The Cisco Kid* shot in Pioneertown would save the producers $10,000. They made over one hundred *Cisco Kid*s, and thus saved more than a million. That's when a million was considered real money.

The town would have probably passed to dust when the Westerns rode into our rear-view mirror, but people moved into the few houses, and they brought a lot of the Wild West with them. The entire town has only a few dozen houses, but sported three bars, long after the salad days of the movies. And that, combined with the absence of a police force, made for a relaxed but eventful atmosphere.

The folks who moved to this outpost had little time for the laws and their enforcers, and the atmosphere attracted others. Musicians and artists joined the rednecks, the cowboys, and the hippies.

A few hours after we arrived, a moonless night fell. Here, where meteorite showers can be observed so closely that *The New York Times* gets its pics nearby, the stars lit the dusty roads, while the pine-clad mountains brooded dark all around.

We entered the saloon. It was a dark and unusually rough-hewn world. The walls were a mixture of weathered boards, bare cement, and handmade earthen bricks. What little light was allowed in came through wine and whiskey bottles laid between the mud bricks. About twenty men and a fair number of women stood around talking and drinking.

Most of the men sported beards, and most of the women didn't. Boo, dressed in LA clothes, attracted the usual attention as she joined me, walking through the crew to a bar of solid, cold, unadorned concrete. By the time we were served, one of the men had broken from the group and made his way over to us.

"Hi, I'm Adam Edwards," was his fateful introduction. We greeted him warmly — it was clearly his turf.

Adam was good-looking with finely chiseled features, shoulder-length blond hair, and sharp blue eyes. There was a wildness about him that might have been scary, but he behaved much as though he was the head of a delegation — which, in a sense, we were to find out he was.

Probably aware that we might be concerned, having entered a place where wildness seemed the order of the day, he moved quickly to put us at ease. Pretty much the first thing he told us was that violence was rare in the bar, but if started there were plenty of people capable of finishing it. As I had little intention of starting a brawl with twenty men all capable of putting me away, I nodded appreciatively. But Adam was more interested in Boo than me, and I let him continue to chat her up while I inspected my surrounds.

Adam informed Boo that he was not the only Edwards, and, nodding to an older version of himself, identified his father, John. Adam, we were to discover, held his father in great respect. In fact, his respect for the citizenry pretty much started and stopped with his dad.

The older Edwards was wearing a flat, round-brimmed hat covered in what seemed to be blue cloth. Its rim was tattered, and a scarf was tied around the base. The scarf trailed down the center of his back. His features were even more stark than his son's. His nose concluded at a sharp point, and his chin was firm and rock-like. His feet were bare, and his hair flowed long from the hat. The effect was part Indian, part *vaquero*. Whatever it was, it was fully authentic. These guys didn't dress up to look romantic — they were what the modern world loses, no matter how hard it strives to find it. Adam, it turned out, was part Sioux or Lakota Indian, with Cheyenne and some white mixed in. John was a thoughtful man, and, on learning that I was thinking of moving to the area, bellowed, being deaf, that I should come out to his truck. With an almost clandestine air he produced, from the bowels of an old Ford, a green can.

"You will need a lot of this," he said, thrusting the thing at me.

"Bag Balm," the can announced itself to be.

"Bag Balm?" I looked at John for inspiration.

He opened the can to reveal a yellow tallow-like substance with a strong odor.

"You will need a lot of this—this and duct tape." John respectfully returned the lid to the can.

"It's a pretty can," was the best I could offer. But John was not a man to wax lyrical about a can that contained what could be best described as wax.

I wondered why I would need large quantities of Bag Balm, and John gave me a queer look.

"For everything," he announced. "Cuts, sores, bruises, bullet wounds, knife wounds, broken bones—everything."

"What is it?" I wondered as we approached the great wooden doors of the saloon.

"Well, it's mostly used to repair cow's udders," John explained. "Cows udders get cut up a lot while milking."

"Rather like tar on a sheep's cut," I yelled. John feigned deafness or indifference, and we returned to the roar of the bar. Later, I learnt that neither John nor Adam nor any of the scores of the Edwards clan who had populated the High Desert eat sheep, and that sheep did not enjoy a good reputation in these parts.

Back inside the bar, I noticed a distinct contrast between the denizens of the desert and another group of drinkers. The latter were obviously the owners of the shiny new Harleys that were leaning out the front. The locals were clearly the owners of a bunch of dilapidated Fords and Chevys parked so close to the bar that they were almost in it. The weekend bikers, in their desperate search for authenticity, had spent a king's ransom on the usual black-leather matching pants and jackets, with the inevitable tassels and chaps with their bottoms cut out. There was something terribly pathetic about the weekend outlaws. They had spent too much money achieving the outlaw look — $25,000 plus on the bikes, and God knows what on accessories. They had come all this way to show it all off, only to be ignored by a bunch who had achieved, without a single visit to a boutique, that desperately sought "untamed" look. The two groups stood apart across the pool tables. The untamed ignoring the tamed, while the tamed pretended to ignore the wild bunch. But they could not avoid stealing glances. Their female companions, in particular, seemed to be futilely comparing their men with these men. The tame crowd also seemed to lack social skills. Boo was already in earnest conversation with Adam, and I was mixing freely with the wild bunch. The Harley riders with their perfect leather gear reminded me of the types that frequent the gay bars of Sydney. It was not the look they sought. They had merely tried too hard and spent too much money.

Adam, the self-appointed ambassador for what is variously known as The Club or The Palace (the official title, "Pappy and Harriet's Pioneertown Palace", being far too unwieldy) delivered a spiel that I was to hear time and time again when other newcomers arrived at this Wild West enclave.

The Palace, we learnt, had originally been a gas station — thus the concrete floors. This tiny town had once supported three bars, but the Red Dog Saloon, which still stands derelict at the other end of Mane Street, was burnt out by the official opposition, The Golden Stallion. The Red Dog was rebuilt, and The Golden Stallion burnt to the ground by way of reprisal. The Red Dog was fired again, and the tit for tat continued until both went out of action.

The old gas station was bought by Frances. Without Frances there would be no Pioneertown. When she came here forty years ago, the place was on its knees, and her plan was to create a bar of sorts. But the place was awash in the filth that will accumulate in primitive gas stations.

Frances and her burly husband, John, went to work on cleaning up, and a biker couple happened by, requesting beer.

"You can have all the beer you want if you'll help us with this filth," Frances, then a knockout redhead, told the bikers.

Much work was done and much beer drunk. The following weekend, fifty more bikers — mostly Hells Angels — arrived, and very soon Frances had her cantina.

The place flourished, and on one occasion four Hells Angels were wedded in a group ceremony that still causes people to shake their heads in wonderment.

Somehow, Frances kept the bar neutral, and warring outlaw gangs drank side by side, always leaving their terrible grievances at the door with their guns and knives. Any fighting was done outside on Pioneertown Road. It was a good place for fighting, dusty but dry, with little chance that an automobile would pass by. Some say five were killed in a fight with the Mongols way back then, and that buried beneath the desert dirt sits a dead man on his motorbike. But Frances laughs off such chatter.

Eventually, the cantina found its way into the hands of Pappy and Harriet, Frances's daughter. Pappy was even more Western in his demeanor than the rest of the wild bunch. If Adam was the ambassador, Pappy was secretary of state, while his wife, Harriet, was president for life. Pappy was somewhere between Wild Bill Cody and a walrus. His facial hair resembled a dried-up swamp. He was less than six foot, but big. His head was big, his neck was big, and his torso approached huge. To help make up the cabinet was Mike, the national security advisor. Mike, a former outlaw biker, well connected with the Hells Angels, had long yellow hair that was meticulously plaited into a narrow tip at his waist. His girth around the chest seemed similar to that of Pappy's, but he was much younger and looked very fit. Pappy was getting on in his years, while Mike, a karate teacher, was still in his prime.

Most of the conversation seemed to concern itself with guns and ammunition, road carnage, trucks, equipment, and stories of outrageous activity. Typical was an exchange I eavesdropped on between two men I had not met. One had been recently kicked by a horse, and had suffered a broken rib. Broken bones were, apparently, a common matter and scarcely worthy of conversation, especially when they were merely ribs. The companion of the man with the broken rib nodded and sympathized. "I broke a rib once," he said. "I broke it farting."

This statement was viewed with some skepticism by his colleague.

"Yep, I broke it farting. Didn't believe it myself until I went to the doctor. He looked up 'farting' — I think he said it was under 'breaking wind' — and said, yep, you can break a rib farting."

The conversations continued, and they continued coarsely. Two women, probably in their forties but short on teeth, were discussing men. One, a tiny thing with tousled hair, was expressing a strong position regarding her man and her desire to be rid of him. The other, a rangy blonde whose beauty appeared marked by the ravages of speed, was interested in doing a swap.

"I'm looking for a new man," the blonde confided.

"You can have mine," her friend replied.

"Then tell me everything," the blonde demanded. "The good and the bad."

"He's hung like a horse, but he's lazy."

"Well ..." the woman said, slowly but thoughtfully, "I could handle some of that for a while."

Evening had come, and the band was starting up. The bar spilled into a restaurant, all old wooden trestles on weather-beaten wooden floors, at the end of which was a bandstand. An extraordinary figure took the stage. Somehow 1964 had been made whole again in a person who sported a bare chest and black-leather cut-off vest. His jeans, low slung on his narrow hips, were as tight as possible, and had been ironed. He gripped his crotch and began hurling insults at the drinkers — clearly his friends — while grinning lasciviously at the few "decent folks" planted in the restaurant area.

"Who in God's name is that?" I asked somebody.

"That's Buzz Gamble," came the reply. Buzz, I noted, had a look that was popular with street hoodlums in the late fifties and early sixties. Tattoos on his arms had faded, but the "WEST TEXAS" which covered his belly was as bold as the man himself. His face showed the heroin years and the jail years and the booze years. Forty out of a total of fifty-five.

He opened up with a particularly direct version of "Little Red Rooster", and the decent folks started calling for their checks. But by the time the checks arrived, these folks were entranced by the sound of this man, who seemed to have Ray Charles and Tom Waits down pat — and then some. By the time he finished his first bracket, not a soul had left, and we listened enchanted as Buzz took us down the road of the blues. The songs washed away some of my fears about moving into the wilderness. The band, Buzz Gamble and the Daily Blues, were, I figured, reason enough to move out here the next day.

We stayed overnight across from the bar at a motel that was once accommodation for movie crews, extras, and the like, run by an odd couple, Ernie and Carole. When Pioneertown was a functioning movie set, Roy Rogers and Dale Evans lived in a comfortable home some seven miles up the road in the tiny hamlet of Rimrock. Gene Autry stayed in one of the small but comfortable rooms at what is now the motel. Here he could mix — that is, drink and gamble — with the lesser lights of the screen, the bit actors and the crews. Sixty years later, Ernie spends his days watching the old movies, seeing these now dead men and women ride into the same sunset he could enjoy if he left his living room and walked outside. The Lone Ranger gallops past the hoardings and shopfronts that exist, in reality, yards from where Ernie watches on his screen. The rest of the time Ernie spends preparing for his weekly event, the shootout. It being Sunday, Carole suggested we stick around and watch the show.

More than anything, the shootout, enacted by a score or so locals in front of the old Western props and houses, epitomizes the difference between the search for meaning and meaning itself, even though it's all an act and the bullets are duds. But the act is real.

Ernie goes to incredible lengths to ensure that the guns and clothing of his gunslingers parallels those of the Old West. So do the movies and the theme parks, but that's all for money. The shootout is free. If no one comes to watch, the show goes on. It exists for the participants, not the tourists. Ernie, the good guys, and the bad guys, and the townsfolk who act out the shooting, are playing out the fantasy of the West. But it's their fantasy, and they do it for free. And when the show is over for the day, the actors resume lives not unlike those of the common folk of the Old

West. They tend to their animals, dig post holes, mix concrete, yarn endlessly on the street or by the post office — the smallest in America — barter, have affairs, tinker and talk of machinery, and lend and borrow small amounts of cash. And when they change out of their fancy Old West clothes, they put back on cheaper versions of the same.

Everyone knows everything about everyone else in this town with no secrets. At the same time, they know nothing. There can be no ultimate truth, because there are so many versions of any event, or collective suspicions about it, that no one can be sure of anything. They police themselves, enforcing reasonable, if not decent, behavior through a code of estranging those who cross the line. Sexual harassment is dealt with not by the courts — for there are none — but in the court of public opinion. Which is worse: paying out the costs on a charge in cash, or, by being shunned and despised, by having heads turn away, by emptying a bar with your presence, being judged by one's peers every day?

It's the code of the West.

8

The source of all evil, the filthy lucre, was the next summit we had to face and, never having owned much more than a lot of books, we were not the sort of people who are given money by financial institutions while still pushing through the bank's revolving doors. On top of that, we didn't want enough. Money, that is. Land and housing were cheap in the High Desert, but a cross between a very large house and a fort, set on fifteen or seventeen or seventeen and one-quarter acres—no one was sure of the exact size of the Boulder House property—a place replete with five garages and two extra living units by the pool would, in LA, cost somewhere between $15 million and $30 million.

But two hours from LA, in beauteous surrounds, we were talking a few hundred grand. That alone was a problem. People don't lend such tiny amounts for houses in LA, especially when one's bank is based in Beverly Hills. Asking for $200,000 for anything but an extension to a toilet was akin to saying we were poor. The Californian property market, following well behind the heels of such cities as New York, London, and Sydney, was taking, as they say, off. The slow start was a product of the city's neglect by the first Bush administration, which had caused riots, mudslides, and even earthquakes, and left the city gasping, her reputation terribly sullied. But the Clinton years had, brick by brick and with infinite care and wisdom, turned languish into hope and eventually a robust return to what one might call wholesale recovery. Especially in the property markets.

News of these events had not filtered through to the High Desert, and did not until after the fateful few hours when those who cherish democracy above all things, five members of the Supreme Court, found it appropriate to stop the counting of votes in Florida and declare another Bush the winner and president-elect.

But in the bright and shining, if last, days of President Clinton's second term, a nice little cottage with views that stretched almost to Mexico could, in the High Desert, be bought for $5,000. To the south, Palms Springs was booming; to the north, even places like Palmdale, a city bereft of palms or any redeeming feature — save a dog pound from which I had rescued our last springer spaniel, Sailor, in the winter of 1999, when the city was still considered a slum — were flourishing. At least the housing prices were returning to and surpassing those set during the George Herbert Walker Bush recession.

So low were the local expectations that the fact, or even the very possibility, that we might spend anything more than $7.80 on a home there set idle desert tongues a-wagging, and soon it was reported to us that we were suspected drug lords; later, winners of some super lotto; and later still, rich Australian ranchers. The land is close enough to LA to be in its sphere of influence, but the vales of Pioneertown, Rimrock, and Pipes Canyon remained unnoticed by the men with bulldozers in their employ and golf courses in their souls. We were, I was convinced, on a cusp that would soon crumble, sending prices as high as the sky, and ending our hopes of ever owning more than a shoe box, leaving us swinging on the rent rope, flying faster and faster and getting nowhere. In fact, all we had was a conviction that this place, though overlooked by the developers, was finer than all the homes in Beverley Hills combined.

It was time to visit Kurt.

Kurt is an accountant whose Wilshire Boulevard firm looks after the money of people who have so much of it that they don't bother to do so themselves. We were paupers compared with his rock-star regular clients, but Kurt had a life outside his plush office — a life dictated by his passion for pool. For years, we had shot together in The Circle Bar on Main Street, Santa Monica, and had become good friends. Kurt was fourth-generation Japanese–American. His family had once been extremely wealthy, but had been caught up in the frenzy of Jap-bashing, perhaps the greatest blight of the FDR presidency. They had been interned in the wasteland of Manzanar Camp in Inyo County, just outside Lone Pine, below the frozen wastes of Mount Whitney and due west of the boiling wastes of Death Valley. Kurt was impressed by the fact that Boo and I had taken time, years before, to wander across the remnants of the internment camp where his family, and thousands of other loyal Americans, had suffered so cruelly for three years. He had been hardened by the family's misfortunes.

He had joined a Japanese street gang as a kid, and had been toughened in a way few accountants ever get to be before donning the designer suits of his profession. He had joined the gang for the same reason all kids do — survival on the hard streets of LA. That life was long behind him, but he had steeled himself, and all that remained of those days was the steel of the knives he kept as mementos from the time when a knife was part of his attire. He had scores of knives, and would sometimes covertly bring them into The Circle, when I would study them in the illicit darkness of the bar.

I went to him for money, telling him of the wonders of the High Desert with the same one-sided passion I had used to sell the idea to Boo.

Kurt was skeptical. He was a city creature through and through. His family had seen enough of the wilds of California, and he was puzzled by why I would seek what to him must have been a comfortable version of the internment camp. He probably didn't relish the prospect of losing one of his regular opponents at the pool tables, but seemed more astonished that someone he believed to be moderately sane would consider abandoning the pleasures and comforts of life by the beach for the wilds.

I explained our explorations of the West and how it had long held a certain fascination for me. Australia once had its own Wild West or, to be more accurate, East, but somehow the colorful killers and cannibals of our lore didn't match up to the untamed madness of the Western United States throughout the 1800s, and especially in the period that followed the formal cessation of the hostilities of the Civil War.

Every week in the tiny town southwest of Sydney where I grew up, we would file into the cinema and be transported to the West as the battle for hearts and minds took place. Down would go the lights and up would come the Movietone News, followed by that week's Western. This was the fifties, and the Ruskies and Americans were locked in a propaganda war. One had Sputniks; the other, Wyatt Earp. It was people enclosed in tiny metal boxes in space versus the lone man against lead-hungry, fast-gunning bad guys. For me, the Sovs never really had a chance.

Australia began as a jail, and never seemed to entirely cease being one. The first Gulag, settled by men in irons, had to compete in my imagination with a land that for one hundred years scarcely knew the rule of law. We had our Rebs, at least *a* Reb, in the form of Ned Kelly, but the US had a whole army of Johnny Rebs captained, in my childish mind, by Jesse James. Ned Kelly's fight against the English was a debacle. The Americans beat the greatest power on earth about the time Ned was being born.

I had devoured the screen version of the Wild West from my first childish glance, and though I saw through the glass or cordite darkly, what I saw — *Maverick, Gunsmoke, The Rifleman* — sure seemed a lot more fun than the jaunts of our bad men: a few highwaymen and a family of Irishmen destined to hang or die in obscurity.

About the time Bob Dylan was writing *John Wesley Harding*, and my father was praying that one day I might find the time to read and even emulate his hero, John Wesley, I was digging around discovering what I could about one of America's first serial killers. How our generation's greatest poet could have written that Hardin never killed an honest man would later puzzle me. His first killings (when he was twelve) were of two Negro kids he found swimming in his favorite water hole in Georgia. Georgia wasn't the West, laws even prohibited the wanton murder of blacks, and Hardin took it upon himself to ride — west — to Texas. He was proud of having shot twelve men dead before he commenced shaving. He killed another forty (not counting Negroes and Indians) before settling at the tender age of twenty-one in a Texas town called, inevitably, Comanche. Comanche was one of the first long words I learnt. At that time, I doubt a soul in the Southern Highlands of New South Wales could name an Aboriginal tribe or people.

I knew far more about the Apache and the Comanche than the Aboriginal when I encountered my first black Australian on a football field. I was nearing fourteen when I found myself playing on a young black, and I remember not wanting to tackle my opponent. I think I was scared. I sure was ignorant. I tried to learn more, but the subject was taboo. Red Indians, as we called them, were, through film, TV, and books, almost family friends. Geronimo was a household name. At night, I would wait for sleep, either yearning to be an Indian or inventing an Indian army I would lead against the white eyes in mythical places such as Arizona and New Mexico.

About this time, I read that back in Comanche, Texas, Hardin had promptly shot the local sheriff. Comanche, I discovered, had six saloons and little else. I wasn't sure what a saloon was exactly, but yearned to wander into that age and through the batwings. Hardin was deliciously shot in the back of the head, and, inevitably, the slug landed in the Wigwam Saloon in a wondrous place called El Paso. The radio about that time was playing a song about the "West Texas town of El Paso", and I figured it was the same place. Hardin, even more delightfully, had just thrown four aces in a dice game at the saloon. I had no idea what a dice game was, but how could a failed Irishman, Ned Kelly — roaming across, of all places, northern Victoria — compete with such men?

Even Hardin's killer, "Old John", was good enough to bite the dust before his trial and right before the same Wigwam Saloon. That was in 1895. More than one hundred years later, I delved a little deeper into Hardin's fate, and discovered that "Old John" was out on bail after Albert Fall, later to be president Warren G. Harding's secretary of the interior, and even later the central figure in the Teapot Dome Scandal, got him off.

Like me, Wesley was the son of a preaching man, as was the other sad and lonely figure of the West, Billy the Kid. Both men terrorized Texas. Both, like Jesse James, were Johnny Rebs, and all three died from a coward's bullet.

As part of my ambition to join the Red (Indian) army, I spent a good deal of time, often with my cousin Bill, crafting bows and arrows from the willows and the poplar trees of the Southern Highlands. The arrows never seemed to fly with the tenacity of the Cheyenne's. They scarcely flew at all. Bill favored the role of the cowboy, his parents being richer than mine, and capable of providing him with bright, shiny six guns similar to those favored by Roy Rodgers. It never occurred to me that, thirty-five years later, I would sleep in Roy and Dale's old bedroom, and possibly in their old bed.

It was a cowboy prank that got me expelled from the Boy Scouts on my first night. Horace Isedale, escaping my coming arrow, threw himself through the scout hall window and landed on his front teeth, both of which were found under a chair. Horace didn't mind terribly, but his parents objected to the cost of providing him with false ones. Horace grew to love his false teeth, and would play tricks with them to scare the girls at school. He would remove them with a swipe of his hand across his mouth and then leer at the ladies, who would scream in fright. Horace, *with* teeth, was not the most handsome of boys.

He must have done his trick too often, as the teeth grew loose. One day, when he was diving into the muddy waterhole that served as our swimming pool, the teeth disappeared when he hit the water. His parents drew the line at a second set, and Horace spent the winter frightening girls without drawing his hand across his mouth. Fatefully, that winter coincided with the purchase of a pool cleaner, and Horace landed the job of sucking the mud from the pool floor and disturbing the habitat of the tortoises that had taken up residence. To his eternal delight, some twelve months later, his teeth appeared in the huge mud-filled bag where the filth of the pool was deposited. Such was his joy that the teeth returned immediately to his mouth, without so much as a scrub.

About the time Horace discovered his teeth, I had discovered the joys of Shakespeare, Dickens, Orwell, and all the other prescribed works for a young man growing up in Australia's version of England's pastures green. Our house groaned with books. The classics, the great works of the Greeks, were merely a grasp away. But other towering literary feasts also caught my eye. I absorbed *Dead in Texas*, *The Bloody Spur*, *Their Guns Were Fast*, and *Montana Dead Shot*, usually from the tranquility of the lavatory seat, and they were to prove a great preparation for our move, many winters away, to Pioneertown and Boulder House. Through them, I learnt the difference between a Colt and a Sharps, which was to be of some value in a place where guns are far more prevalent than books or even newspapers, and where the sound of gunfire is so common that it causes no alarm.

9

Kurt, our accountant, shook his head with something akin to dismay when I suggested he find a bank that would pony up a few hundred thousand dollars for us. Though the banks couldn't give money away fast enough at the time, Boulder House was a most peculiar property, and Bill a most peculiar man. The combination was about to get volatile. The initial problem was Bill. In his unfettered confidence, he had extended the house into his neighbor's land, and we soon discovered that a portion of Boulder House, including part of the kitchen, was actually on land owned by one Floyd Salazar. Right slap-bang in the middle of this parcel of land stood the "murderer's cottage", usually inhabited by Floyd's son Danny when he wasn't serving time in prison. Normally, the matter could have been resolved for a small sum, the land itself being worth a few hundred dollars at the most. But nothing was normal here in the desert, and things tended to get less so as the months passed.

The differences between the violent Wild West and the carpeted canyons on Wilshire Boulevard were getting wider. And so began the longest escrow in the history of Yucca Valley and environs.

I might have anticipated the banker's problems. They were of the sort that city bankers have when dealing with highly unusual buildings in the middle of the High Desert.

At first, the suits were unhappy with the well, as I would grow to be. The paperwork on the property showed it pumping eight gallons an hour, which is a pitiful amount of water, but better than none, which was what it actually pumped. The banker called from his office in Beverly Hills and informed me that we would need to pump more water.

"The amount of water that can be pumped," I told him, "is determined by forces even more powerful than banks — God."

I pointed out that the water, which seeped from the mountain into the cracks and fissures in the granite over a period of many years, was all that could be pumped. There was little that I, or even the world's largest bank, could do to speed it up. But such problems were cropping up with every aspect of the house, and the sale was moving at the same pace as the water. And with the question of water came the question of fire. We were miles from the nearest hydrant, and county regulations stipulated that we had to have sufficient water to put out a fire — a difficult thing to calculate indeed. Eight gallons an hour would scarcely put out a barbecue. In endless tedious conversations, days of telephone tag, I argued that the property consisted almost entirely of rock, and that rock didn't burn. The threat of brush fires was minimal, as there was very little brush. And, if the house caught fire, there was little hope that 20,000 gallons of water would put it out. It had burnt once before, and it had burnt fast.

Bill, in the meantime, was getting toey. He had found the exact place he wanted to move to, and he wanted the money. A year had passed since escrow had commenced. It was again

Christmas, Boo was again in Australia, and I decided to head for the high plains and personally assure Bill that we were doing all we could.

Naturally, I stopped off at The Palace, and even more naturally ran straight into Adam Edwards.

"I thought you'd have moved in by now." Adam had fronted up in the otherwise deserted Palace, and roused me from my musing.

"So did I," I said forlornly.

Adam's aunt Saundra—a *Playmate* calendar girl of 1958—had owned Boulder House when it was a small cottage. Adam had played in the rocks as a child, and slept in the house many times. I understood his desire to return, and felt he had had every right to be interested in the house's destiny.

"Tell me about Saundra," I said.

Bill had remarked that she was "a damn fine-looking female," and any time her name was mentioned other men shook their heads ruefully.

"My dad tells it best," replied Adam, beckoning for the older Edwards to join us. "He's the one who built the house."

I told John I was intrigued by why such a beauty as his sister had left a Hollywood career that included biggish parts in biggish movies to settle on Coyote Road.

"She had some kids to this big, burly guy," John began, as I settled into hearing how Boulder House came into being.

"He was a friend of lots of movie stars—his best friend was Steve McQueen. She was living on Laurel Canyon and I was living in Hollywood, and the guy was violent. She called me one afternoon, and said that he was going to kill her and the two children, and she wanted me to come and look after things.

I said I couldn't because I was bowling that night, but I took her a 12-gauge and told her, 'When he comes, give him some of this.' Then I went bowling.

"Well, he came. He couldn't get through the front door, but he smashed his way through the back — screaming how he was going to kill her and the kids. She emptied the 12-gauge into his chest, blowing his heart right out of his chest. A 12-gauge can make a mess, especially from a few feet."

It appears the authorities were aware of the deceased's propensities, and as it was clearly self-defense, Saundra was examined, counseled and, after a few weeks, given her freedom.

She fled to the desert.

"And you joined her, and built her a home," I said, thinking this a fitting, all-in-the-family end to a tragedy.

"No," John replied. "There already was a house. One of her boyfriends blew it up."

An ex marine, a munitions expert, had been living with Saundra and the kids until he began behaving weirdly. She asked him to leave, and he told her he'd fight her with hate. That hate was stronger than love.

"Hate can never win over love," she replied, and he said, "We'll see."

Saundra, fortunately, was away on a trip when the angry boyfriend laced the place with explosives. He lined the fuse to the telephone line and, late at night, assuming she was home, made a phone call that set off the charges.

"The fire brigade arrived in time to hose off the concrete slab," said John.

Lying on the ground among the ashes was the old painted peyote wheel that had marked the entrance to Coyote Road.

It still had the rope tied around it that Comanche, an old Indian who wandered the desert, had found and given to Saundra. She chewed on the rope to stop the pain, and only then was she able to look at the destruction. All that was left was an old iron fireplace. Someone had even stolen the crystals that hung from the Ten Years Ago Tree.

Then, visiting one day, she spotted a sprout of green—a Joshua tree—coming up through the ashes. She told her kids, "As long as we can stand in that yard feeling love and goodness for one another, it will never be gone."

She decided to rebuild. John, a fine builder, agreed to do the job. It took him six months and cost $712. Saundra worked right alongside him, and at the end of the day she washed off the grime, put on a long dress, and drove into town to work as a cocktail waitress. The kids slept in a big tent, and Saundra dragged a double mattress up onto a huge flat boulder for her own bed. When we moved in, we christened it Playmate Rock. But that was still a long way off.

"It seems," I said miserably, recounting just one of our escrow nightmares, "that Bill Lavender somehow managed to build his kitchen into the property of his neighbor—a guy called Salazar. That's the house where someone got shot."

"I know," Adam replied with laudable nonchalance. "It was me."

He proceeded to draw back his blond beard, and even in the thin light of the bar I could see where a hole had healed.

"What happened?" I inquired.

"The asshole had been fighting in the bar, over there," said Adam, pointing to where the pool tables lay. "He got thrown out and went to his truck to get his gun. I followed him. I was trying to stop him." Adam sounded aggrieved.

"I had some beer, and the bar was closing, so I talked him into going home, and went with him.

"We were just sitting in the cabin shooting at stuff and I said, 'You couldn't hit the fucking wall,' and he said, 'I can hit you,' and put the gun up to my face and shot me point blank."

"Shit," said I.

It is next to impossible to ascertain the exact truth about events minor or major in the high country, but it appears the bullet proceeded to bounce around Adam's mouth and then exited to lodge against his spine. Adam was somewhat sobered by this development, and staggered out of the shack, blood streaming from his lips and from the hole in his lower left jaw.

The bullet seemed to have done its damage. The question was where it now resided. Adam was spitting blood, but seemed to have stabilized by the time he reached Ernie and Carole's, insisting he didn't want a doctor, and would just lie there and die. Danny was, by all accounts, a small but troubled Latino with strong Hopi Indian roots, and had informed Adam that if he went to the cops he would finish him off.

Adam was reluctant to go to the cops for reasons of his own. So he did what any half-sane lunatic would do under such circumstances — he woke up Ernie and Carole at the motel. It was Carole, not Ernie, he was seeking. She had once worked for the AAA, and although that wonderful organization exists to help repair cars, there was a widespread local belief that anyone with such a background (be it clerical) could be trusted with things like a bullet that had gone missing somewhere in Adam's head.

Carole could not find the bullet, and considered the task of removing it slightly beyond her skills. At 4.00 a.m., Adam took some beers to bed, and Ernie contacted his father. John Edwards was no stranger to bullets or wounds or cops, and found his way to the motel, where Adam was adamant he would not go to hospital.

Thereupon, Jerry Edwards, John's brother and Adam's uncle, an extremely competent ironworker and former LAPD officer, was summoned. He brought his tools, and, as Jerry does fine and delicate ironwork, it was hoped that he could remove the offending slug. But even Jerry could not track down the bullet that seemed to have disappeared without leaving an exit wound.

So John went to the police, and negotiated on his son's behalf. When the cops heard the story, they assured John they were more interested in Danny.

Adam was finally taken to hospital, where a lot of surgeons passed on removing the bullet. It was right on the spine, and no one wanted to make the handsome young man a paraplegic. Finally, a young female doctor opened him up and took out the slug. Danny hadn't had the sense to leave the shack, and when the cops arrived three days later, he was found in the possession of chemicals that the police and the courts found to be used in the production of methamphetamine.

"When," I asked Adam, "is he likely to be released?"

Adam stared at his beer. It was a subject that had obviously occupied him.

"Next October."

"With any luck, we should have moved in by then," I said in a carefree tone, while thinking that we had signed an agreement to buy a house at the end of a very lonely road with a psychopathic neighbor who was completing his fifth year in prison. All this to get away from a psychotic neighbor.

From the frying pan of Venice into the fire. Vicky, The Palace barmaid, made a rare appearance, and I ordered a rare whiskey.

10

The next day, I journeyed out to Boulder House to placate Bill, assuring him that after the Christmas delay a check would be in his hands — remembering I had told him the same thing the previous Christmas. I returned to LA. In that tiny prism between Christmas and New Year, a time when no one expects anything to happen, especially in Beverly Hills, the bank called to inform me the boat had come in, and I was free to pay Bill. I turned around and headed straight back to what would be, in a few days, our home. So keen was I to take possession that when I slowed for the sharp turn onto Pipes Canyon Road, a police car managed to catch the speeding Jetta, and I was booked for doing 89 mph in a 55 mph zone.

"But the locals said there were no cops," I told the cop. The cop nodded, and admitted I was unlucky.

Bill was packing. Like almost everyone within fifty miles, he carries a faith in guns that borders on the religious. Bill is hardcore NRA, and proudly showed me his distinguished membership award — a beautiful limited-issue duck decoy that was far too grand to ever grace a stream or a lake. Bill was moving out, and we were moving in, when I noticed seven or eight rifle butts protruding from a blanket on the big cypress bed.

"I see you're right for arms, Bill," I remarked.

"I've moved my guns already," he replied.

"Then what's all that on the bed?" I asked.

"Oh, them," Bill said absently. "Just a few I haven't moved.'

He then recounted the details of his armory. Most of the weapons were rattled off at such pace and with such detail that I merely caught words like magnum, hollow-point, semi-automatic, and the like. I did, however, count, and Bill, I reckoned, owned a total of twenty-one guns. "You expecting royalty?" I inquired.

After a year of nothing happening, the New Year brought an explosion of activity. Just by moving in, I had set off a series of events most people don't experience when buying and taking possession of a new house.

Strangers arrived, bearing gifts.

Tony immediately joined me in renovating, and we were pulling down interior walls when a bearded man — the rule rather than the exception in the desert — arrived to present me with a Dream Catcher. This was a long stick with eagle feathers hanging like scalps, some beads, and a woven net-like device that was supposed to catch dreams. A very useful object indeed, I thought, after the necessary ritual of gift-giving had been observed and I could return to a furious Tony, who seemed to think that being polite to the locals was merely a way to avoid work.

Tony had taken to staying at Boulder House, even though he had a free room at Ernie and Carole's.

"This way," he said ominously, "we can get more work done."

While many of the residents of the High Desert seem committed to the eight-hour week, Tony works because he loves working, and is bewildered by the fact that others suffer work and some abhor it. Tony was further incensed when, an hour later, two prominent local hippies arrived to "cleanse" the house by wandering through it waving burning branches of sage. They then wandered through the property as well, and declared it to have "very good energy," on account of it being situated in a vortex. I wasn't exactly sure what a vortex was, but was prepared to agree with their hypothesis that the bowl-like shape of the land could well have been caused by the crashing of a meteorite many millennia ago.

The cleansing of the house reminded me that the house was more construction site than home, and that I was to be picking up Boo once again and soon. Some physical cleansing was in order.

I had momentarily met a small, pretty, dark-haired girl called Lil Debbie, who had slipped a note into my pocket with an assurance that she was the best house-cleaner in the High Desert.

Lil Debbie arrived with some unusual props: a mop, a quart of vodka, scrubbing brushes, orange juice, 409, and such. But soon, like Tony and me, she was hard at work. Tony has that effect on some. He makes one feel guilty about not working. This is a feeling not shared by Adam, or by most of the locals, but Tony is from Wisconsin, where work as defined by Marx (labor) is looked upon differently than in Southern California, where work is the accumulation of other people's capital.

Although I was the owner, and therefore the boss, Tony had decided that he was the foreman and I was a very junior apprentice. We had spent the day dragging immense boulders onto an old Ford truck I had purchased from, inevitably, Adam

Edwards, driving them across that small part of the property that the truck could manage, and then barrowing them through the house where we laid them in one of the courtyards. It was not pleasant work. The flat "rimrock" boulders all weighed more than 150 pounds. Some weighed over a ton, but Tony had a knack of moving boulders.

It was the laying of the stone that we found the most offensive. We were paving one of the courtyards where Bill had let the dogs go for their ablutions, and as we dug into the decomposed granite dust we were greeted by the smell of twenty years of urine from some of the best Rottweilers ever bred. We employed lime in vast quantities, sixty-pound bag after bag, but it was only when the great rocks were finally cemented into place that the smell passed.

Some of the local handymen made their appearance. These were the work-shy, looking for work. Tony was like a bantam rooster, small but protecting his turf—my turf. This was his job, and none would come between him and work.

I discovered that he lived in a forest in Wisconsin, and that even his father did not know exactly where. Dad, if he needed to contact Tony, would walk into the woods and leave a sign explaining himself. Every winter, when the ground froze in Wisconsin, Tony packed a small bag and headed out to California. No one ever knew when he was coming. He liked to just appear, and surprise them, like an attack of poison ivy. Officially, he stayed at the motel with Carole and Ernie, but took any opportunity that presented itself to sleep outside, preferably on the hardest rock he could find. Sleeping bags were for sissies. When the first signs of summer appeared back up north, Tony would vanish from Pioneertown as quickly and unobtrusively as he had arrived. The trick was to nab him while he was here, and make sure no one else got him.

Gina, a close friend of Tony, and a neighbor of ours, arrived next, bearing a mint-condition 1950s pinball machine as a house-warming gift.

"I couldn't possibly," I protested, plugging it in and watching the scuba-diving motif with attendant mermaids light up and start zinging.

"If you don't want it, I'm taking it to the dump," Gina insisted. "I've wanted the damn thing out of my house for two years."

It was a beautiful machine. A classic. Even Tony paused momentarily to admire its silvery wonder.

"Is he always like this?" I asked Gina. "A maniac?"

"The thing about Tony," she replied, "is we're always pleased to see him arrive, and we're always pleased to see him go again. Not that you actually see Tony arrive. He materializes. Nor does he leave. He disappears."

Gina and Debbie, old friends, were chatting away about a party Gina had attended down in San Bernardino sometime back. What caught my ear was Gina saying that of seventeen women at the party, only she and her boss had not been in jail. Lil Debbie nodded sagely.

Gifts continued to appear. Deeming that we needed better eyes, Krystoff arrived from Poland, via LA, with an excellent set of field glasses made in the old East Germany for use in the defense of Warsaw Pact nations. It seemed odd that a house built with a view to defend itself against forces of the Soviet Union and her allies would be protected in part by an offering from that nation's most important military alliance.

It was 11.00 p.m. when I threatened to call the police. We had been working since the break of a frosty morn, and Tony seemed determined to enter some record book for the longest continued bit of what Australians call "hard yakka" since the forty-eight-hour week had been passed by the House of Commons in the 1800s. I had tried being polite, informing Tony that I was employing him, and therefore could determine when work started and stopped. After all, I was footing the bill. As a journalist I had earned many a friend in the trade union movement, exposing bosses who drove their workers half as hard as I wasn't even trying to drive Tony. There was one weakness in my brilliant scheme to capture Tony and exploit him. It was a simple but unusual dialectic. The boss assumes that the laborer will work for his pay and do his allotted hours. I had stumbled onto a new dialectic the first time I had ever seriously employed someone. That someone, Tony, had no interest in money. He had whatever he needed, and was only interested in work. For work's sake.

Years before, when I was covering the building industry, I had heard whispers of people like Tony, people who liked to work. At first, they were given subtle warnings to the tune of "Get off the fucking site. It's three o'clock." If that didn't work, veiled threats followed, often accompanied by something falling from a crane and landing near the offending member of the workforce. Failing that, the union official would approach the employer and threaten to "pull the lads off the job" if nothing was done. If that didn't fix the matter, and it usually did, there would be a terrible accident, something horrific enough to ensure that word would spread throughout the industry about the perils of pushing oneself and therefore, possibly, one's workmates too hard.

During that very day, we had moved and laid some tons of rocks, and only when I had refused to continue working by flashlight had Tony consented to come into the house. Then he proceeded to launch an all-out assault on some pretty substantial walls that I had suggested, some days before, the house might do without.

Lil Debbie, who had decided it might be best to stay overnight, looked askance as drywall dust flew and walls fell to our hammers and saws. Apart from the occasional cigarette that I stole with Debbie (Tony does not approve of smoking), the only breaks had been to receive guests and presents. I felt that I was being unfaithful, not only to my friends in the trade union movement, but to those who had fought to end slavery. The irony was that I was in charge and was unable, due to my disposition, to allow others to work on my house while I was idle. Finally, I hit on a plan, which I sprung a few moments before midnight.

I laid down my hammer, and pulled the cord from the Sawsall with which Tony was merrily removing a wall. Silence's reign was short. Tony, indignant, turned from his efforts and menaced me with the tool.

"Tony," I said, "I am in charge. This is my property. If you don't stop work, I will call the police."

Debbie looked alarmed.

"My house! We are stopping work. I will call the police," I reiterated.

Lil Debbie didn't like work, but she apparently didn't care much for the police. "They'll think we're on drugs," she protested.

That was a point. It would be unusual indeed for a police officer to be called out by a property owner to escort a worker from the employer's property for refusing to stop work.

"But I am not," was my confident reply.

Tony had dumped his Sawsall and was threatening to leave the site. He headed for the door and his truck, but promised to be back, ready for work, at first light.

11

Not only had Bill built the house around the needs of dogs, but he had fashioned huge runs behind the garages so the Rotts could express themselves by hurling their 100-plus-pound bodies against the hundreds of yards of six-feet-high steel fences. He had also built a small apartment at each end of the garages so that prospective owners could stay near the animals and get to know their individual charge. In fact, Bill so cared for his breeds he made buyers sign contracts that would allow him, at any time, to come to their house to ensure that the dog was being properly trained. If Bill was unhappy with the dogs' circumstances he could, and would, take the animal home via the courts.

But all this was behind him by the end of the twentieth century. Age may have not caught up with Bill, but time, or the times, had. Although people from all over the US would spend large sums of money on his award-winning Rotts, more and more failed to treat the huge beasts according to Bill's iron laws. A well-trained Rott is as safe, perhaps safer, than any dog, but a poorly treated one was both an insult to Bill's Herculean efforts at producing the finest Rottweilers in the land and an extremely unsafe creature to have around the home. Bill cared for both his dogs and his reputation, and had reached the conclusion that he could no longer trust people with his babies. The poor treatment of Rotts and other potentially dangerous dogs had led to so many attacks on people that most insurance companies no longer insured households with Rotts, Dobermans, or pit bulls. Bill had ceased to breed them some years before we met, and had been trying, reluctantly, to sell Boulder House since making that decision.

The problems attendant to buying a house built for dogs that came with hundreds of yards of fenced dog runs, all cemented in place, had clearly deterred wiser men than me.

Neither Boo nor I had the skills or the desire to go into the breeding business, especially if people could not be trusted with the end product.

We had agreed that the runs had to go, and be replaced by a cactus garden. But cactus costs. I had, in an advanced state of delusion, imagined we might grow agave, distill the hearts and make tequila, and had mentioned this in passing to Tony, who preferred the extremely unpleasant task of working with cactus to the merely unpleasant task of laying rock into urine-infested, decomposed granite. A fully grown agave cost more than $100, and I would need acres to go into tequila production.

The next day, Tony was blessedly late, and I lay in the huge waterbed, recalling falling asleep beneath the brilliant stars I could see through the skylight above the bed. I savored the luxury for more than an hour until I heard the unmistakable deep thudding of Tony's truck muffler, and rose.

I knew Tony was a cactus freak, but did not know he was familiar with pretty much every cactus within forty miles. He had arrived with a deal.

"Come on," he said, indicating the front seat. "We are going to see The Lizard Lady."

I had heard talk of The Lizard Lady, and knew she was an odd soul (who out here wasn't?) who lived with iguanas and slept with her favorite. From what I knew of iguanas (almost nothing), they might be related to the Australian goanna, a particularly ferocious lizard, who you would no more sleep with than the Bush twins.

Tony had no interest in lizards, but explained that he had located a considerable amount of agave at the Lizard Lady's home, positioned atop a nearby mesa. The Lizard Lady, Tony informed me, had a dog problem. Her animals had taken to roaming, and needed to be enclosed before they were hit by cars, joined a pack of wild dogs and got shot, attacked someone who would sue, or a combination of the above. The Lizard Lady needed fencing, and was prepared to swap our dog-run fences for agave.

I was impressed, but wondered if things weren't moving a little fast. The tequila venture was no more than an idea. Now I was about to be committed to a dramatic, and I knew fantastically difficult, enterprise without thinking it properly through.

Tony had no such reservation, and would not be deterred. We pulled into a yard, and his truck was immediately surrounded by baying hounds of every type. The Lizard Lady came out in her dressing-gown, sporting a huge bandage on her forearm — the result, she explained, of a misunderstanding with her bedfellow, her newest iguana, Elizabeth, a male.

She hadn't always been so relaxed around lizards. At first, she explained, she was scared to death of them — even tiny, little ones. Her daughter had bought the first of these ghastly reptiles home, and had chased her around the kitchen with it. Then it became ill, and the daughter had to go away, leaving her with a sick iguana. She bonded with it and kept it close until they shared the bed. In these comfortable confines it grew. And grew. Now it was five feet long. Other lizards (all iguanas) found their way to her house out in the windswept flats on the other side of Old Woman's Springs Road, deposited there by lizard lovers who heard she would care for them. By the time I met her and her flock — what does one call a collection of iguanas? — they had taken to sleeping with her, and her boyfriend had taken to the couch. I would have moved to Italy.

To look mean and ferocious, these huge, scaly primitives puff themselves up, apparently in the belief they are not ugly and frightening enough. That might have been necessary when the giant sloth, the mastodon, and the hairy mammoth walked these lands, but seemed unnecessary in the presence of me — and even Tony. Bubba, her favorite, is about sixty years old. She takes him for walks on a harness. Elizabeth — the male — is the biter. And bite her he did. Hours of microsurgery were needed to get the tendons reattached, followed by six weeks in a cast.

Sean, a Palace regular, recalls waking up in the Lizard Lady's bed one morning to find Bubba stretched out on him, savoring his warmth. I asked him what lizard breath smelled like.

"Pretty bad," he said. "Like rotting vegetables."

While Tony looked restless, determined to commence work, I inquired after her hand, and she removed the bandage. The bite was horrible and, although a few weeks old, still a sight. The effect was strangely lizard-like. That is, the Lizard Lady's arm looked like part of a lizard. In fact, in the same way that members of the British royal family have come to resemble horses, the

Lizard Lady resembled the prehistoric beasts in her care. Was this what Blake meant when he observed that we "become what we perceive"?

But she took us into the house, and offered us beers while introducing us to her large family of lizards. One, the biter, was enjoying the warmth of her bed while his mates were lazing around a house that had accumulated strange objects over many years—the type of things one would expect to find in a Lizard Lady's home.

The formalities of meeting these four- to five-foot creatures from the age of dinosaurs over, we returned to the yards and the agave.

Perhaps thirty years ago, when the house was built, the owner had planted agave under the windows so that when they grew no one would try to gain entry, as nothing on earth is worth climbing over agave spikes to attain. The plants, perched against the house, enjoyed both direct sunlight and light refracted from the white walls, and had prospered. There were five windows and five clumps, and each clump consisted of twenty or so plants. The main plants were all over five foot, and many of the lesser plants above four. I had done a little research, and knew that the plants over four feet tall could be harvested, their pineapple-like hearts cut out and distilled, and, hey presto, "tequilas all round".

A man, woken by our presence, came from the house blinking in the bright light. This was Dan the Lizard Lady's man, and in his hand rested a beer can. The can was Milwaukee Best, a cheap drop, but not necessarily any worse than Bud or Coors, and certainly preferable to Michelob. The Lizard Lady explained that Dan would be erecting the fence when we brought it over, and he didn't seem enthused by this development.

Tony was tiring of all this standing around, and looked menacingly at the huge agaves.

"We had better get started," he stated.

"Now?" I exclaimed.

Twenty minutes ago, I had been tucked up in bed contemplating my contemplation of the galaxy the previous evening, and now I faced the ferocious spikes of one of the kings of the cactus family.

"Now!" Tony scolded. He went to the truck and removed sundry objects, spades, a long machete-like knife, hand saws, and other objects I didn't feel like holding, let alone using. But Tony threw himself amongst the spikes, and soon the two of us were digging, cutting, and tearing at the plants.

Though winter, the late-morning sun was strong, and would get stronger, especially in this unshaded spot up against the house, which beat the heat back at us. In deference to the spikes and the thousands of insects, spiders, and scorpions that were furiously swarming from their ancient nests, I suggested we obtain gloves at the hardware store. Tony clearly considered this a cowardly piece of time-wasting, and informed me that gloves were useless when dealing with cactus, as the spikes pierced the toughest leather. Good news for my hands, I thought.

Most, but not all, cactus can be removed from the earth without injury by dragging them by their roots. Agave, growing singularly, can be dug up, and when the roots are exposed, picked up and bundled, with great difficulty and care, into a truck bed. But when they have clumped, with twenty growing from the same single plant, their roots intertwined and home to vicious crawling things, the task is decidedly more difficult.

One cuts, digs, drags, claws, and tears, and inevitably is spiked. The first three spikes entered my right arm, the one most used in such endeavors, within ten minutes. The pain was erased by numbness, and soon the arm was both swollen and useless. I was drenched in sweat, and covered in dirt and bites, but we had managed to fill half the truck with smaller agave taken from the outside of the core plants. Tony hacked away at the clinging roots, informing me that there was virtually no way to kill a cactus, especially an agave. This came as a disappointment, as I had already developed a hatred of the things, and was wondering whether all the tequila in Mexico was worth the effort.

Tony, perhaps aware of my misgivings, stood and stared furiously at the mother of all agave that stood before us.

"You take that side," he suggested. Tony apparently intended to start the serious part of our work immediately, regardless of my condition. "We will need digging bars," he added, heading for the truck.

And need them we did.

By the time my left arm was rendered inoperable, the giant agave was loose but still *in situ*. Tony suggested that while he prised the thing from the dirt, with which it had coexisted for so long, I use my boots to push it out of its nest.

"Your legs are stronger that your arms," he remarked. We had been hosing the soil as we worked to soften it, and so I sat down in the mud, and we prised and dug and kicked and strained until the agave gave up its hold, and rolled onto its side in defeat.

"Gotcha!" I lay panting proudly beside the plant, savoring the victory.

"We will need a ramp to get it on the truck," observed Tony. He went off looking for a suitable plank, leaving me to contemplate that the job was far from done. By the time I got to my muddy feet, Tony had found his plank and positioned it at the back of the truck. Cactus is mostly water, and he rolled this one, which must have weighed in at 350 pounds, to the base of the plank, coaxing, dragging, and pushing it into place. All that remained was to push the thing up the plank and onto the bed of the elderly Ford and drive it home, dig a hole in the granite, and roll it off the truck and into its new home. We had planted twenty agave by sunset. But the torture, I believed in my folly, had at least passed. Tony looked pleased.

"Tomorrow we will get some really big ones," he exclaimed. "I know where there are a lot more. Some of them can be vicious, so we'll have to be careful."

12

The desert is so hard, its occupants have to be harder. If it doesn't scratch, bite, or sting, it should be somewhere else. That's a fair call when describing the human inhabitants, but was directed by John Edwards at the fauna and flora. Aside from the people, almost everything — plant and animal — can and does kill or inflict pain.

The toughest of all life forms is, of course, the cactus, and the toughest and most unpleasant of the cactus are the various members of the cholla family, a family that is nature's version of The Mob. The common cholla, or Jumping Cholla, is an ugly plant that produces little but spikes. In the spring it manages a small green flower, but, as cactus flowers go, it lacks luster. Other cacti, even other members of The Mob, strive to justify their existence by offering beauty for a few weeks in spring, but the Jumping Cholla has its reputation to defend, and does not err on the side of beauty. Even the animals of the desert shun the plant, except goats, which will enter a cholla patch and graze on the blooms. But goats are notoriously stupid animals, prone to stink, and their value is principally their ability to eat things that are spurned by the rest of the food chain.

The cholla has a few uses—all defensive. Humans will climb over walls, no matter how high they might be, ignoring spikes and broken glass. But a cholla, even more than agave, is a barrier that only the most foolhardy will try to negotiate. The desert is full of stories of those who have tested their talents against this terrible, ugly curse.

We live near Anza-Borrego, the largest wilderness area in California, which is probably the cradle of evolution for what we now call the goat. Horses, camels, and llamas definitely evolved in this wasteland, but as the climate changed from temperate to blinding heat, they had the good sense to migrate over the land bridge to the steppes of Russia and parts further abroad. The llama fled to Central and Southern America. Millions of years later, the Spanish reintroduced the horse, to the alarm of the locals.

But the cholla, not being fleet of foot, stayed. As the land grew harsher, so did the plant.

My first experience with it occurred in Anza-Borrego, about fifty miles south of where we are located in Pipes Canyon.

Anza-Borrego is terrain that makes Death Valley look like rural England before foot-and-mouth—an arid area of little commercial use, and therefore preserved. It is as it is because the Colorado River once ran through it, and deposited the immense wash from what is known as the Grand Canyon in this dramatic and fearful terrain.

The good folks who tend to our national parks have erected warning signs for those who are foolhardy enough to traverse the place. The first, I noticed, stated in plain English (and in Spanish) that death by dehydration lurked in the arid land we were about to enter. Temperatures on the desert floor, it informed us, could reach 180 degrees in mid-afternoon, during mid-summer. Which was exactly when we entered this forbidding place.

The other dangers were the usual ones, such as snakes, scorpions, and flash floods. Rain in the nearby mountains can fill the immense network of gullies and tear through the land in minutes. As it is impossible to know that storms have hit the mountains, we were told to be wary of the possibility of thirty feet of water arriving in a boiling crest. The only warning of the imminent arrival of the wall of water is a white froth seeping from the soil. The racing tide beyond forces moisture from the soil, and the bubbles give the wary a few seconds' notice and a slim chance of finding high ground before the wave, carrying with it boulders and tree trunks, hits.

Boo and I approached our sojourn into the badlands with caution forewarned, we thought, of the desert's dangers. One merely had to keep water at hand and stay on high ground.

Before we had traversed a mile in the withering heat, I discovered another danger. It was one that the appropriate department had failed to warn us of: the Jumping Cholla. The creature sprung at me over a foot, and a sizeable portion attached itself to my leg, screwing its way through my jeans, and deep into the inside of my left calf.

Amazement was quickly followed by pain. Pain by a kind of panic. The clump had attached itself firmly and was, I felt, digging in. Digging into my skin.

The first reaction to a cholla attack is to grab the cursed clump as it screws its way deeper into the flesh. It is, as are most first reactions, exactly the wrong thing to do, being just what the cholla expects. The hands of the uninitiated are rendered inoperable as the cactus gives up its outside claws. My fingers were immediately thick with treacherous barbs while the clump on my leg sank its teeth deeper into my calf.

I had somehow left my knife in the car, a way off, so I asked Boo to find me a suitable stick as I tried to pull the barbs from my hand. After a few minutes of prising, I managed to remove the main clump and hurried away from it, fearing that it might strike again. A dog was crying nearby. It, too, had been attacked, and had tried to remove the barbs with its teeth. Its mouth was full of spikes. We tried to give it and its owner comfort, but my leg was swelling fast. I pulled up my jeans, and discovered a psychedelic pattern swirling up my calf.

This was all a bit disconcerting, and was to get more so. I began to feel dizzy as we made our way back to the car. When we reached it, my leg was so swollen that my jeans were stuck above the knee, under which extended an increasingly bloated, brilliant calf. It was so bad I allowed Boo to drive. She found a bar in this godforsaken stretch of untempered ugliness, and I staggered into it, dragging my horrible leg. The assembly was sympathetic, and delighted that something had happened to enliven their day. They explained that I was a victim of Jumping Cholla, going so far as to point out that the bar itself was called "THE JUMPING CHOLLA", something we had not detected in our haste. One chap was kind enough to offer me a T-shirt advertising the bar and its famous barb, but little useful advice was forthcoming.

"Kerosene is best. Rub some kerosene on it," suggested the barman.

It was one of those rare days when we had ventured out sans kero, so I inquired whether there was any on hand. There wasn't. "Beer might help," a customer suggested in a forlorn tone.

I took him at his word, and drank two. Even in this dark place, it was evident that my calf was continuing to grow and to increasingly resemble an album cover from the late sixties. We were due to return to LA that day, so we departed henceforth. By the evening the fever had passed, though the swelling remained for a few embarrassing days while I waited to remove the wranglers.

I was luckier than many others.

The Jumping Cholla has, since the horse, camel, and the llama fled, developed an ability to detect the movement of humans and other animals, and to spring its barbs upon the unfortunate passer-by. This is how the ghastly things procreate. In the furious heat of mid- and late summer, the white spikes, which grow to half an inch, become so dry that clumps become electrified with tension. The clumps can detect the passing of a creature from its reverberations in the dirt, and, like a science-fiction monster, detect the exact position of the passer-by. With unnerving accuracy, the plant slings a portion at him.

Men have been known to ride (on horses and, more recently, motorcycles) into cholla country, and not come back, nor go on. A skittish horse sees a rattler, throws the rider, who lands in a cholla bush and stays there until he forms a skeleton. Even the buzzards will leave the flesh from fear of the cholla. Down the road a few miles from Boulder House in Yucca Valley is a stand of cholla so thick and tall that no contractor would agree to remove it, even though the cleared land would have had some value.

There are trails through the Cholla Park that were once popular with motorcycle riders. Then, a few years back, a biker, traveling at a good pace, lost it (the bike) on a bump, while racing though the forest of silent killers. The unfortunate man went sailing some twenty feet into the middle of a cholla thicket. Some of the cactus stands ten feet tall, and the poor chap landed in the gentle caresses of a giant Jumping Cholla cactus.

In this case, the cholla had not jumped, and the plant could be excused for assuming it had been jumped at. The cholla took the assault poorly, and as the man struggled to get free, clutched him more tightly. Help, attracted by the unfortunate man's screams, arrived, but it was no help at all. No one could penetrate the thicket to get to the man, who stopped screaming after five or so hours. That was when the helicopter failed to rescue him. Bulldozers were brought to the scene, and some argue they are what killed the hapless biker by pushing the cactus deeper into his person. If so, they did the man a favor. He might otherwise have remained crucified on the cactus and alive for days.

The poor chap died after about seven hours. The cholla has the embrace of someone only embraced every few centuries. It doesn't like to let go. It is the most thoroughly obnoxious of all the plants and animals on earth, and I hope one day to rid the Boulder House property of the giants that grow by the gates.

More likely, I will get Tony to move one that has grown too heavy to support itself, and has collapsed down where the dark water line has broken, causing them to grown so thick and tall they fall over. We might move it to a gap in the fence that introduces one to Boulder House, and so plug it. Might. I also might continue to ignore the monsters. The dogs are learning to do just that. The one that fell continues to grow from its new angle, and thrusts its deadly spikes towards the sun, as dangerous as ever.

There are, of course, uses for even this most despicable example of God's handiwork. They are said to have healing qualities. They certainly have the opposite. Our friend and builder, Crinkly Jim, if he loses a cat or a dog, or, for that matter, a friend, buries his acquaintance with cholla dispersed through the dirt. No animal, not even a goat, will battle through cholla to chew on the dead. Hunted Apache braves were known to tie a leather strip between two good-sized cholla plants so the pursuer, usually a white man on a horse, would drag the fearsome creations down upon him, or him and his horse, or both. Either way, the pursuit would cease.

13

The week after we moved the agave, I repaired to bed with a savage chest infection playing havoc with my asthma, or vice versa. The infection was, I reckoned, the result of tearing out insulation black with mildew where water had traveled through the roof and into the room next to the swimming pool, which we were attempting to convert into a guesthouse.

I had been warned about the quality of health care in the surrounds, and advised, when possible, to seek self-medication. This is a common approach to matters concerning wellbeing and I had, in the early stages of the illness, driven to a local feedlot and purchased some antibiotics, claiming Sailor, our new springer spaniel, had my infection. I must have looked ill, and the man in the feedlot summed up the situation briskly. If such a problem occurred with "his dog", he confided, he would recommend Amoxicillin. The good man proceeded to count out one hundred 250-milligram tablets, emphasizing that if it were "his dog", he would provide two capsules in the morning and two at night.

I was somewhat concerned when reading the antibiotic instructions to discover that the cure at hand was for the treatment of infections to the gills of fish. I figured that as my infection was about where my gills would be — had my forebears not struggled from the primeval ooze and cast their gills aside in favor of lungs — this stuff might do the trick. And I was happy in the knowledge that I had saved $70 on a trip to the doctor and a good $50 at the druggist (the one hundred antibiotics costing a mere $29). So I let the battle for control of my breathing apparatus take its course, which finally resulted in victory for the dog or the fish.

The upside of being sick nigh to death and sleeping fitfully, if at all, was being awake when the gray of dawn began pushing the blackness of night out to the Pacific.

The first streams of sunlight hit the very top of the mountains twenty miles to the west. The gold light quickly drives the dark into the valley, and the band of light, high and wide, turns the world into a great golden band above the absolute blackness that awaits the sun's cheer. For a few moments, when the snow is fresh and heavy up high, the early morning light touches the pure white and mingles it with golden rays, creating a jeweled effect that lasts ten minutes.

When the sun finds enough height to peer down on the pines, and the mountains turn a bluish green, the white of the snow recedes, and the valley begins to feel the rays and starts to shine. During the day the sun falls evenly, and the definition of the ranges is washed out until it is well into its descent. Then the ranges and peaks are outlined from behind and seem to stretch forever, range after range, higher and higher, sharp even in the light haze that appears most evenings. It reminds me of an old record cover, the album being, I think, *Pipers at the Gates of Dawn*, though in this case it should be dusk — which doesn't sound nearly as good.

The granite dominates the day. When the sun is high, and even when the moon is at its fullest, the pink stone with its many mossy mottles is master of its world, and dominates the perspective. That and the vegetation which, except where the dirt roads form their lines, seems to cover the earth like a green fur.

Closer up, and especially in the higher land by Boulder House, the appearance of uniformity gives way to a never-ending display of difference.

The trees, except for the yucca, which is a member of the lily family, are sparse. Pinyon pine, scrub oak, mesquite, and the silvery-green mountain mahogany grow where there is water close to the earth's surface. Few grow high. We have oak and pine that stand above sixty feet, but only because cliffs provide them with run-off and protection from the harsher winds and the hottest sun. The ancient twisted and gnarly junipers with their gray berries — eat one a day for good health, say the locals — are reputed to be older than Christ. At least older than Christ would be if he was still with us.

The washes are poor relatives of the High Desert. Few stop to admire them, and as they will carry the flooding rains, they are also feared. Dreary, full of sand, and treacherous.

But during the last hour of the sun, the washes tear off their homely apparel and become as pretty as the girl next door. When the sun stops staring down on the white sand and bends its devotion elsewhere, the washes come alive with life and color.

Because the topography is so diverse, the range of shades and colors is constantly changing with the movement of the sun, which, for at least three hundred days a year, shines above. Mostly the only cloud cover comes from the vapors of the F18s, F16s, and F14 Hornets from the nearby (by desert standards) US marine and air force bases. The yuccas, the creosote, and the gamma grass are far enough below us to take the appearance of an immense meadow, depending on the direction of the sun. In the afternoons, the mountain ranges appear misty in the sun's refracted light, while in the mornings they are distinct and bright. Yet the light never totally washes out, no matter how hot and direct the sun, because the range of colors—black and brown on the buttes, green below, white in the washes, and pink where the granite imposes itself—provides such stark differences.

14

Not long after my recovery, I began to see — if that's the word — a gentleman, Ed Gibson, who lives about a mile from Boulder House as the crow flies, and not much more by road and rut. Soon, when I entered The Club or the bowling alley, I would head straight for Ed if he was in evidence at the bar.

In a world where cowboys, hippies, and 'necks fuse, Ed is king of the kids. Almost the father to a valley desperately in need of fathers. There is absolutely nothing phony about the man. His cowboy hat sits upon gray locks that hang almost to his waist, as though it was placed there at birth. His white walrus moustache is as full as any man's, in a world where such facial accompaniments border on the compulsory. Sitting next to him, one could be sitting next to Buffalo Bill. Or John Wesley Harding. He looks like a gentleman rancher who started as a cowboy and made his way to the top. Which, in a modern sense, he did. He looks good in suspenders, but being a cautious man wears a belt as well. At nearly seventy, he is good-looking, and his style attracts the glances of women thirty years his younger. He probably gets more stares from tourists than all the other wild-looking types, and is so much like the person you expect to see in the Wild West that you have to look again.

Ed worked for many a long year in the energy business before our utilities became criminal conspiracies. He had traveled America as a linesman, and had come, before his retirement, to understand how the giant power plants work—an achievement apparently yet to be matched by Governor Davis, or, to my reading, the *Los Angeles Times*. Or, for that matter, me. In the course of his work he had strained the muscles in his right hand to the point where two of his fingers were permanently frozen, as it were, to the palm of his hand. Frozen they may be, but at least they are still attached to his hand, unlike so many residents of the High Desert. Many handshakes involve grasping one finger, or perhaps two, and the remaining stumps.

The cause of my bonding with Ed was initially the cause of International Labor. His union, the International Brotherhood of Electrical Workers had been good to Ed, and he retired at a level of comfort few working men enjoy. But Ed was as comfortable with the International Brotherhood of Electrical Workers as he was with the International Brotherhood of Love, the organization established in the mid-sixties to promote, amongst other things, the evangelical movement to distribute LSD. His travels had taken him to many of the right places at the right times, and he had been fortunate enough to happen to be working up around Big Sur when the hippie movement was in its salad days. Ed became a crossover redneck. Naturally intelligent, he embraced flower power and, more literally, women, while keeping the state's electrical power running. Ed straddled the two worlds, and their women.

The first few times I ran into him at The Palace he was gruff. People who handle enough electricity to power cities, who hang from poles high above the earth, and have seen friends turned into cinders, have a right to a certain gruffness. I doubt anyone would describe me as gruff—at least no one has to date—and in style we were most dissimilar.

But our shared history of organized labor united us, and soon Ed was bringing his monthly union journal to The Palace and slipping it, somewhat surreptitiously, I thought, to me.

There is something comforting about the papers that unions publish. At one stage in my life I would arrive at a desk in the Labor Council building in Sydney, and scour them, looking for something that could be turned into a story for the national press. The union tabloids no longer arrive at my desk, but when Ed slips me his copy I feel a link to a world I will never be part of again. It's a world, for all its warts, I have loved. A world where men with sticks stand side by side before the guns of the cops and the dogs, and sometimes the armed forces. A lost world.

I was honored to be invited to Ed's home, which is situated at, or about, the convergence of Roadrunner Rut—itself more a river during rain, and definitely little but a dusty rut in the long summer—and Coyote Road. Here Ed lives amongst his guns and knives, his collectibles, and his memories. He likes to sit at his bar, pouring Gentleman Jack, one of the better bourbons, reflecting on labor history, the international order, national politics and the economy, and the crooks who have taken over the country.

We sat amongst the guns and knives and whips (ones suitable for driving cattle), sipping the proud bourbon and discussing the market. Once, in an extravagant mood, I told Ed I thought there was a great big bear out there. An ugly, stinking bear worse than any that prowled the mountains above us three hundred years ago. I predicted that the Great Bear would soon be upon us. Ed nodded, sipped. Enough said. Ed is not the sort of man to invite a neighbor over to discuss his financial future, and the conversation moved to the familiar themes of the past. Of memories Ed did not want taken, unheard and unknown, to the grave. Most people in the High Desert think of bears as real, live animals, creatures that can be and are seen. Ed knows of the other bears, the bears of Wall Street's imagination.

A superb listener and a determined talker, Ed has found that happy convergence where one respects the rights of another to hold the fort of conversation if they will yield equal time. This is not the norm in Southern California.

Of late, he is inclined to intimations of mortality, and this depresses me greatly.

"Seventy ain't old, Ed," I say when his thoughts turn to Old Man Time. Ed looks a bit like Old Man Time.

"Ninety is old," I add.

Ed lets the matter rest. But something in his eyes reminds me that almost seventy years for a working man who has pushed his body hard at work and play is a long time. It scares me, this thought. Without Ed, I would have no deep male soulmate in the High Desert—just a lot of mates.

The conversation turns to the heartier topic of the expected arrival of Danny, the little Indian, and Adam's shooter, who is soon to return from jail to the cottage closest to Boulder House.

"You still don't have a gun, do you?" Ed inquires on one visit.

"Nope," I reply in half-hearted defiance. I have long worn the absence of a gun in the house as a badge of honor. To my knowledge, ours is the only household bereft of guns within ten miles. But a violent criminal would soon be very near our property. The prospect was vexing.

"Would you like one?" Ed inquired whimsically.

"Well," I started, then stop, remembering the nights when I lay awake and pondered our vulnerability, convincing myself that my concern was for Boo or Sailor, that I was not getting armed because a half-crazed criminal with marked recidivist tendencies and an apparent collection of like-minded men and women who made their trade in the manufacture and sale of "ice" were about to descend upon our happy haven.

"I suppose I would, I guess."

Ed rose slowly.

A few minutes later, he returned carrying a very large and powerful shotgun: a long-barreled 12-gauge Remington Magnum 87. I almost blanched as I took control of a weapon more than half my size. I had shot the same model at Adam's a few months before, and almost lost my shoulder. I remember Adam saying a slug from this creature could pass through the block of an old Chevy truck. I also remembered the bruises to the shoulder. Adam's shoulder was black, and he was more than familiar with such weaponry. But Adam had bruises on his bruises.

"Got any ammo?" I wondered out loud.

"Not for you. You will have to get that yourself."

I lugged the thing out to the car and drove it home.

Ed is the titular head and co-founder of "DILLIGAF" an organization that has no head. DILLIGAF (Does It Look Like I Give A Fuck) is a collection of some fifty men and women who meet at The Palace around three on Friday afternoon, and about the same time on the Christian Sabbath. The women have seen fire and rain, and some have ridden behind men whose jackets carried the Death's Head.

In the absence of a police force, matters of import, such as they are, are attended to by the DILLIGAF, the motley band that Boo and I had first observed when we entered that establishment on our first visit to Pioneertown.

Though it is one of the most informal organizations on earth, its roots lie in better-known company — that of the Hells Angels. At one time, The Palace and Pioneertown itself were controlled by the "Red and White", as the Angels are known to insiders. At the mention of DILLIGAF's antecedents, Ed and other prominent members of The Club turn particularly reticent, muttering things about "those days" and giving one every reason to believe that in a distant time they had what people out here call "connections".

Here I have to be pretty careful and not too specific, for the dead are many. When Pioneertown was a movie town, it boasted two bar-restaurant-bloodhouses. One was the Golden Stallion, presumably named in honor of Trigger, who was actually white, but perhaps Roy was reticent about the place being called The White Palomino. The other was the Red Dog. As we have learnt, a tit-for-tat burning, rebuilding, and re-burning finally left no trace of the Golden Stallion, and the Red Dog fell into decline.

Back then, The Palace was a gas station, but one with a license to sell beer. It was purchased in the early sixties by Frances, then a heart-stopping strawberry blonde who took advantage of the absence of a proper drinking hole, and turned the gas station into a bar. Thus the concrete floors, which once housed petrol pumps. Frances had "connections" with the "Red and White", and the place was ideally suited for weekend runs for two of the nation's largest Hells Angels chapters — Barstow and San Bernardino — both a couple of hours' ride from town.

It was decreed that what we now call The Palace be neutral. Outlaws from any club were welcome as long as the internecine warfare between clubs stopped at the doors. Outside those doors, anything went, and at times men bled to death in the dirt a few yards from the bar.

But Frances and her powerfully built husband, John, kept order within the premises, and as the years passed it developed a reputation for being as peaceful a place as one could expect, given the clientele. Frances's daughter Harriet had been a beauty and something of a sexy singing sensation in LA and Vegas in the sixties and seventies. She had toured Vietnam extensively with her burly husband, Pappy, but her public career was drawing to a close as the years passed, and Frances, starting to get on in time, thought it was time to hand over the reins.

Harriet and Pappy became the new owners of the cantina. They renamed it Pappy and Harriet's Pioneertown Palace. But the outlaw image frightened the respectable citizens who were slowly discovering Pioneertown, and so a deal was cut. The gangs collectively agreed not to come to town, at least in their colors. As the years passed, so did the outlaw bikers, and though they still make appearances, only those with a skillful eye can detect a current, fully fledged Hell's Angel. If, for instance, a wild-looking tattooed bunch arrives wearing T-shirts that read "If it don't look right — start a fight — and support your local Red and White", it is fair to assume one is dealing with the real thing.

Ed scoffs at any suggestion he was a Hells Angel, but admits that he rode with the gang, and remains in contact with the former president of one of its US chapters. He rode with another outlaw gang called The Nuggets, a gang out of Anaheim.

"We were affiliated with the Hells Angels, but all gangs are. The Angels make the rules of the whole organization."

I was surprised. All my journalistic life I had assumed, when I wrote the phrase "rival outlaw gangs"—a not-uncommon journalistic expression—that the gangs were in fact rivals.

Mike Bristow, a senior DILLIGAF man (women make up almost half the organization), did concede that formal "connections" exist—and he informed me that it was okay to have a DILLIGAF badge sewn on your jacket, as "the Red and White gave us permission".

"Only," Mike added, "if we do not use their colors."

Thus the DILLIGAF patch I wear, on my hat, is black and white, and I wear it partly because it shows an attachment to the old industrial society and the kind of solidarity that once expressed itself in the trade union movement. But it is the least formal of organizations. When I learnt of its existence, I asked Buzz Gamble, a long-time member, how one joined. Buzz replied that I was already a member. The ethos seems to be that of Our Lord's: "When two or three are gathered together in my name—there am I in the midst."

Buzz never rode with a gang. Buzz was more a one-man gang bent on a course of destruction. "Give me three of him, and I could destroy the world" might well have literally been inspired by Buzz's life of astonishing criminality.

Buzz began his crime-and-dope spree having been "honorably discharged" from the army, a fact which itself suggests that reform of the institution was greatly needed thirty years ago.

He attended every jail in Texas, but based his early curriculum at Huntsville, and as he talks about the place, one pays quiet tribute to the makers of the film *Cool Hand Luke*.

Buzz can't just sing. He can act. His whole life has been one great Shakespearean folly. Folly, but not all fun. With a few people around him, Buzz's stories will take you to the places that wise men try hard to avoid. And just as when he sings I can close my eyes and believe it's Ray Charles, so when he tells his tales, he takes his audience into his world.

One Friday afternoon, the DILLIGAF has gathered at The Palace for its get-together, and Buzz is holding center stage — his favorite and rightful place.

Survival in jail requires skills, and one of the fundamental skills in a world where boredom is punctuated by brutality is storytelling. Buzz has had a lot of practice. The DILLIGAF have all heard the story before, but they lean forward, eager to hear it one more time.

Buzz is on a road gang, hoeing weeds from the roadways with his colleagues. THE MAN, straddling a horse, watches the crew through the sort of sunglasses associated with Latin American despots. The guard is nursing a rifle and wearing a pistol, and he's bored.

"Gamble," he shouts, "you take a run. I'll give you half an hour."

"No, Boss man," Buzz replies. "I ain't runnin, Boss man."

"Gamble, I'll give you an hour. You can move a long way in an hour."

You listen to Buzz, you close your eyes, and you hear James Lee Burke.

But Buzz knows he can never escape. The Boss man and his good ole boys will get their guns and dogs, hunt him down, chase him up a tree, and "shoot his ass".

"You can't escape from a Texas jail," Buzz explains. "You can escape from one, but only to enter the grounds of another."

Prisons like Huntsville were always an extension of the slave system, but whites were allowed to join. In the Civil War, one and a half million yards of cloth were produced at Huntsville in a single year. The cloth was desperately needed by the increasingly ragged Confederate Army, but little of it ever reached them.

Huntsville, Buzz recounts, is just part of a vast prison system that is distinguished only by the fact that "It's where the chamber is."

The white, black, and Latino inmates were totally segregated, and the inmates work long and hard. The cotton planted during the Civil War is still picked, and it's processed at the jail's textile mill.

"Everything you eat, everything you wear, the mattress you sleep on, the pork, the meat, the vegetables, it's all produced here—nothing comes into Huntsville 'cept prisoners. And no one escapes, not for long."

Texas tired of Buzz, and he of Texas. The authorities indicated he should take his one-man crime spree to sunny California, otherwise the consequences would prove fatal. He moved to California to get away from the cycle of dope and jail, but things came horribly unstuck.

He talked his way into running a bar in Salinas, and booked country and Western singer Johnny Paycheck, writer and singer of the redneck international anthem "Take This Job and Shove It" to perform.

"All Johnny asked for was some money, a fifth of Jack, some pills, and a young girl," Buzz recounted.

"I got him the Jack and the pills, but couldn't manage the girl. After the show, I got to drinking with Johnny, my half-brother, and his real brother, and we drank and drank and drank until about four in the morning. I was counting the money while we drank. I stuck $1,800 in a money belt and put it on."

Buzz had a '69 Dodge Charger with a transmission that slipped so bad he had to get it up to about 4,000 rpm to get it moving at all. He was on his way home to his wife, who lived in a trailer park. He hadn't seen her for a few weeks, and needed to smooth things over. But he was hungry, and the only thing open was a Winchell's Donut House with a Wally Cox–type guy behind the counter. He was about five foot one, and had thick glasses. Buzz asked for three plain glazed donuts.

"He looked at me and said, 'Three plain glazed donuts. That's it?'

"I said, 'Yeah. I want three plain glazed donuts.'

"He said, 'You're a real big spender. Real Diamond Jim Brady.'

"I said, 'What did you say?'

"He said, 'You really gonna spend some real money. Three plain glazed donuts.'"

Buzz was particularly irritated. He was carrying $1,800, and some four-eyed geek was sneering at him for being cheap. But he also had, stuck down the back of his pants, the great equalizer — a nine-millimeter Beretta.

Buzz asked the donut man to "Repeat that, please."

He said, "Yeah. You're a real big spender."

"I pulled the pistol out, cocked it, and stuck it in his face. I said, 'See all those donuts you got out there?'"

Buzz waved his Beretta at the next day's donut supplies. And the man, much humbled, replied, "Yes, sir!"

"Load em in my car."

"What are you talking about?"

"I said, 'Load the fuckin donuts.'"

The only thing disturbing the tiny mall that night was a vacuum-cleaning truck, which circled about the parking lot sucking up a day's trash. The man in the truck watched in wonder as the donut man carried box after box of donuts out to the car. Buzz, who had assumed a firing stance, with both hands clasped around the Beretta, followed the donut man's movements.

"I made him fill up the entire car with donuts — until there was just enough room for me to get in and drive.

"We went back into the store, and he says, "What about the money — aren't you going to take the money?'

"I said, 'Fuck the money.'

"Then I shot the cash register and blew it sky high, and told him to lie on the floor."

Buzz squeezed in amongst the donuts, started the Charger, revved it to the required 4,000 rpm, and screeched away at almost five miles an hour. The little electric truck took chase. It was probably the only getaway car ever to be chased by a vacuum truck. Buzz made it to the highway, and finally to the trailer park and into the arms of his wife.

But the vacuum man had his license plate.

The smell of donuts that had spent the day in the sun greeted him as the amazed rocker opened the door of his Charger the following afternoon. Buzz, with no memory of his drink-fuelled exploit, concluded that his half-brother — a prankster — was responsible. He squeezed in amongst the donuts, and headed to work. A few miles down the highway, police cars materialized behind and in front of him. Cops came at him, training shotguns. Buzz was lying spread-eagled on the ground when the events of the previous night came back to him.

In a case that was to be known as "The Great Donut Robbery", Buzz was charged with the theft of 169 dozen donuts and the use of a firearm in the execution of a crime. The latter charge proved to be the more serious of the two.

The next day, "Peanut" Anderson, who owned the bar, bailed Buzz out. Peanut had determined why Buzz committed the robbery.

"It was for the dough, huh, Buzz?"

Buzz's legal strategy was not to relinquish the evidence, the donuts, and at each appearance over the next eleven months the size of the evidence diminished as the donuts shrank. The plan was two-pronged. The donuts had shrunk to the size of golf balls, and what once filled his car could now be produced to the court in a few small bags. The crime became pettier with each passing month. Rats and mice had also taken their toll, and the police stolen-property rooms were attracting a good number of rodents. They were causing distress amongst the law-enforcement agents. Buzz's lawyer hoped that by not relinquishing the evidence, the police would grow so tired of the guests that they might offer a deal.

"He called it his bargaining power," Buzz explained.

By the time Buzz was sentenced, the 169 dozen donuts, which had started off being wheeled in — in three large laundry carts — could fit into a shoebox.

Buzz was tried by his peers, who laughed a lot during the case. Jury duty could be worse. Even the judge was unable to maintain a stern countenance, and Buzz would probably have walked had the new "Use A Gun — Go To Jail" laws not recently been enacted. He was given five years to life. The prison was Soledad. The sentence was for armed robbery, and no mention was made of the donuts. So, when asked, Buzz informed his fellow inmates that he had robbed a bank.

But the mood in Soledad was vicious.

"Black, Latino, Mexican mafia, Nuestro Familia, Aryan Nation, I was locked in a city with nothing but criminals, and everyone was expecting a riot. The tension gets really high," Buzz recalls.

The blacks, whites, and Latinos were busy preparing, as ever, for the next phase of the great, never-ending American race war. Buzz almost made it before the real trouble came. He was only a few months from getting out when the word came down that there was to be "a big major race riot".

"For two days, the tension on the exercise yard was really heavy. Everyone was grouping up, and you knew they were fixing for people to die, and you didn't want to be one of them.

"You can't understand the sound of seven hundred men running towards each other at the same time. It sounds like an explosion, like a stick of dynamite going off. Anyway, the riot lasted in the yard for two days, and I knew what was fixing to happen. I didn't want to get killed, so I wrapped magazines around my body and tied them with bed sheets. Then I put two sweatshirts on and a jacket. Most of us had weapons, but they were buried in the yard.

"When it did come down, the fucking explosion, there was burning, there was windows breaking, there were shots being fired from the towers. They were shooting at groups of us — I've got scars from the shotgun pellets where I didn't have the magazines down low enough."

Buzz pulls up his T-shirt to show his rapt audience his scarred flesh.

"I was lucky."

Buzz has had his share of luck.

"I only got hit twice by the knives and some shotgun."

After the rioting came the inevitable lockdown. Six and a half months of it. Total lockdown. No movement at all, except for solitary visits to the shower. During the lockdown the tension rose, and word spread that there would be reprisals. The word went down, and the word was that the blacks were going for three hits, and one of those hits was Buzz Gamble.

"In the yard, during the fighting, somebody got screwed up really bad. Someone who was trying to kill me."

The man was killed, and whether Buzz did it he couldn't exactly say. Prison riots are confusing affairs. In the mad frenzy, it was impossible to know who did what. Buzz thinks he might have killed the black man, and his tone softens. He is not proud or ashamed of what he might have done. But the blacks had determined that when the lockdown was lifted, Buzz would die.

"They told us that lockdown would end on Tuesday morning at ten o'clock. Someone was going to kill me, and it was all happening over 169 dozen donuts. I had already taken my radio apart, and made two knives out of the handle.

"I stayed in my bunk, and the doors opened and the adrenaline started pumping so bad that when these two black guys showed up at my door and charged me, I jumped up and stuck one, and I stuck him here."

Buzz places his finger under his jaw and makes a thrusting upwards motion. The knife, he indicates, entered the man through the soft tissue under his jaw, and continued until it had finished the opponent's time, not just in jail.

"The other one was still coming. He was swinging a sawn-off baseball bat. He hit me in the jaw and knocked out all my teeth. He ran back to his cell, but the guy who I had stuck was laying half in my cell and half out — and the doors couldn't close.

"I couldn't get him out, so I pulled his legs in. So I've got a dead black guy in my cell with my radio handle sticking in his neck."

The guards and the higher echelons knew exactly who was going to be hit, and as long as Buzz didn't leave his cell it was self-defense.

He got an extra fourteen months for possession of a prison-made weapon. Buzz collected his teeth and pulled out a few that were just hanging on, and flushed the lot down the toilet. The prison was locked down again — for four months — and Buzz had lips "like beer cans". He was fed soup, which he took through a straw, and lost thirty pounds. Finally they took him to the dentist over in the central unit.

Buzz is a vain man, a showman. Not the sort of man who would take kindly to the loss of his teeth. So he slipped the dentist a few twenties and told him he wanted to look like he used to — with the gap and all between his teeth. Without that distinctive gap, Buzz wouldn't be Buzz. The old dentist told him to bring a snap of himself smiling — something Buzz does more than most — and by the time he walked out, he had a perfect version of the teeth that had accompanied him all his life. Probably better.

Buzz left prison and took a house in Salinas. Derelicts and junkies populated the block, and Buzz had vowed in jail that he would never go back. He was on parole, and he knew he could never make it in a town full of dope fiends. So he spun a globe and stopped it wherever. Where he would live. The finger stopped the map at Palm Springs — which is only fifty miles from Pioneertown. Buzz was getting closer to what — for the next twenty years and doubtless the rest of his life — would be home.

He found peace and safety in Pioneertown, partly by chance. A friend who cultivated marijuana asked him to mind a crop of sensimilla high up in Pipes Canyon. The friend brought food and booze, but no money. When winter came, Buzz packed eight pounds of weed into his backpack, saddled his horse, and tried to ride out of the mountains. The snow was thick, even down low in Pioneertown, when he rode into the village. It seemed deserted, but Harriet's mother, Frances, who then owned the bar, found him shelter in a sort of barn down at the corral. Back when the town was founded, it was named the OK.

To the amazement of the entire parole board of California, Buzz has not seen the inside of a cell for nine years. Giving up heroin was a good career move.

Buzz is a master storyteller — a skill he has honed through twenty-eight years in county jails and state prisons. It's a skill much in demand here in the High Desert, where there can be as little to do as in prison, especially in the summer months when the heat drives locals from whatever work might be available. An hour passed as Buzz told his tale. Most of the listeners gathered in the weak winter sunshine hadn't interrupted even to get fresh beers.

15

In three weeks, Tony and I had, I thought, created a place suitable for Boo, and I drove to LA to bring her, bride-like, to her new home.

The pool was humming in a contented fashion, but the late-winter weather ranged from cold to icy, and swimming would prove difficult as an inch of ice had formed and seemed to have settled for the season. But I had stocked a cord of avocado, a fine hardwood that left little ash, and hoped to keep the entire house warm by mastering the complexities of a wood-burning stove that projected immense heat a good three feet into a house of some four thousand square feet.

I had taken to sleeping in front of the wood stove, wrestling on the couch with Sailor, our spaniel who was mighty efficient at spanieling the fire. Boo and I would be sleeping upstairs in the room carved from the rock, in a water bed that I would soon discover — courtesy of Sailor's claws — carried almost a thousand gallons of water, most of which was to flow down into the dog's den and through to the kitchen.

But just as water flows downwards, hot air rises, and I figured that after exiting the stove it would make its way to the rock room, and ensure us a comfortable first night.

My principal concern was rats; my secondary fear, mice. Perhaps Tony and I had disturbed a nest, or perhaps the animals were emboldened by the absence of Bill's cat, Elvis. I had noticed, a few days before driving to LA to pick Boo up, that the animals had taken to partying all round the house, and behaving in a most cavalier fashion. One rat I had dubbed "King Rat" was most objectionable. He had taken to watching TV, and seemed to be particularly interested in the stock market, avidly viewing *The Money Gang* and *Street Signs*. A rock shelf runs through the dog den that houses the TV, and King Rat had taken to reclining on the shelf and keeping an eye on his portfolio when not scampering outrageously about with his extremely extended family.

Sailor viewed the activities of the rodents with benign neglect. Although bred as a multipurpose thief supposedly capable of catching birds, pheasants, quail, rabbits, and all manner of animals, he had a single, catholic interest in tennis balls. No junkie could be as hooked as Sailor to his balls. The rats and mice would only incur his bated wrath if they strayed in the direction of a favorite ball. This, they soon learned not to do.

Otherwise, they were free to party, and such was their abandon that I dreamt of King Rat wearing sunglasses and smoking a cigar.

Apart from bringing Boo back to a frozen, rat-infested house, I could see nothing but clear skies — through the rain.

And so we arrived to quickly discover there was water everywhere, save in the faucets. I had offered a cup of tea as I stoked the fire, and Boo donned shawls and scarves. The response of the tap was a loud splutter, and silence.

In the city one does not contemplate running out of water, and until recently I had spent the last thirty-five years in a city, never even considering where the water came from. Years back, some smart consortium had decided the High Desert could be developed and fortunes made if a regular supply of water was introduced. As water was plentiful in the alpine stretches thousands of feet above us, the principals proceeded to lay pipes for the seventeen miles from Big Bear to the canyon. A cloudburst, from a very large cloud, ended the scheme. The land that some claim receives more sunlight than any other place on earth and was forever desperate for water was foiled by too much of it. The pipes were torn apart and scattered, and the project abandoned, leaving nothing but a name for the place — Pipes Canyon.

Even though I knew that our water principally came from the two thousand–gallon tank at the back of old Ron Hopkin's exceedingly old truck, the knowledge was, until that moment, without form. But the void was now filled with the realization that water was finite. That we had run out at such a crucial and embarrassing moment was not material. There is, as many before me have learnt, no good time to run out of water. All the cleaning and preparations done to smooth Boo's arrival had backfired. In doing it, we had exhausted the most essential comfort.

I ran to the bathroom and tried the sink: it barely managed a fart. The pool, I thought: frozen and full of chlorine. The well: frozen. The stores: miles away and closed.

"I know," I said with the air of unlikely optimism. "The water in the toilet tank. The ones we haven't flushed."

It didn't wash. Boo was not going to drink tea made from boiled toilet water, even though I explained that it was no different from that in the tap.

I had filled the dog bowl high before leaving, and, in the cold, Sailor had ignored it. Boo caught me glancing at the bowl, as did Sailor, who wandered across and took to drinking from it.

"Have you noticed Sailor drinks by putting his entire snout in the water?" I said, by way of diversion, then added, "Would you like a beer?"

There was plenty of beer, a drink that Boo has no affection for whatsoever.

"The hose — there's water in the hose. It's frozen, but once the fire's going, I can wrap the hose around the stove, and as the water melts we can fill the kettle."

But frozen hoses don't bend, as I soon discovered, and the stove wasn't exactly setting the world on fire, due no doubt to the fact that much of the rain that continued to fall seemed to have landed on our wood pile. The only dry wood was a stack of four-by-two beams, all eight foot long, that Tony and I had removed when we took out the wall. The rain seemed to be clearing when I donned gumboots and stumbled and slid down to the garage to a good-sized saw that Bill had kindly left. It screamed fearfully in the total silence of the desert, but soon I had a fine bundle of dry wood and the promise of heat.

I took some pans outside, intent on collecting some water, hopefully before it froze, and returned in time for the rats and their little friends to make what looked to Boo a triumphant appearance. Verily did they dance and sing and parade upon the floor.

The rats didn't seem to mind the cold or the absence of water, but Boo did. She is not a girl overly bothered by rodents, but she sorely wanted a cup of tea.

I scurried into the frozen wastes, and collected the pans. Tea at last.

A truck pulled up out the front. It was Gina, carrying a steaming casserole that Carole had prepared for our first night. Gina herself presented us with a bottle of excellent Californian chardonnay before disappearing into the dark. But our mood was much improved.

Boo suffers from a peculiar aversion to sea travel, due in part to a wave that somewhere in the Indian Ocean washed over her on the ship bringing the four-year-old to Australia back in the mid-fifties. She has a less peculiar dislike for the water bed, an invention, if putting water in plastic and calling it a bed dignifies that word, that, like its sixties cousin, the geodesic dome, never fulfilled its promise.

But it was the only bed properly set up, and as the rodents had taken to warming themselves by the stove, we had little choice but to make our way upstairs to sleep, or at least huddle together, and try to find the warmth that had eluded us thus far.

We climbed up the stairs, and then climbed up the granite on which the bed was perched high on a rock slab some four feet from the rock-room floor, and which had no steps. Having reached the wooden frame around the bed, we hurled ourselves up and into it, into the roiling water. Then we sank, down to the cold wood-on-granite base. En route, Boo lost a significant amount of skin from a shin that did not quite make it past the granite.

We adjusted to the movement of the water, and warm air from the fire penetrated the room to the background of furtive scurrying noises. As we had left the rats and mice by the fire, I wondered what other creatures we were entertaining. We were soon to find out.

The sky cleared, and through the sunlight came the stars,

which seemed to be almost in the room. The night was moonless, and the stars brighter than any we could remember seeing.

I went to sleep reflecting that Tony didn't like the moon because it stole the light from the stars. Tony was the first person I have known to dislike the moon. It's a funny old world.

16

The moon's greatest admirers are the coyotes, and, Boulder House being the last outpost on Coyote Road, we had inherited a goodly number of packs or "troops" of the animals.

Most of "our" coyotes live in what we came to call The Hilton—a range of rock, studded with large pinyon pine, oak, deep gamma grass, juniper, and buckwheat that separates the Hidden Valley from the vast sweep of Pipes Canyon. It's the wildest part of the land, furthest on all sides from human habitation. Here, nestled in caves against rocks under some of the biggest trees in the region, where the grass grows tall and brown, they have made their dens. The only beast that threatens is man—white man. The Indians, to whom the coyote is sacred, would not consider killing the animal that they view with fear and with the sort of sympathy they have for all living things. Nature, as Stephen Powers, California's first anthropologist, says, "was the Indian's God. The only God he knew; the coyote was his only minister." Tonight, its song—"the saddest and most beautiful and most triumphant music in nature"—haunted the skies above Boulder House as they met to forage or socialize, or just to have a good old howl-in to the full moon.

Our coyotes live well. Deeper in the desert, where the land is hard, they have a more wretched appearance, and to the north, where snow covers the ground far more than here, they are more magnificently coated. Locally, they are the color of the land at twilight: gray-brown and reddish, with a little white.

I watched one evening as they took up positions around Sailor, who wandered down into their main drag a few hundred feet below on the desert floor. They were particularly organized, one fleeting shadow after another moving out of a canyon with what appeared to be precision, taking positions around the young dog. Sailor might not have been their planned dinner, but he stood between their pack (perhaps pack is the wrong word, as the coyotes live in small family groups) and the food that The Blade Runner leaves out some nights. They stood silent sentinels, five or six of them visible in the fading light only if you knew they were there. Sailor seemed not to. They were all around him, but Sailor was young and stupid. He would probably have fought, and, as he was on the way to their food, would have lost.

The cliché that most wild animals will only attack if cornered is not accurate. If their food is threatened, they will fight. Sailor didn't know he was in their way, so I clambered and slid down the ridge, and, as boldly as I could, walked past their points, calling to him. They watched, knowing exactly what I was doing, but I shivered in the evening air when I saw one flick behind me, potentially cutting off my retreat. There are stories of coyotes attacking man, but I couldn't see them attacking a large male. As a rule, they will not mess with domestic dogs either. They know that an injury can mean a slow and painful death. Instead, they will watch and wait — wait until they have identified an easy target. Then they will send a female in heat out to lure a healthy young dog into an ambush.

It was darker on the desert floor, and I lost sight of them. They were all around me, only yards away, watching, maybe just interested. Sailor came to me, and we returned through their ring.

Inspection of their droppings suggests a good life. There are few seeds, indicating a good deal of meat in their diet. They rely on meat, mostly from rabbits, vegetables and fruit, and berries and roots if necessary. The white man put bounties on them, ignorant of their capacity to control rabbits. So the rabbits came in plagues, ate the grass, and starved the cattle. The Navajo, who lose thousands of sheep to the coyote each year, generally accept their deprivations in what has been described as a "spirit of religious tolerance". An analysis of the contents of the stomachs of fifteen thousand coyotes has shown that rabbit amounts to 33.2 per cent of their diet.

Rabbits were most evidently in abundance around Boulder House through late spring and early summer, but there are fewer about now in the winter. The coyotes, their friends the eagles, the hawks, and the snakes have consumed almost an entire generation. But the rabbits are in their holes making new families, more fodder for the food chain.

Our coyotes are strategically positioned for the good life. There is food at Pioneertown, leftovers from the trash. The Palace is only a mile on the other side of the wash, and Sean, when he was the bar-b-q chef, would take great trays of leftovers out to the animals when the restaurant closed for the night. They came to await that treat, and would form around him in the dark. That was their Saturday-night outing — across the butte, through the wash, and into town.

The mind of the coyote must be like a map. Every rock, stream, clump of grass, every bend in every stream, every water hole, every hideout and cliff, is exactly mapped. The map's dimensions include smells, sounds, the direction of winds, and even the whereabouts of the moon and the stars—all the information from long before man came here. It is said that the coyote came first and made man, gave him fire, taught him how to hunt, and introduced him to death.

"The Apache say that in pre-human times coyote created 'a path' in which man is doomed to follow—a path of gluttony, lying theft, adultery, and other wrongdoings," says J. Frank Dobie, who set out early this century to write a tract on the animal and who, over twenty years, wrote a large book. Powers, the anthropologist, noticed an element of "practical humor and slyness" in the Pacific Indians that he had not observed in those of the Atlantic. He believed the Indians had acquired this from interaction with the coyote.

That an animal could be responsible for an entire human attribute is a remarkable suggestion. Only a man like Powers would have made it, as he wasn't the Smithsonian style of anthropologist. He was much attacked when his *Tribes of California* was published in 1877, but remarked he had "waded too many rivers and climbed too many mountains to abate one jot of my opinions for a carpet-knight who wields a compiling pen in the office".

All the human attributes lend the coyote characteristics that appeal to cartoon creators. Added to this is his ability to imitate. This may be the base of the common Indian belief that the coyote can talk. Ernie and Carole recently heard a dog yapping in the night. Skylar, their small dog, apparently recognizing a friend, leapt up and ran out into the dark to meet it. It was a bunch of coyotes, and Skylar escaped to make a trip to the vet.

Another night, they heard a loud meowing. At first they thought it was their cat, but White Kitty was draped over the sofa. Ernie went out to investigate. The meowing was coming straight out of the mouth of a coyote half hidden behind a Joshua Tree.

The coyote legends of the Indians mold the creator with Coyote Man. Coyote is God the Father and God the Spirit plus the Devil in one. Each tribe has an Old Man Coyote, Old Man, First Creator, Chief Coyote, Coyote, and Coyote Man who came first and procreated earth and man.

From the day of the arrival of the white man, the coyote has endured a bad press. So significant was he to the denizens of the Old World that the Spanish found it necessary to remove him as a religious symbol. In their zeal to erase pagan strivings from the souls of the conquered, they burnt and destroyed almost all depictions of the animal. Their records leave only enough to show that coyote worship was rife.

Mexico City was once Coyoacan (meaning Place-of-Coyote Cult), and nagualism—the belief some humans could transform themselves into animals—was at the heart of its citizens' beliefs. J. Frank Dobie speculates that this was a form of the werewolf belief. In the Aztec pantheon, three gods were represented by or represented the coyote. The Spanish suppression of pagan histories such as those pertaining to the coyote lasted nearly three hundred years, and reflected the church's belief in the "diabolical" nature of the coyote. This lasted until 1830, the very time when English-speaking people were moving into the southwest and coming into contact with him. The Anglo-Celts named him "Prairie Dog" at first, but the Aztecs' name continued to dog the animal like no other. Indeed, no animal name from all of North America has so penetrated both English and Spanish as the coyote.

Even before the advent of television and the cartoon characters, the word had become so widely used as to include the following: a thief, a broker, a fixer, a mix of beer and brandy, a smuggler of people, an exploitative lawyer, a half-breed Caucasian, a bastard child, the woman's last child, and a man with a skill in attracting women. This is merely the downside, the bad press from the Spanish.

Before the Spanish, the word referred to a wise leader, a horse that never gives up ("the bayo coyote"), a tireless trot, hidden water (coyote wells or holes), to drift around, to sing well, and the sense of understanding direction through stars, winds, and landmarks (coyote sense). Thus the saying "*El Indio y el coyote nunca se pierden.*" ("No Indian or coyote ever gets lost.")

Perhaps the sound of men, of the screams of saws and the crashing of the truck over the rocks, perhaps the mere presence of Tony, had quieted these desert spirits. Until Boo's first night at Boulder House, I had heard them only from far away. Tonight they put on a right welcome for the woman of the house, yipping and howling from one "troop" to another.

On the first night of Boo's presence at Boulder House, as we swished about in the waterbed, Boo vowing never to sleep in the thing again, Sailor pattered up to attempt, unsuccessfully, to sleep at the end of the bed. He settled for a rug on the cold floor, seemingly unconcerned by the coyote cacophony. Above us, the skylight delivered the stars into the room, and as the water warmed (I had discovered that it lay on an electrically heated pad that, if pushed high enough, would bring the water almost to the boil), the plagues that attended Boo's arrival seemed trivial. For who else was laying in a bed the size and scope of a swimming pool, the Milky Way brilliant above, while the souls of the desert sung?

By the time we woke, the coyotes had long retired to their dens, and we lay for a while listening to the silence.

True, deep, complete silence is something few who live in the civilized world ever get to hear. Pipes Canyon Road was too far away to hear a car pass, and the area is pretty much off limits to airplanes. This is due to a heat vortex that had caused those who charted flight paths so many years before to direct them away from the area. The only source of sound is the wind, and the fire down below must have lasted throughout the night, as the rock room was still warm. But it was the silence, the complete absence of noise, the silence of the deaf, that reminded one that all modern life involves constant eternal noise. Not since I had left the Australian bush had I heard such silence. Boo and I listened to it until it was time to rouse.

17

It was to the great four-poster cypress bed that we repaired the next evening, and it was here we were to stay.

It had a medieval feel, but we were to discover a post-modern comfort level. Though not blessed by a skylight, the room looks onto one of the many courtyards, and one could lie in bed admiring the rising sun bathing the rocks — in particular, Hamburger Rock, dubbed thus for very obvious reasons by Adam Edwards when he would camp out here as a little boy twenty-five years before. Hamburger Rock — two great buns and a giant patty — would be, if it were a hamburger, sufficient to feed the multitude. A blue jay takes up residence on top of the top bun each morning, admiring the world and wondering what is for breakfast.

The well had produced no water during the night, but Bill had left us the numbers of all the relevant help, including the two water-delivery services. Wishing only to be diplomatic, we called both as the water tanks were good for twenty thousand gallons, and the water trucks carried only two thousand. This for $40 a load. They were vague about when they could come out, but assured us it would be as soon as they got through with their other deliveries. As that could be another day off, it was necessary to drive to a store on Old Woman Springs Road, some four miles away, for bottled water. The toilets could be flushed with water from the pool (the ice was cracking), and it was too cold to contemplate a shower.

We returned, made tea, and heard yet another truck pulling up. Rodney and Harriet arrived, bearing more extraordinary gifts—two chandeliers, from the old Pioneertown sound stage. Rodney, who knows about such things, having spent his life in construction of one form or another, deemed that only our house was big enough for the monsters, and was built strong enough to hold them. They had been made down in Mexico, and had featured in old Western movies depicting saloon scenes until the Western wore out its welcome. Since then, they had sat idle in the cavernous 8,000-square-foot sound stage that was slowly crumbling on Mane Street.

We unloaded them in one of the five garages that grace Boulder House, as I figured there were more immediate tasks ahead than importing scaffolding and support beams, and installing these black, wrought-iron objects of illumination. Given they were four feet in circumference, three feet high, carried over forty lights a piece, weighed a few hundred pounds, and had been collecting dust for sixty years, I figured they could rest a little longer while Tony and I got the house shipshape. Besides, Boulder House already sported a chandelier, albeit a modest one.

Rodney, a huge, hearty man with the walrus look that seems to be a popular personal statement in these climes, was delighted to be taken on a tour of the house. He builds houses and designs gardens, and I felt more than a little pleased when he declared it to be the best house anywhere in the region.

The conversation soon turned to water, as most desert conversations will. Rodney can design things, has a superb eye for interiors and exteriors, and has handled big operations, casinos and the like, in Las Vegas. He had long learnt that the secret to success in the desert was abundance of water. As ours clearly had none, we would have to try an alternative approach to desert living. I told Rodney I was ordering the household to shower less frequently, suggesting Tuesdays as a suitable day for washing the entire body. After all, Boo had spent much of her life in England—whose people commonly go their entire lives without the aid of a shower, and the deserts of England are few indeed.

"Americans are picking up diseases because they are no longer exposed to dirt and germs. They lack the immune systems of their forebears," I announced.

Rodney has the heartiest laugh in the High Desert, and wasn't particularly concerned about his immune system. He had been working in dirt, dust, and sand for a good forty years, and no doubt had the constitution of an ox—which in girth he faintly resembled.

"But the expression 'cleanliness is next to Godliness' has clearly been distorted upon translation from the Hebrew," I continued.

Rodney, spotless in a crisp white-linen starched shirt that set off a magnificent wide-brimmed Mexican hat, looked blankly back at me.

Boo and Harriet were touring the house, and I heard Harriet from upstairs insisting that Boo would need a maid.

As originally framed, the expression meant "cleanliness will bring you closer to God," I explained. Our Lord and his disciples lived in a desert quite similar to the one we inhabit, but we have no evidence that God Almighty was or is clean. Jesus, we know, once had his feet washed and did likewise for others. John the Baptist was given to frequent trips to the river. But neither is actually God. God (The Father) is probably clean. It's hard to imagine him up there in his many mansions all filthy with a matted beard and dreadlocks, and looking like John Walker. God (The Spirit) is no doubt spotless. Anyway, if avoiding the shower does increase one's life span, I may live to see Baltimore win a Super Bowl. Or even longer.

The question of bathing was one long close to my heart, and I had been heartened to discover that the British writer Frank Muir had written a history on the subject — an item that Boo had brought back from her last trip.

I try to remind locals, incessantly complaining about the cost of water, of the strictures of the sixteenth-century English proverb to "wash your hands often, your feet seldom and your head never".

Facts are facts. Of the seventeen million people living in Southern California, some sixteen million live in a desert. Deserts are defined by the absence of water. Yet Californians are showering as never before. A far-sighted leader would order residents to shower perhaps twice a week, thrice during summers. The order could easily be enforced by providing incentives to children to inform teachers if their parents were ignoring the edict. The teachers could report offenders to a Water and Power Czar, who would sentence them to labor in the state's marijuana fields.

Such a system would crush the power and water cartels, save everyone thousands, and wipe out much hair loss, a product of applying unnatural amounts of water and absurd concoctions to the head. Perfume, an age-old and pleasant alternative to body odor, could be freely dispersed at street-corner vending machines.

William Vaughan observed around the turn of the sixteenth century (in *Naturall and Artificial Directions for Health*) that the head should be bathed with hot lye made with ashes four times a year. He was, by the standards of the day, somewhat obsessed with washing. Vaughan also made the sensible suggestion that the application of cold water following the quarterly lye hair-wash keeps back baldness and quickens the memory.

There is also the question of lost time and productivity. Our current mania for cleanliness can be dated to the later part of the nineteenth century, and the idea of bathing alone is even more recent. The concept flourished when America became an industrial nation and most engaged in manual labor. Regular bathing was suitable for those such as coalminers, people working in offal factories, the oil industry, mechanics, and the like. Unhappily, these people were often so poor they could scarcely afford plumbing, so dirt and stench were so commonplace as to go unnoticed. Thus the absence of dirt or of smells was seen as a sign that one was from the better classes. Only the very rich and powerful—Howard Hughes comes to mind—could afford to be dirty. Balzac's ambition in life was to become so important that he could fart in society. But I digress.

Seventeen million people spending, say, ten minutes a day in the shower represents a loss of 170,000,000 minutes. The widespread disappearance of the bath means that this time is entirely wasted, as the productive functions that can be achieved in a bath—reading being the most obvious—are eliminated. It is possible to read a newspaper in most showers, and I usually fold the *Los Angeles Times* along the glass and read a feature from the bottom of the op-ed pages. If the bottom of the op-ed page is a piece written by someone from the Heritage Foundation on the need for more nuclear-attack submarines, one simply puts the shower off for the day and waits for a Robert Sheer or even an Arianna Huffington article to appear in the right spot.

Perhaps the oddest justification for washing comes from Mark Twain's mother, Mrs. Clemens, who wrote that "people born to be hanged are safe in water". That might be true of hanging, but, as John the Baptist discovered, is ineffectual when it comes to beheadings. Besides, if one had to spend one's entire life in water, hanging might seem a good career move. Mark himself called the Turkish bath a "malignant swindle. The man who enjoys it is qualified to enjoy anything repulsive to sight or sense."

Bathing can lead to other unpleasant experiences, even if one doesn't actually take the bath.

Lillie Langtry, while visiting an English earl, was asked whether she might cavort in a bath of white wine while he and his landed companions watched. The good lady complied, and playfully splashed around to the delight of the audience. The earl ordered the wine, believed to be an Esterhazy-Pierpont-Gluckhauser (a hock) to be served with the salmon mousse that evening. It was greatly enjoyed, but after the meal the earl was approached by his butler and told that while he had poured eight bottles of the wine into the bath, he had bottled eight-and-one-half.

Plutarch tells us that Archimedes, the genius who gave us geometry (or quite a bit of it) had to be dragged to the tub by his servants.

We don't exactly run to servants, but if we did I'd give them little chance of getting me to tub or shower. We are fortunate enough to have both, but the bath, a nineteenth-century steel affair with claw feet, is yet to be troubled by water, or wine for that matter. It resides in the old "bordello" bathroom at the foot of the stairs, painted red to match the red-flocked wallpaper and other bathroom features from days gone by. One always expects or hopes to see Claudia Cardinale soaking in it, bubbles rich around her breasts.

All this was probably double-dutch to Rodney, a man who works hard physically and earns his shower rations. But he knows his water, and, like Buzz, is a master storyteller. As we wandered the grounds, he recounted landscaping Sly Stallone's mansion in Malibu, an area devastated by fire every decade but always rebuilt in time for the next inferno. Sly wanted his house to be surrounded by high-pressure water jets that would blast a wall of water into the foliage around the mansion at the first sign of a spark. But Rodney was forbidden to consult a water diviner, even though he and many others swore by this method of deciding where the well should go. In fact, one of the recurring themes of desert conversations is the usefulness of employing a water diviner or "witcher".

People one would normally place on the practical side of the ledger are commonly great believers in this mysterious practice, and Rodney, as practical a man as one could meet, was a firm believer in witching, and in particular the prowess of one particular old Indian.

Sly Stallone, very much a product of The Enlightenment, did not. He forbade the construction crew from consulting the old Indian. Sly's brother was building another mansion across the road. He had consulted the Indian ($100 was the going price), and the man had arrived in the back of a big white Cadillac with his wife doing the chauffeuring.

The Indian was blind, but he alighted from the caddy and said, "Squaw, fetch me my rods."

"The old Indian walked around for a while, the squaw directing him, and suddenly started to shake all over, and the copper-wire rod just seemed to bend and drag his arms down to the ground," Rodney recounted.

"That's where he said the water was, and that's where they found it. Plenty of it."

Sly's crew continued to drill, consulting maps and geologists, and coming up dry every time. As wells are expensive to drill — about $20,000 a shot — knowledge of the whereabouts of the water was extremely useful.

"We waited until Sly was gone, and brought in the old Indian," Rodney continued, laughing like a naughty schoolboy.

"The next time we drilled, we hit water, and Sly got his wall of water."

I wished Bill Lavender had done the same. Bill's well goes five hundred and ninety feet into the granite, and produces about enough water to provide a comfortable shave every other week.

18

I had managed to establish a "workstation" on the second floor of Boulder House overlooking the amphitheater, the Ten Years Ago Tree, the rimrock ridge, and the pine-clad San Bernardino Mountains a few miles beyond. Below us — beneath sea level — lay one of the harshest deserts on earth. Above, the terrain is alpine. Both are a mere twenty miles away. As "workstations" go — "job sites and offices" tragically banished from the lexicon — one could ask for little more.

The computer, printer, fax, scanner, the laptop, the other computer, and what passed for a filing arrangement were all in place, thanks to Ed, and Boo could carry on her magazine editing as she might have in Beverly Hills. Except for the 760 area code. Californians are very tuned, one might say, to area codes, with our old one — 310 — being the most desired. Giving one's phone number prefixed by 310 had been a down-payment on civility. Folks returned 310 calls before 323 (Hollywood at the best, LA at the worst) but no one knew what to make of 760. That, followed by a mailing address which placed us squarely in a joint called Pioneertown, bordered on the embarrassing.

But Boo, with her tape recorder connected to the telephone, is able to toil away as though she actually is in a smart Beverly Drive office. She could just as well be in Alice Springs or the more settled parts of the Antarctic. The population density in both places would be extreme compared with this office, set high amongst the giant rocks.

As she mostly interviews celebs and models, interest in where she actually is located is limited, and when discussed considered "way cool". Otherwise, most probably assume 760 is a "way cool" exclusive nest of Beverly Crest, or Beverly something, and that the editor they are spilling all to is fielding secretaries and fat-free lattes with a flick of her Armani-suited arm. Instead it is Boo, often in her underwear, surrounded by animals, warmed by a groaning gas heater, her nearest neighbor about to be released for the pointblank-to-the-face shooting of the wildest of the Edwards clan, short on water, with a troublesome septic tank, at a dead end of a barely sealed road called Pipes Canyon. Beverly Hills it ain't.

While the "work station" was working, Tony had decided I was poorly equipped with life's essentials, which for Tony were objects sharp and blunt and comprising steel. These included shovels, digging bars, crowbars, mallets, and rakes. All manner of things. Some of these I had purchased at the local lumberyard, and Tony had no trouble breaking them. He muttered darkly about me buying tools made in foreign countries. Fact was, I told him, such instruments are no longer made in the US, but by coolies in Asia.

"You cannot get them anymore, mate," I said with some satisfaction.

Tony objected to any work not done in the US and not done by him. So it gave me some pleasure to point out that one of the joys of globalization was that cheap tools that broke when strained could be purchased from far-off lands that Tony, a hardcore Republican, disapproved of.

"I know where to get them," he said with equal satisfaction.

Soon we were bumping along Gamma Gulch, named after the gamma grass that covered much of the southwest before the introduction of cattle. When the beeves had arrived here they had consumed most of the gamma, but it was now making a comeback forty years after the cows had been moved to lots. The rate of the return was startling. Now the stuff was everywhere, especially on Gamma Gulch, but also all round Boulder House. It seemed to have grown in stature as well as scope—some of it being three foot high.

The grass, almost white when the sun is high, turns golden as the light plays upon it from an angle. By late afternoon, the clumps take the appearance of thick stands of half-grown wheat; and where the stuff is thick, a newcomer could be excused for thinking he or she was driving through wheat fields, albeit ones dominated by the yuccas. As the gamma is the plant most devastated by cattle, it seems that nature has returned the last of her players to the field and that this tiny section of the West looks like it might have when the Serrano Indians wandered the land, oblivious to the coming holocaust. Some say that with the going of the grass the creek beds disappeared, choosing, I expect, to flow underground now that there was nothing left to tie the water to the land's surface. Perhaps the water will return to the surface. Either way, the golden gamma brings yet another touch of beauty and completeness to the land.

We passed the place where Erle Stanley Gardner, the creator of Perry Mason, and one of America's most prolific writers, lived, and I mused on how the return of the gamma grass would have pleased him.

He had described the place well in one of his modern Westerns, *Pay Dirt*:

> There it lies, miles on miles of it, dry lake beds, twisted mountains of volcanic rock, sloping sage-covered hills, clumps of Joshua trees, thickets of mesquite, bunches of giant cactus. It has the moods of a woman, and the treachery of a big cat.

Gardner's name is linked to the neighborhood for another reason—his rescue of one of the High Desert's best-known and most loved historical figures, Bill Keys.

Keys came out from Arizona, where he had been cowboying in 1903 after a gun fight, and found his way to the Desert Queen Mine, the remains of which now rest in the midst of what, nearly one hundred years later, William Jefferson Clinton would dub the Joshua Tree National Park.

The mine was being run by the notorious McHaney brothers, whose rustling activities had taken them into the hidden valleys far above—two days' bullock drive—to the fledgling town of 29 Palms. A miner had located gold a few miles from where they had relocated some cattle, and the McHaney brothers shot him "in self-defense" and claimed the claim. It was probably the richest of the many High Desert gold mines, but the McHaneys managed to blow more money than it made. When it was worked out, Keys claimed it for back wages.

In 1917, Keys obtained the keys to the Desert Queen Mine. He wasn't as interested in what was left of the gold as in a stream that ran through the section. After marrying Frances Mae Lawton in 1918, he established a highly productive farm. His wife was equally productive, and soon the family numbered seven. The authorities, never happy when someone establishes a life away from its prying eyes, demanded the family move to a township where the kids could get schooling. Keys searched the statutes, and found that it was the responsibility of the state to send him a schoolteacher once the number of souls requiring education reached five.

"Not true," said San Bernardino County.

The law stated they need provide a teacher only if there was a schoolhouse. Keys would have to move his bairns into town. Instead, he proceeded to build a school, and a reluctant county dispatched a teacher.

But trouble was in the offing. Our Christian president exhorted us to love our neighbors like we would like to be loved. This is easy enough in the cities, where one typically barely knows one's neighbor, unless he is the Man with No Brain. But in the High Desert, while it is impossible to not know one's neighbor, it can be hard to love him or even her.

Worth Bagley was a man deemed too violent to remain in the LAPD, which in the late 1930s was something of a distinction — as it remains today. He was pensioned off, and took his ninth wife to the now national park, and promptly went to war with the only target on the horizon, poor Bill Keys.

The issue was, superficially, cattle and water rights. Bagley proceeded to slaughter sundry livestock belonging to Keys and then, in 1943, lay in wait for him with a pistol, opening fire while Keys was reading the details of a "no trespass" sign that Bagley had erected. Bagley's shot went wild and he ran towards Keys, who in turn ran to his old jalopy and his rifle. Keys aimed at his assailant's gun arm, which he hit, a remarkable feat. But the bullet deflected into the body cavity, causing considerable shock and death.

Evidence that Bagley was stark-staring crazy was not admitted, and his wife, who told all and sundry (save the jury, before whom she was never allowed to appear) she had left her husband because of his incessant threats to kill a perfectly peaceful neighbor, was likewise ignored.

Keys went to prison, and may have died there had Gamma Gulch's celebrated writer, Erle Stanley Gardner, not come to his aid. The two men were friends, but could hardly have been more different. Gardner, a lawyer, employed as many as six secretaries at a time as he churned out novels, screenplays, and novelettes by the score. On a good day, he would dictate fifteen thousand words, and over fifty years he wrote eighty-two books featuring Perry Mason, out of a total of one hundred and fifty-five published books. He also knocked out hundreds of articles and travel tomes. At the height of his popularity (in the mid-sixties), twenty-six thousand of his books were sold — every day.

In the meantime, he had visited China and come to speak fluent Chinese, maintained an ardent involvement in fishing, boxing, archery, tennis, and golf, raised his horses and cattle, and became an authority in, amongst other things, geology, archeology, engineering, astronomy, forensic medicine, and the breeding grounds of the California gray whale.

This amazing reach made him a superb lawyer, and, aware of the injustices of the US legal system, he established the Court of Last Resort, where he would study and fight to reopen cases he considered unjust.

Keys had been in jail for some years before his wife, not one to ask favors, wrote to Gardner, telling him of the plight of his old friend he had lost touch with.

Keys had been offered immediate parole on arriving in jail, but would only accept a pardon, and Gardner went to work to achieve just that. This great champion of social justice let loose a large team of legal experts, and Keys was pardoned by Governor Goodwin J. Knight on 26 July 1956, after serving five years. Keys joined seventy other innocents freed because of the work of Erle Stanley Gardner.

The rancher returned to his homestead in the rock-bound canyon. There he was buried beside his wife in 1969.

Today one can visit his old ranch, the Desert Queen, but only on restricted tours. Bill would be surprised to discover a sign at the entrance informing visitors that they too would be off to jail (for six months) if found trespassing.

As we swirled through the fine sand of Gamma Gulch, I hoped the Wild West would be better personified at the Parsons Ranch — our destination.

I had heard talk of Parsons Ranch in the past, and assumed it was the ranch of one of the far-too-many parsons in the area. I had avoided it in the same way that right-wing Republicans and Democrats try unsuccessfully to avoid sin.

But Tony informed me we were heading to a ranch occupied by one Jean Parsons, an elderly lady who lives at the last of the outlying High Desert settlements. She is, Tony explained, the stepmother of Gene Parsons, who found fame and fortune with the popular sixties band The Byrds, and less of both with the Flying Burrito Brothers.

This was all a little confusing. I knew only of Gram Parsons, who also played with both bands and introduced The Rolling

Stones to the steel guitar. They, in turn, allowed him to record 'Wild Horses', or he allowed them to, depending on whom you believe.

Gram Parsons overdosed on morphine and booze in 1973 at The Joshua Tree Motel, a pretty little whitewashed adobe hotel fifteen miles down the road. It was there that Gram took his last hit. Room number eight is now something of a shrine, and fans, before they visit the Joshua Tree National park, a favorite haunt for Gram and the gang, stop and leave flowers, poems, and other tributes at a little shrine.

Gram spent a lot of time in Joshua Tree teaching the Stones, particularly Keith, country music. When the greatest show on earth finished "Wild Horses", Gram was given the honor to be the first to record it.

I knew a good deal about one of the Parsonses, but could remember almost nothing about Gene, who was, I think, the drummer in The Byrds. It struck me as odd that I was about to visit the stepmother of the one I didn't know about, whose Christian name was pronounced the same, while all three shared the same surname.

So much did Gram love the rocks and yuccas, and maybe the gamma grass, that he and his road manager, Phil Kaufman, had sworn, while at the funeral of ex-Byrds guitar player Clarence White two months before, a solemn pact with each other. The last one standing was to burn the other's body in the Joshua Tree National Park.

It's not easy to burn a body in the middle of the national park under the best of circumstances — especially when the corpse has already been taken to LAX and is in the hands of Continental Mortuary Air Services. These folks do not make a habit of handing over stiffs, especially to a couple of drunks wearing touring jackets with "SIN CITY" emblazoned on their backs. But Kaufman — or "The Road Mangler", as he is more fondly known — having borrowed an ex-hearse from a friend, had somehow convinced a clerk to free Gram into his sweaty hands.

With a mate called Martin and a bottle of Jim Beam, he took the body back to Highway 62, past the motel where Gram had died a few days before. In the dead of the night, they drove to a place called Cap Rock, not because of its supposed spiritual significance (the myths were to come later), but because they were both too drunk to go any further. Besides, it was the middle of the night, and neither had the slightest idea where they were.

The coffin slid out on the hearse's wheels and crashed to the ground. Gram was inside, naked, save for a strap that covered the slit on his chest where his organs had been removed. Five gallons of high-octane petroleum were applied, and Kaufman recounts the effect:

> When high octane ignites, it grabs a lot of oxygen from the air. It went whoosh and a big ball of flame went up. It was bubbling. You could see it was Gram and then as the body burned very quickly, you could see it melting. We looked up and the flame had caused a dust devil going up in the air. His ashes were actually going up into the air, into the desert night. The moon was shining, the stars were shining and Gram's wish was coming true. His ashes were going into the desert. We looked down. He was very dead and very burned. There wasn't much left to recognize.

Headlines around the world screamed things like "Rock Star's Body in Ritual Burning in Desert", but, as Kaufman points out, it was merely "a couple of piss-heads taking care of business for their mate".

I told Tony some of this as we skidded along the long, sandy, deserted road, and he was suitably disgusted. So I got back to the more wholesome matter of tools and asking him how a visit to this woman's ranch would assist in replacing the worthless tools Tony had broken.

"You'll see," was all he said.

And see I did.

We finally came to a large iron gate that Tony had called ahead to have opened, and wound down a ravine to find ourselves in a glen. Here every imaginable object from the industrial age had been deposited, apparently by Jean's husband, Gene's father, before he passed away in the early 1990s.

Trucks dating from the 1920s rested in the sun. Bulldozers, long decrepit, stood beside them. Old windmills lay on the ground, their wings still elaborating, in faded paint, their origins— "Chicago Illinois." On one wing drenched in seventy years of sunlight, the faded yellow, red, and blue face of a clown smiled up at us through weeds. When we left, I took him home.

A few acres were covered in a jumble of machinery, winches, pulleys, old iron gold carts, and tools—hundreds, perhaps thousands, of them.

Mrs. Parsons emerged from a cottage little bigger than a desk, and offered us beer. She was a sporty woman, well into her seventies, kept fit and hale by the actions and spirit that come with surviving at the end of a road that makes our humble dirt affair look like the intersection of Hollywood and Vine.

We can, from Boulder House, see the lights of a few neighbors and friends, and that is a comfort. The only lights that Jean can see are the magnificent crowning lights of the firmament. She has no electricity and no neighbors. The ravine towers some eight hundred feet above her tiny settlement of the little house and even littler outhouse. The escarpments that surround her do provide something more essential than all the things she lacks — a constant supply of the purest water.

Around the settlement grow great cottonwoods that shade her outdoor tables with dappled light, and a continuous breeze wafts through the ravine, air-conditioning her home. She owns a section, a square mile, and on it is gold and fine quartz. The quartz mine is abandoned, but Tony and I climbed the cliffs, and found its remnants and some fine quartz. The quartz is valuable, and at times Jean has had to stare down half-drunk would-be miners hoping for an easy penny. It's a hard life for a well-spoken graceful lady.

The three of us wandered through the acres of steel. The collection seemed to end at about World War II, and included primitive Geiger counters and short-wave radios. It is a collector's paradise, but we had come for tools. Tony quickly located two enormous shovels once used to fill furnaces with coal, which Mrs. Parsons believed came from a train line. She wasn't sure about the antecedents of the pieces, as her husband had been collecting them from before their marriage.

Jean left us to scour for objects sharp and blunt, and we later found her under the cottonwoods, sipping red wine. She produced more beer and some of her stepson Gene's latest CDs, as well as some remixes of the original Byrds albums. As I knew next to nothing about Gene, I asked her if she knew anything about Gram.

She recalled that not long before he died, she was invited to go and listen and hang out with Gram and company at some

Joshua Tree gig. She called Gene in Northern California, and asked whether she should. Gene replied that she shouldn't mix with that crowd, and she took his advice. As well she might.

Having exhausted all we had in common, at least as far as the musical Parsons were concerned, we got down to business. A good shovel, if such a thing can be obtained, costs a good fifteen dollars. The huge things Tony located had lasted sixty years, and were going for two bucks. I snapped them up. We filled the truck with enough equipment to bring a gleam to Tony's eyes, and after an hour of gossip we made our way to Boulder House and some serious work.

19

Some places — Melbourne, Australia, comes to mind — enjoy all four seasons in a single day. Here in the valley we can experience them at the same time. A few days ago, the sun shone in all its glory while heavy snow fell. Here we are in the High Desert looking at what are damn near alps. Snow and sun have mingled delightfully for weeks now, and already, a few months into the year, more rain fell than in all of last year — which is not saying much, as last year was as dry as an Englishman's towel.

Working outside is intolerable to all bar Tony, who last week I observed toiling away in the snow and freezing wind. I didn't stop the F100, considering it too cold to wind down the window, but Tony, under his snowy crust, waved and smiled cheerfully. The rest of the workforce — if that is not too strong a word — were ensconced with their bourbons and beers in The Palace, huddled around the various stoves. One is an old square steel contraption and the other a large steel drum, and both, to Harriet's consternation, were being fed and re-fed with costly avocado wood — an excellent fuel producing great heat and virtually no ash. Rodney arranged for six cords (at $170 a cord) to be delivered, and I snared one, which I figured should last the winter. Which it didn't, but winter had a peculiar fury that year—the year Our Lord was to smite us down for failing to see the great portents and flee in the face of Y2K.

During the Y2K scare the radical Christians and the radical hippies spent small fortunes—up to $30,000—on self-sufficiency. Solar panels, generators, wind power, all of which are not entirely "sufficient", do provide for a certain smugness (common amongst those who were right for the wrong reasons). But both radical hippies and God-bothering militia types are as one in the belief in the coming apocalypse, and I kept a close watch on my tongue when the "logic" of leaving the grid altogether was expounded. And expounded it was. One had to be careful to avoid all manner of folks until well into May, when even the most determined of the fanatics conceded that the whole matter might be related to Our Lord's arrival some years after his estimated time of arrival circa 2000 BC-AD?? or thereabouts. And by then rumors of something odd in the largely unknown world (unknown to the denizens of the desert) of dot-communaires were causing ructions as the pigs and goats and rabbits were purchased by yours truly and eaten in a great feast where Buzz Gamble and the Daily Blues played till dawn before one hundred or so debauched locals who cared neither for the Y2000 scam nor the biggest rip-off on the Dot-Com front.

Meantime, it was best, I considered, we keep connected to the grid and called my friends at Enron.

The night after the biggest snowfall in years (a pretty paltry affair by mountain standards), it was still snowing in the mountains beyond my "office" window while sunshine rendered the rest of the valley and foothills a glorious white.

I called Buzz early at his early opener. He is supposed to spring the locks on the Joshua Tree Saloon at 8.00 (a.m.) but likes to get there at 7.00 to warm the place up and cater for anyone particularly needful of an early drink—himself. I asked Buzz how we should handle the "blizzard" (a whole two inches of snow), and Buzz, obviously playing to the bar—at 8.00 a.m. he might have five or six drinkers—bellowed, "Hell, that ain't no blizzard. That's just Texas Tea."

I told him I figured we were snowed in, and he found it hard to believe we could be snowed in by two inches of snow.

"You sure it's snow? Is it white?" Buzz asked.

"I'd be damned worried if it was black," I replied. "We could be dealing with a volcano."

"Volcano! You're a crazy motherfucker."

"I'm not saying I can't drive in two inches of snow, Buzz. The problem is finding the road. I guess we can rely on airdrops. We are quite low on beer. Will the air force drop beer?"

"You are one crazy motherfuckin' Australian. It's not the air force—it's the National Guard. And they are sure as hell not gonna drop beer to a crazy Australian trapped in two inches of snow."

Buzz, clearly enjoying this performance, loudly pointed out that the purpose of the markers on the edge of the road was to define the road so "crazy motherfuckin' Australians" could get their own beer.

"Well, they'd probably refuse to drop Tecate anyway," I replied. "If they dropped Michelob, I'd tell them to take it back. I doubt even Adam would drink Michelob. I'd rather drink Lily Langtry's piss."

The reference to the esteemed actress was lost on Buzz, and I left him muttering "motherfucker" into the phone.

But apart from Tony's exertions, no outdoor work would be done today. The snow made things too cold and slippery, and to my mind life was dangerous enough without challenging the howling elements. But Tony never slips or stumbles. He has no place to fall. Tony plays Seneca to the scores of Petroniuses that make up the remaining workforce. They would prefer dining with Trimalchio, and their work could well be described as *The Fragments*.

Instead, Boo and I decided to drive down to Yucca Valley, our nearest big town for supplies, just in case more snow did arrive. Bill had shown us photos of Boulder House under several feet of the stuff some years before when he had been cut off for days.

The back roads to Yucca are dotted with old ramshackle deserted cabins and shells of cabins that once were someone's dream. After the Spanish war of 1898, president Harding made sections (360 acres) available to veterans, and later World War I soldiers took up parcels of the arid land. At that time, the area attracted victims of TB and poisoning from mustard gas. The remnants of a TB clinic remain a few miles away where Pipes Canyon Road meets Pioneertown Road.

These men and women replaced the cowboys, the cattle, and the cattle-rustling that dominated the economy after the passing of the Indians until the Depression of the 1890s, when beef prices fell so low that the game was not worth the candle. But in the boom years following the gold rush, when a single beeve could fetch seventy dollars, knowledge of water sources and familiarity with the scores of hidden valleys turned a pretty penny. Cattle could be stolen in Mexico, eighty miles to the south, or from the Ranchos based in Los Angeles and San Diego, driven through the passes, hidden in land where whites had scarcely traveled, and then herded north. Alternatively, stolen cows and horses from the Californian settlements could be given fresh brands in the hidden valleys, and then driven to Mexico for sale. In Mexico, rustlers deployed an early time-and-motion technique, stealing Mexican stock and running it north. Some of the poor beasts spent much of their lives being chased back and forth across the border.

Reading through the history of the early days, one is struck by the numbers who met an early and violent death. Like in the rest of the West, rustling, hard drinking, and gambling were practiced by men openly brandishing hand guns or shooting irons, but today the churches are far more numerous than the bars, and far better attended.

In fact, the Desert Christ Park became a leading tourist attraction after Christ's first physical manifestation in this part of the Eastern Mojave.

Taking the back road into Yucca to avoid the ugly strip, we passed this extraordinary park, one of the desert's great blessings. Boo insisted on inspecting it.

It is perhaps appropriate that the Christ Park and the Cholla Park are adjacent, as some argue that Our Lord's Crown of Thorns was manufactured from cholla—proving that when Christianity is involved, people will invent any manner of things. The Christ Park became a leading tourist attraction after Jesus's first physical manifestation in this desert, in 1951.

A God-fearing pattern-maker from Inglewood, Frank Antoine Martin, had "sculpted" a ten-foot, four-ton statue of Christ in his driveway in 1947, intending it to be placed at the rim of the Grand Canyon. Due to the extremely liberal position that the National Parks Service took at the time, this truly inspirational and wondrous monolith was deemed to contravene the division of church and state—the park being the possession of the feds. Martin argued that a cross was displayed at Easter sunrise services on the Canyon Rim, but the secular authorities countered that the cross was taken down after this annual service. Raising and lowering the 6,300-pound, ten-foot Christ might have proved to be as difficult a task as the resurrection itself. So the ten-foot Christ was rejected of men, a statue of sorrow, and, as Martin liked to tell newspapers and magazines, "not wanted".

Not wanted by all accept Eddie Gardner, a desert missionary who was later to achieve national fame as the Desert Parson. Gardner found it fit to base his ministry at the head of Yucca Valley, at Apache and Santa Fe trails. And with the flair of an early Pat Robertson, he saw in the four-ton statue a chance to draw attention to the spiritual needs of the folks of the desert and, perhaps, to himself.

Moving Christ to the desert was a more complex operation than the Son of Man's efforts prior to his Temptation. In fact, it required the skills of the Harbormaster of Balboa Bay, Los Angeles—one Tommy Bouchey, who brought in cranes and heavy rolling stock to raise up Our Lord. By the grace of God, on 28 March 1951, Christ was lifted up once again in the wilderness, hair and robes flowing, arms somewhere between beseeching and crucifixion. After being dragged fifty feet up a steep incline behind one of the scores of churches, he was placed upon a knoll in time for the 1951 Easter sunrise service on 8 April. *Life* and *Time* magazines both featured the miracle, although *Time* noted that Christ's finger had broken off during his move. This would seem to diminish the statue's spiritual status, as the Bible makes much of the prophecy that "not a bone of his body be broken," and definitely does not suggest that an entire finger be lost.

But so taken were the people of the desert that Mr. Martin immediately moved other artistic endeavors, including the moving "Jesus Blessing the Children" from Inglewood to the more biblical desert environment. The works, which can truly be described as "larger than life", soon spread to cover five acres of hardscrabble desert.

Over the following decades, Martin created a virtual New Testament down on the Pioneertown side of Yucca Valley. His works multiplied until he had, in hundreds of tons of wondrous cement, recreated "The Betrayal of Christ in the Garden of Gethsemane" (lest anyone wonder where he was betrayed), "Christ at the Home of Lazarus", "Mary and Martha" (who apparently lived together), "Christ's Blessing of the Little People", and "The Scene at the Holy Sepulchre", replete with three mourning women staring into a tomb that Martin had dug into the hillside, and where he sculpted "The Shroud". Martin further beautified the desert with what has been described accurately as his "most magnificent and ambitious work", a carved facade of the Last Supper with the head of Christ, framed in an open window, cut in three dimensions. The remaining figures are in bas-relief, and the whole box and dice, the facade, stands three stories high and thirty feet wide.

A nation aching for meaning during those days, when Godless communism threatened from within and without, poured cash into the work, and donations reached $3,000 a month. All manner of scenes from the New Testament soon dominated not just the hillside but a good part of the township.

But all was not well in the new Holy Land. Perhaps it was the surprise appearance of Eddie Gardner, the Desert Parson, as one of the twelve disciples that caused a rift amongst the true believers. Rifts, akin to that of the nearby San Andreas Fault, appeared not only in the "immortal" concrete statues, which stand gleaming white in the desert sun to this day, but also in the flock. Due to a "misunderstanding", one parishioner bought the five acres upon which the handiwork had been brought forth, and proceeded to sell it back to his parish at a decent profit. The Reverend Gardner was described as "very saddened" by this turn of events and left the parish, preferring to live and die on the Navajo Indian reservation in northern Arizona than remain in the world of filthy lucre.

Alone, with nothing but a cement mixer, Anton continued his work tracing the Biblical fables, from the manger almost to the cross. But the constant effort, in boiling heat and icy winds, caused Anton to sicken and die on this hillside so far from Galilee. A mile or so from the Christ Park, he sculpted a saber-toothed tiger by the highway. The stark beast is truly fearsome, in contrast with the meek and mild figures of Christ, the Apostles, the Wise Men, Mary—everything but the crazed swineherd—that stare "Christ like" down at the highway. All are overlooked by today's connoisseurs of fine art who would prefer the works of Mapplethorpe to these uplifting scenes.

So overlooked, so unwanted, are they that, though built to endure the blast of an atomic bomb, they have been unable to withstand the march of time. Heads of the apostles have rolled, and outstretched arms as big as a child have had their cement and rebar steel exposed. The children that Our Lord is beseeching to "come unto me" seem to be suffering from terrible diaper rash, and look somewhat flyblown.

Unhappily, on sultry summer nights, sordid things happen, even in this place of innocence.

Young men, and men not so young, seeking not salvation but sex, are drawn to the place. Holier visitors began hearing noises coming from the men's toilets. The park ranger commented that Christ Park had become a veritable "Sodom and gonorrhea".

The police chase them away, through the nativity scene, past the manger, and into the cholla thickets.

20

Whereas Pioneertown is almost embarrassed by its authenticity, Yucca fails entirely. It is not the ugliest city in America, but is well named.

Not long after our arrival, Ernie introduced me to Tom, one of his gun-fighting cronies, who also happened to be mayor of the city of Yucca Valley. For reasons I never established, Tom promptly asked me what I thought should be done to "beautify" Yucca. This was akin to being asked for the definitive explanation of the origins of the universe, and I demurred.

Finally, it came to me. "Get a bulldozer," I told the mayor.

Yucca is a horrible example of the American blight — two Chevron stations, a Taco Bell, the mandatory McDonald's, and endless other fast-food drive-throughs. Car yards pile alongside ghastly Walgreens and Shop Rites, and every other abomination a city should hide in shame. In its defense, Yucca boasts the magnificent snow-capped San Gorgonio Mountain as a backdrop, and still has feedlots with huge Trigger-like horses standing guard out the front. There are no parking meters and no traffic officers, and it does have one of the finest signs in the history of capitalism from a local realtor: "Your nest egg will be safe with Betty Henn". A row of antique stores in "Old Town," with names like Horse Feathers, are cheap, and jammed with Old Western relics that ten years of lying out in the desert sun have rendered desirable.

Every weekend, one of the world's great swap meets converts the old Sky View drive-in into a wonderland of irresistible junk sold by cowboys and mountain women from the backs of their cars. Here, between stalls laden with snakeskin walking sticks and 1940s newspapers, Patti Page pauses in mid "Mocking Bird Hill" while the intercom loudly announces, "David, your bacon and eggs are ready in the Sky Café. Come and get 'em while they're still nice and hot."

Lately, the fingers of the New Age have touched tiny portions of the strip, and there are a few stores, like The Cactus Garden, that my mother might describe as "tasteful".

But few they are indeed, and a visitor with the slightest semblance of refinement would be challenged to see anything but uninterrupted ugliness.

Humanity somehow overwhelms this godforsaken dreariness, and indeed Yucca advertises itself as "the friendliest place on earth". The "girls" at Vons discuss health and family problems with the customers at the checkout at exasperating length. Milo bags the food, and greets his customers and us with an embrace. The flower girl fills in my checks if I have forgotten my glasses. They are a merry crew at Vons. It is indeed odd to walk into this giant national enterprise and to be greeted as an old family friend.

The Valvoline operation on the highway once worked on my car for two hours and refused any payment, as they had only established the cause of a leak from some part of the thing.

The Palestinian men who run the local store offer credit with an alacrity that would have me short-selling the store's futures. Buzz has credit with every liquor store in town.

But none of this makes Yucca any less ugly. It's a place to stop, stuff some poison down the kids' throats, and drive on to someplace else.

One attempt to pretty up the place has occurred near the Palestinian liquor store, and opposite the Jelly Donut — a landmark of almost anthropological importance.

Many winters ago, the aforementioned wondrous artist and sculptor Anton Martin created a perfect rendition of a saber-toothed tiger, a creature that once walked or stalked these lands. The saber-toothed tiger has been described as the greatest killing machine nature ever invented, and the alabaster tiger of Yucca is a fearsome-enough-looking beast, even if the stark white paint he is dressed in detracts from his beastliness. The most terrifying animal nature ever created — at least in the Northern Hemisphere — stands on a tiny isthmus by the highway, hidden from the tourist view by cactus and a sea of American flags so dense one could mow them.

The town is blessed by fine eating houses where a patron is helped through the complexities of sophisticated culinary delights. At Jerry's Bar and Lounge, a waitress was good enough to inform us that "The Chablis is the white one. The Cabernet is the red one."

"They are nothing like each other," she added helpfully.

They are nothing like wine either.

The purveyors of battery acid dressed up as drink have done well out here, and seem to sell the most rancid of their products exclusively to the haunts of the upper desert. Wine in such places is not drunk for the betterment of the palate or the gastronomic juices, but for the hit. These are wines that in LA would only be drunk by winos. When asked for something kinder and gentler on the palate, a bottle of Pink Zinfandel is invariably produced with the sort of look that suggests "We have culture in this town." The Zinfandels taste like — and probably are — a thin mix of bad Chablis and some rotten red with just a suggestion of urine. Or bad apple.

At the same time, Jerry's offers steaks so superior to those we were accustomed to in Venice, Santa Monica, and Hollywood that after a few mouthfuls even the urine starts to taste reasonable, and one is reminded that an Indian prime minister — was it Desai? — used to drink his each morning. Perhaps he still does. We don't hear much from him these days. Pity.

Tuesday night is fifty-cent taco night, and a good many residents of Yucca — and much of Pioneertown — descend on Jerry's for their fill. Three and even four generations of families loll around the big wooden tables while toothless babies and toothless great grandpas stuff their gobs with the greasy cheesy delights.

Yucca Valley — population twenty-five-odd thousand souls — may have more fat people than any other town in America. So great have they grown that the supermarkets provide electric golf carts so they can drive themselves around the aisles — loading fat food into the baskets attached to the front. Fat couples ride along side by side, blocking entire rows. Boo has renamed it Fat Fucca Valley.

As we made our way along the shelves past a man with a cart stuffed to the gills with frozen pizza and nothing else, she zeroed in on an item of unusual houseware.

"What do we need those for?" I protested, staring at the rolls of sticky, rubbery shelf-lining prominently displayed in the kitchenware section.

"We'll need it for earthquakes," she announced, snatching up enough to line the *Titanic*.

The coming big one — the mother of all disasters — The Quake, is one subject so absolutely terrifying from both a personal and a financial aspect that it is not often discussed. Two of the world's largest and best-known fault lines run damn near through Boulder House's bedroom. San Andreas is twenty miles to the south, and Landers is half that distance to the north. San Andreas has yet to pop, but the experience of the Landers affair is instructive.

At 5.45 on the morning of 28 June 1992, a 7.6 quake shook the desert awake. The entire populace fled their homes in terror as roads changed course, school buses bounced about like broncos, fences moved thirty feet, and huge underground water tanks sank so deep they were never to be found again. The earth became a sponge, and the shaking lasted for three terrible minutes. Tough desert men will attest to the terror. Eric, a man who loves nothing more than a good fight, and carries many a scar to prove it, remembers screaming as he and his roommate tried to open their Yucca apartment door. Finally they crashed through into a dawn full of the cries of the fearful. A wheelchair-bound neighbor was thrown from his bed and could not make it to the chair. His toilet exploded, and water raced through the apartment, threatening to drown him as he floundered on the floor. Eric dragged him to the uncertain safety of the street — a new world of wrecked houses, many fit only for the bulldozer. A couple visiting from the Dakotas had left their baby girl with a sitter for the night, and a chimney collapsed upon her cot, killing the child. It was the only death from the Landers quake, but many still talk of miraculous escapes.

The townsfolk were waiting in clusters for the authorities when, three hours later, another quake—this time centered at Big Bear, thirty miles away at the top of the San Bernardino Mountains—let loose its power. This was a mere 6.6, but it shook Southern California as hard as the first. A great rumbling roar like a train thundering towards the huddled masses. Rockslides in the mountains caused massive eruptions of dirt to fly, like clouds from a bushfire, high into the air. Six hours later, the mountain sky was still thick with dust. Many reported fires. As the quake rolled out along the desert, the small crowds could see the wave of energy coming. The Joshua trees, named so because the early Mormons thought they resembled Joshua in prayer in the wilderness, bowed before the wave as the terrified residents watched the quake race towards them.

"It was like watching the wave at the baseball," Eric recalls. "As it approached, a line of trees would shake and bend. We just stood there watching it come like a tidal wave. Everyone was yelling and screaming. I was yelling, 'Here it comes,' and then it hit. Everyone was knocked around like a bunch of drunks."

Then it passed, leaving whole communities picking through the rubble that had been their lives. In the wake of the quake, new and wondrous fault lines were discovered. One, the Kickapoo Fault, lies just to the north of us and is illustrated in maps by the Department of Civil Engineering. The black line stretches across the map from Landers and swings to the west, which is regrettably close to Boulder House. Ominously, it also ends with a series of question marks. No one knows where it ends at all.

As no one knew this huge fault even existed until the "Big One" hit, perhaps the map should be comforting. What is not is the naming of the fault. The Kickapoo were a hard-fighting bunch of Indians and should not be remembered as a fault line — or a major intersection in Yucca. Naming roads and fault lines after Indian tribes that are located a thousand-or-so miles away is not as tasteless as calling a football team "Redskins", but one would have expected academics in the 1990s to have come up with something more relevant. They could have named the streets and faults after local tribes annihilated by white occupation. The Serrano Fault would be more appropriate. But the streets and the faults of our environs are too often named after a mythical people, a tribe from far away. Who wants to be reminded of the local slaughters? This is the West — the land of cowboys and Indians. There are about as many cowboys as Indians. Approximately five.

"Right lateral and vertical displacements were of 1.2 meters," reads the official report. It is one of those government-academic reports that sometimes turn out some interesting sentences. Even bureaucrats can find something approaching language when writing of a big quake — and nothing could be more demonstrative of the power of such things than that government reports can, at times, be made interesting. A layman struggles with "lateral and vertical displacement", but wonders if he might be correct in gauging that the land moved almost four feet to the west, and that same amount up — or down. In parts of Landers, "ground rupture" was one mile wide. Typically, a home not being designed to move in such a fashion split in two, and "the center of the house rotated clockwise in respect to the foundations."

I have been in a situation where houses rotate clockwise and anticlockwise, and it's not a lot of fun.

There was a time I rather enjoyed earthquakes and made fun of those who feared them. We had enjoyed a good number of them in LA, and in Venice — one hundred-plus miles away — had felt the rolling from the great Landers Quake. It was just a gentle rocking by the time it hit us, just like the ones before it. The next day, we pored over the pics in the *Los Angeles Times*. One showed a road near the marine base that stopped abruptly, only to start again twenty yards to the south. One got the impression that people could have been swallowed alive by the earth — something that few people wish to experience, to my knowledge.

But like all earthquakes in those days, the damage was far away and not part of our lives. If we had not felt the rocking, it might have been in Japan or Turkey.

It wasn't till the Northridge quake in 1996 that I changed my mind on the question of earthquakes. We were still in Venice at the time, and were fortunate enough to be living in a small wooden structure — beside the Man with No Brain — which had enough flexibility to give with the shakes. Shake is not the right word for a big one. Shake, rattle, and roll would be an appropriate phrase. For a minute or so, it seemed a giant had picked up the house and was tossing it in the air. Up and down, left and right meant nothing. Walls became roofs; roofs, floors. Boo totally ignored my demand that we do as we had been so often told and get out of the house. So we rode it out in bed. It turned out that she was right. It was impossible to get out of bed. The floor had become the wall, and it was necessary to climb horizontally. While the world shook.

The power was gone with the streetlights, and for a while the city was black and silent. The house settled, and I ran into the spare bedroom where an Australian woman was supposed to be. But she had found a flashlight and made it to the bathroom, where she was busily making up her face.

"Get out of here," I cried.

She turned to me, waving what seemed to be a great tube of lipstick, and replied, "Not until I have done my face. You never know who you might meet in an evacuation."

As it was, she met half the neighborhood, but, as the streetlights were out and the darkness was complete, no new love was in the offing. The next thing we knew — without so much as a "fare thee well" — she was gone. Home. To the safety of Australia, which pretty much finished with its eruptions many millennia ago.

The city shook for a few days as we all cleaned up. Glasses, plates, and Boo's pretty things were smashed through the house, and the chimney had collapsed.

The Biblical exhortation to build upon the rock was followed by Bill Lavender in such a manner that the Dirty Old Man Of The Desert could, or at least should, be granted sainthood.

Needless to say, nary a boulder dared move at Boulder House during the Landers affair. Indeed, right before we were to take possession, a quake hit Yucca Valley. Its epicenter, we learnt from the TV, was practically smack in the middle of the big bedroom. Boo got straight on the phone to Bill to see if there was anything left of the place.

"Well, the dogs barked," came Bill's drawl. "And a cup did move on the bench. I think I popped a water pipe," he let out with a yawn.

"That's amazing," Boo exclaimed, having expected catastrophe.

"Nothing amazing about it," Bill retorted. "That's how I built the house. To withstand all that bullshit."

But the "Really Big One" should be interesting. As blasé as Bill might be, a walk around the property and a glance out to the back courtyard is a mite nerve-racking. Huge boulders, some of which must weigh ten thousand tons, are cracked, and seem to totter eighty feet above the house. Bill built his house *in* — rather than *on* — the rock, and who knows when they all might come tumbling down? Every other day I stare up at these broken giants and wonder if it will be a year or one hundred thousand years before the "Really Big One" comes. Perhaps these precarious pinnacles will hold, and Boulder House will be saved.

Bill is philosophical on the question, as are the finance companies that, while showing scrupulous attention to detail over all manner of unlikely risks, never mentioned the "Really Big One", or even a little one. Bill explained the matter.

"Don't get earthquake insurance," he counseled. "The deductibles are horrendous, and FIMA will cover you anyway."

So we rest safe in our beds.

In the time following the Landers and the Big Bear quakes, the area received a mere forty thousand aftershocks. The land shook for months, but it has stopped now. However, there is a disturbing remark buried in the seismologists' report.

"Boulders," it says, "greater than ten feet in diameter" crashed down almost one thousand feet, and trees were "toppled", suggesting that the boulders were bouncing ten to fifteen feet off the ground. Strangely enough, people moved out of the area, and the population, ten years later, has only recently returned to its pre-quake levels. But when the Big One comes, most of those who live will rebuild.

21

Remodeling Boulder House proffers something of an epistemological problem. Almost. That is, not only do I not know what I am doing, but most of the people who do know don't know either. So I proceed, sans architect, plans, color schemes, and often sans Tony. Tony is an outside man—rocks and cactus, pipes and wires, trenches, concrete.

Despite our efforts at ripping out walls and installing skylights, Boulder House was still somehow managing to outsmart us. It was as if the house was used to being dark, and intended to remain so. Bill, being a practical man, had thought out, with exactitude, the best way to keep sunlight at bay and thereby keep the house cool. Such had been his success that for much of the year the place was not only dark but cold. The natural granite that made up a good part of the walls regulated the heat in the summer, but as the winter months passed those same granite walls would turn deadly cold and stay that way well into spring and even early summer.

We decided that I should drywall all the dark deep-brown wood walls and then adobe it with a rough but white look. The theory was that sunlight combined with white walls would drive the darkness and attendant cold from the place.

This whole huge house will need the services of someone more skilled than I, or even Fleet—a jack of many trades and a good new friend. Fleet claims his nickname comes from some confusion with Fleetwood Mac during the time they and he were living in Topanga. It is my belief that Fleet is called Fleet for the same reason that all huge Hells Angels are called Tiny, and that people with red hair are called Bluey.

Adam is, of course, the finest drywaller in many a mile, but has taken to cards. He was broke on Saturday night when he realized he had seven gentlemen turning up at his home, and not a dollar to bet with. He approached Tony, hoping Tony might give him fifty bucks for his pool cue, which he claims to have paid $200 for. Tony and I were enjoying a smoke in Tony's room at the motel when he recounted Adam's woe. Adam was opposite, in The Club, and in a foul mood. It's a sorry situation when a man has guests around for poker and can't afford to play in his own home. Usually he wins, maybe enough for a week's supply of Bud. Which is a lot of Bud. Adam scorns coffee, starting and ending his days with Bud—an activity he seems to think is his patriotic duty. How he wins at cards is a matter of universal wonder. Adam, if he is anything, is confident, especially in the evening when a box or two of Bud have made their way down his gullet. So confident is Adam that when playing, say, five-card draw, he refuses to look at his cards.

"I know they are good," he says, smiling his damned handsome smile, for Adam and his father, John, and Uncle Jerry are nothing if not handsome.

So he sits at the card table beaming his confidence with no idea what cards he is holding. It is a little off-putting for the other players. especially when Adam doubles the bet and one stares at him through the smoke as he repeats, "I know they are good."

He looks at his cards with the affection some have for their children. Adam has one rule at his table, and it is a measure of the man: "No limits." It is also a reason I attend the sessions infrequently. I have forgotten much of what I knew of the games and am constantly dealing cards up when they should be down. Last time I played, I quickly lost $40 and pulled out. I lost it to Tony, so I made it double or nothing on something I know something about — football. Backing Baltimore against the Rams with a fourteen-point start in the Super Bowl is about as easy a way to make money one can find.

But one can lose a lot more than $40 at a no-limits table. Suddenly, one is sitting on a decent but not great hand, needing $100 to stay in the game. And there, opposite, sits Adam, happily doubling everybody back, with still no idea what cards he is holding. The first time I played, I was sitting on two color pairs — a good five-card hand that beat the players who hadn't folded. All except Adam, who, oblivious to what he "held", turned over two worthless cards and then three aces. He scooped up the pile of chips gleefully. In other circles, one might have searched him, but Adam is scrupulously honest, at least when it comes to cards. But there is not a man in twenty miles who would trust him with his girl.

Learning that Adam was prepared for a cash-for-cue swap at very reasonable terms, I left Tony and hurried through the cold to The Club. Sure enough, Adam was in a foul mood until I approached him. His eyes lit up — and when Adam's eyes light up, girls tremble.

"Wanna buy my cue?" he asked before I could make an offer.

"Tony mentioned it was for sale," I replied as demurely as possible.

One doesn't want to be seen taking advantage of the local hero in his misfortune. But the cue was soon mine, Chuck the barman providing the cash, as I had only a few dollars myself. The cue is a beauty. Not pretty — too flash — but it sings. I should make the money back in no time and still possess a stick that plays like $400. Adam had his money and was off to meet his guests. I didn't attend the game, but Slovakian Pete, the snake man, did, and the next day morosely told me that Adam had won handsomely without, again, looking at his cards. One wonders just how good a player Adam would be if he looked at his hand before betting, but his attitude seems to be that such actions are a sign of bad faith, in which case the cards might turn against him.

Adam hosts regular poker games at his historic cabin throughout the winter. The house is tiny but, having been built by a famous architect, has architectural significance. It won't for long, though, if Adam doesn't repair the roof. On those rare occasions when it rains, the water pours through the single bedroom and the living room–kitchen, and Adam moves outside until the place dries up.

The cabin is not hard to find. One merely follows the empty Bud cans, which Boo refers to as "the trail of beers", till one comes within sight of a huge black-and-white skull and crossbones flapping merrily above a corral. A great swirl of dogs bounce around in greeting — the number of which seems to constantly vary, as they enjoy a nomadic life. The latest acquisition Adam named Honey so he can cry, "Hi honey, I'm home," when he arrives back after the bar closes.

Inside, a big poster of Jim Morrison dominates the room. Next to it are Butch and Sundance shooting their way out of town, curiously mingled with various South Sea artifacts. It is dangerous to admire anything in Adam's house. He is likely to immediately give it to you.

Everywhere are photos of all the Edwards. Adam was a parachutist. There is a photo of him in his red beret. In his early twenties, he was a major heartthrob, not just handsome but beautiful.

Which brings us by a circuitous route back to the drywall problem. While Adam is making money at the table he is loath to make it sanding mud off my walls. And Adam with money is Adam with Bud. More Bud than usual. In my experience, Budweiser and the finer touches of the difficult art of drywalling a house that has bent and twisted in heat and snow, been rocked by earthquakes, and was built on angles in the first place don't mix.

Rodney could do the job. He's nearly as good as Adam. But Rodney gets a nice check from his union each month, and while not shy of work will have enough on his plate keeping Harriet happy now they have bought a new cabin.

So the ball lands in my camp. It's either that or live in a construction site forever, so I must rise from the pleasures of staring at either the keyboard or the blizzard up in the high pine-clad forest of Big Bear and start sanding.

22

No one out here wears a watch. It doesn't really matter if one is on time or not.

Sean, who has come over to grade our road, and stayed on for dinner — which he cooked himself, being a gourmet chef as well as an expert grader — claims to be able to read the moon as easily as the sun, a claim I consider downright impossible.

"How can you read the moon on nights when there is no moon?" I scoff.

"I read the stars."

I look at the moon, a thin wedge of cheese above Rimrock. Off towards the marine base, Venus fades. According to Sean, it's nearly eleven. I stride into the house. Sean is about eleven minutes slow.

There is no point in taking this to the Supreme Court. The time of day means little, and the time at night, nothing. Who cares what time it is? Does the burrow know the time?

As the great Banjo Patterson observed, townsfolk — he meant city dwellers — have no time to wait. Here the opposite is true. Time is free, and there is a lot of it. The road from the gate is strewn with danger. Lurking everywhere are people with plenty of time. The three other occupants of Coyote Road, The Blade Runner and his wife, and an eccentric artist directly opposite them, are in a constant state of unarmed conflict, a battle that has its roots in one party kicking up dust onto the other's guest's shoes. The Blade Runner is a great lover of machinery, and an avid reader of *Rock and Dirt* magazine, if it's possible to read a journal that prints only advertisements for machinery, and boasts of having the largest collection of iron on earth — since 1957.

Russ is in his eighties. He spent his salaried days working in San Diego overseeing the movement of sand and gravel to construction sites, and is never happier than when telling stories of the movement of same — usually the same story. He must have been a bull of a man in his day, and he still carries a hard demeanor. When we met, I thought he was dying. Blood seemed caked around his mouth, but on further inspection I determined it was chew, a wad of tobacco being his companion from dawn to dusk. He owned three tractors until he sold one a few months ago. Now he is reduced to two machines, and one — the smaller tractor — is operated by his wife. Until we moved out here, I didn't know that the people who make tractors make a ladies' model.

The perils of the road extend all the way to the bottom of Pioneertown Road and even beyond. A trip out for breakfast, even to clear the mailbox, is perilous, and may take two hours. Recently, I ran into five friends just getting the mail, almost the entire male population of Pioneertown. Some locals consider it rude not to visit. Ernie and Carole consider a week without a visit a snub. Carole can talk about their dogs, past and present, for an hour, barely drawing a breath.

This did not sit well with my experiences of life in Los Angeles. There I learnt the ultimate purpose of civilization, its overwhelming drive, and the reason for the striving of the soul. It is not the pursuit of happiness, but the elimination of patience. The pursuit of speed, and the speeding up of pursuit. The great goal of our culture is to banish that bane of true happiness, that most undesirable of human requirements — patience. LA is teaching the world that a wait for half an hour on a freeway off-ramp to purchase a burrito in an instant is a giant step for us all.

Monday nights are taco nights in Pioneertown, and with Boo in LA on business, I ventured forth with Ernie and Carole to acquaint myself with the old Pioneertown Bowling Alley. We had no intention of bowling, and few that attend this establishment trouble the perfectly maintained 1940s ten pin-bowling joint. They prefer to trouble Ron, the proprietor, in the forlorn hope of obtaining a drink and even a spot of food. Ernie and Carole sat, wisely it turned out, at tables, but I waited at the bar in the hope of purchasing my new friends and myself a drink. Realizing my intention, Ron scuttled away into the bowels of his establishment, leaving me alone and impatient. The minutes passed. I looked at Ernie and Carole, expecting that as locals they would have some explanation of why a proprietor was unable to serve his three customers — the bar being otherwise empty.

For a few more moments, I admired the place. Roy Rogers smiled down at us from walls adorned with him bowling (in cowboy boots), smiling at Dale, smiling at Trigger, and doing Roy Rogers things. There was even a signed score card from the great man, and I had time to reflect that this was the only time I had entered a bowling alley without being repulsed by the smells attendant to human activity. There was no sign of human effort whatsoever — neither on the floor nor behind the bar. I tried a plaintive "COOEE", the cry that, according to Australian

Aboriginal lore, is the human sound that travels further than any other. Ron, a tiny man who was incapable of standing still, returned. He bounced about behind the bar, reminding me of a flea, and ten minutes after we entered the bar inquired whether we would like a drink.

"We would," I told him, "sometime today."

Ron took the opportunity to disappear from the face of the earth, even though all the prerequisites of beers, a limited range of hard stuff, and an even more limited array of mixes stood right before me. Eventually, he returned and took our orders, and disappeared again. I ordered a margarita and then sat down, realizing why Ernie and Carole had done so some twenty minutes before. Ron returned and started making a grand disturbance, as though assembling a motor car rather than three margaritas.

We waited. My margarita, when it arrived was, I told Ron, "unspeakable". It was pink, and the salt, rather than lining the rim, seemed to have been included in the drink.

I turned to get a fresh drink — a simple bottle of beer — but Ron had disappeared again.

My cooees turned to bellows, and Ron bobbed up from somewhere, wondering whether all was well. It wasn't, I told him, asking, perhaps brutally, for a simple bottle of Bud. Ron disappeared again. There was no possible task he needed to attend to. There were only three people in the bar, and Mane Street was utterly deserted. I stared at Carole, bewildered.

"It's the desert, David," she said with relaxed indifference, sipping on her drink.

In LA, even in better restaurants, food is ordered "to go". And drink is made available instantly. Los Angelenos live to go. They talk all the time about leaving. They are impatient to go. But they never leave. People don't leave Pioneertown, nor do they talk about leaving.

Patience is the ability to wait without suffering. But for denizens of the modern world, waiting is suffering, and suffering should not, we all know, be part of the human condition. The city has turned the struggle for greater speed — what the eggheads once clumsily labeled instant gratification— into its ethos.

The life of the hunter was hours, maybe days, of patience, followed by a burst of speed. The patience was far more important than the speed. Los Angeles is reversing this arrangement, and creating a society where life is a long burst of speed, followed by a moment's patience. This, again, is most evident in its eating habits.

From our last apartment in Hollywood, I could walk to the elevator, descend to the "secure" underground parking, simultaneously start the car and open the security gates, fly along Rossmore Avenue, cross Melrose, cross Santa Monica Boulevard, cross Sunset, pull into an Indian restaurant, order, pay, pick up the food, cross all the aforementioned streets on the race home, and serve a warm curry to ten people in about ten minutes. That's a minute a person. To achieve this in a pastoral society would take many hours. A hunter would be lucky to provide enough food for so many mouths in days, if at all.

The hunter would spend most of his twenty or so years of maturity in pure patience, waiting for prey. The food, once caught, would be eaten collectively: a communal act that evolved into what used to be called a meal. Los Angeles families are so well supplied in foodstuffs that they have been freed from eating together. And who has time for such an awkward arrangement? Instead they graze, at the refrigerator door if time permits.

Otherwise they grab something, and eat while pursuing a higher goal than that of getting to know other members of the family. They make money. As the family disintegrated, psychologists invented "quality time". Time spent with loved ones has been institutionalized.

"Quality time" has not been a complete success. The very title implies that this time is more important than time spent making money, and that's a hard sell to a five-year-old in LA. The old-fashioned meal brought us together for primeval reasons. To eat. Quality time is forcing a bunch of people united only through biology to meet and get to know and, hopefully, like one another. As a bonding mechanism it's got a long way to go. It's a speed bump.

If Los Angelenos have to wait, they do it at traffic lights or on the freeway. They will spend about three years of their lives waiting at traffic lights.

But the elimination of patience has not corresponded with the extinction of patience's closest cousin, waiting.

Forced waiting and the elimination of patience lead the city's citizens, primates of a new culture, to other occasional malfunctions. Road rage is the most recent, and one of the more graphic manifestations of the daily battle waged between patience and waiting. To the years they spend waiting at the lights, we must add the years spent stopped, or crawling along what are called, in remembrance of things past, "freeways".

Residents of the High Desert have great patience, as they rarely have to wait, especially now that Ron has sold the bar to Stephanie, who, having worked a bar in New York, knows that there is something of a relationship between service and cashflow.

But they have no traffic lights, or traffic. Not a single stop sign adorns the town, though there is one on the corner where Pipes Canyon departs from Pioneertown Road. Thus we don't get a lot of road rage, and the closest thing to a traffic jam occurs at the Post Office. Here, at about 10.00 a.m., up to five trucks and as many as two cars can be found, their occupants yarning and gossiping and avoiding commencing what they have to attend to.

Ed, who first drove me to Boulder House, became a frequent visitor and has bought sixty acres off Roadrunner Rut — a longish rifle shot from Boulder House. He and his wife spent many weekends at Boulder House while finding the right place, and another half-dozen getting a trailer to the site. But it was much-needed therapy, as Ed had come to suffer from chronic road rage.

He lived in Marina Del Rey, but worked in Seal Beach. That's only fifty or so miles, and in his Le Baron convertible Ed should be able to jump on the 405 freeway, after a quick run along the 92 (The Richard Nixon Freeway, as it is no longer called), and be at the office in an hour. Max!

But Ed, whose lack of patience exceeds the city average, usually spent two and often three hours making his trip — the 405 being the least free of all the city's freeways. The road home was neither shorter nor quicker. Averaged out, Ed spent five hours a day fighting his way through traffic to get to and from work, and eight, nine, or even ten hours running computer systems that were designed to speed the movement of information. That left him less than ten hours a day to sleep, eat, and have fun. Ed likes his fun.

He likes to go to bars and get "a nice buzz up", beat everyone but me at pool, and then head home. Once home, he will eat, and after a few hours rest it's back to the freeway.

Naturally, his work suffered.

Ed is way above average intelligence, and he found a way to stack the deck in his favor. Realizing the five to six hours in the car were the cause of his social limitations, that his principal "recoverable hours" were those spent on the freeway, he decided to turn his convertible into a mobile mini-bar. Ed reasoned that he could kill two birds and still get stoned. The trick was to get to The Circle, for that was his preferred bar, with a sufficient "buzz" that he could immediately join in the spirit of the place without wasting an hour or two catching up with all the other drinkers.

Although Ed disapproved of drink-driving, he did not consider drinking while driving an offence. That it was against the law did not necessarily make it an offence. Smoking marijuana is against the law, but few would consider that an offence. Only a few years ago, cops in Texas would describe the distance of a drive by the number of beer cans required to complete it. A "two-can" drive was maybe forty miles. A six-pack drive, one hundred and fifty miles. Ed's driving record was, until he made this decision, impeccable.

Ed's preferred drink, like Buzz's, is Kessler, a cheaper whiskey that requires a decent dash of coke to be rendered drinkable. Ed took to buying bottles of Kessler and to stopping at a nearby McDonald's, where huge Cokes, enclosed in plastic tops, can be purchased in an instant.

Ed had outsmarted society once again. He would pull out of the McDonald's and, stretching his arm out of the convertible, empty half the gallon or so of Coke and ice into the nearest gutter. The container would be refilled with Kessler, the plastic top returned, the mix shaken, and the straw inserted. Ed would cruise onto the 405, sixty miles from The Circle Bar. A favorite recording of The Rolling Stones would boom out his rebuilt super-duper music system, and Ed could get his evening started at about the same time that his friends were making their way to the bar. As the drive could stretch for three hours and the ice died in the Coke and Kessler slush, he often found it necessary to pull off the freeway, flash into a McDonald's, and be back on the freeway, level with the crawling cars he had just left, holding a fresh, cold Kessler and Coke.

Ed carries a confident air that can accompany people who have worked for the higher reaches of the US government. If a police car was stuck beside him for ten minutes, he would sip his Coke and Kessler concoction, and smile. Ed has a large head and a large smile, one of goodwill to all men, and he would cast it at the cops stuck a few feet away as they waited for the traffic to edge them closer to their drive's end. Once he obliged the bored cops by turning up "Sympathy for the Devil" and a few other favorites while he sipped in absolute security.

It was a system he was to utilize until he was finally brought down, after a fabulous example of road rage, which led to his eventual involvement with Alcoholics Anonymous.

Tom, who was working that night at The Circle serving Ed and a few others, later calculated that Ed drank a bottle and a half of Kessler before deciding it was time to drive home. This, coupled with the half-bottle he had consumed on the freeway, caused Tom some concern, but he figured Ed was capable of his usual drive home, a mere trip through Venice. And Ed made it home without effort.

He was about to park when someone cut him off, stealing his spot. Ed openly admits to suffering from bouts of road rage, and taking a parking spot someone else has already located is a serious social offence in LA. The rage came upon him just a few yards from his apartment, but attracted the system of justice he so admired, and he was asked to walk in a straight line. The police directed Ed to a section of pavement that was severely cracked. Ed suggested the cops try to walk straight along it, but they declined. Ed walked a crooked ten yards, and was taken to the Venice police station, was found to be three times the legal limit, arrested, and handcuffed to a steel rod in a holding area. There he joined a half-dozen men who were also inebriated.

He was naturally demanding the right to call his then girlfriend so he could be bailed out. He had to be at work in six hours, and as the situation at work had grown tense, non-arrival because of a DUI test would make things even more difficult. But the cops ignored his righteous demands and left him in the tank.

Deep in his jeans pocket was Ed's cell phone. He began to wiggle, and after almost half an hour of furious wiggling, his phone slipped into his lap. But Ed's hands were cuffed to the steel rod behind him, and it was impossible for him to use his fingers to make his call. This deterred him but a little. He had been, in the service of his country, in more testing situations. He didn't have to punch her number, as the phone was programmed to dial. But he did have to get to the automatic dialing button, guide it to her number, and press the little YES that would hopefully wake his beloved, long deep in sleep. He achieved this by maneuvering his body and the phone so his elbow touched the appropriate button. Miraculously, she was aroused, but the phone had slipped, and he could hear nothing. Seeing that the call had gone through, he bellowed "I'm in the Venice police station, bring $500!" He did this for a few minutes, not knowing whether she could hear him, and even if she could whether she would be in the frame of mind to come to his rescue.

Then he sat and waited as his cellmates speculated on his chances of gaining freedom.

About a half-hour later a large contingent of police officers entered the tank, all expressing astonishment and wonder. His phone, still on, was in his lap, and the cops, greatly impressed by his feat, released him and escorted him, with the respect due to a commanding officer, and handed him over to his unsmiling girlfriend. It was the last time they were to go out together, but he had time to race home, clean up, borrow a mate's car—his being impounded—hit the 405, and arrive at work with a relaxed air, on time.

The judge ordered him to attend Alcoholics Anonymous. This made his short day even shorter. Now he had to spend an extra two hours, three days a week, listening to the "confessions" of others, of lost souls baring their sordid secrets to strangers so they could continue to drive vast distances to pursue tasks that usually involved making things go faster.

His drinking time was even further eroded. Mandatory breath tests were made on all entering the sessions. But, Ed noticed, after a few of what was to be three months of this tedium, the tests were not taken on these poor souls as they left their session. He took to buying bottles of Kessler and jumbo-sized Coke containers again. He reported that from there on in, he always left the meetings with a "nice buzz", and by the time he pulled his blue convertible up outside The Circle, was ready to play.

187

The ending gets happier still. Soon after, Ed was "headhunted" by a major corporation only a few miles from his home and even closer to The Circle.

He had been freed from speed's grip. But for every free Ed, there are a thousand still in speed's clutches.

23

Ernie and Carole are the sort of citizens that Norman Rockwell would prize. Citizens very much in the traditional sense of the word. They care for all and sundry, especially the sundry. No matter how badly their trust is abused, they will offer more. If everyone in the world had the goodness of these two, TV stations in Somalia would be advertising weight-loss programs. When their tenant didn't pay a lick of rent for years, she was never threatened with eviction. When she had no money for the power and water, Ernie and Carole paid for that, too. The list of those who have enjoyed their largesse is embarrassingly large. Cars are lent—never to be seen in any worthy shape again. Rooms are granted free to those they know will never pay. Carole devotes herself to historic causes; Ernie, to "The Gunfighters" and the weekly enactment of Wild West shootouts opposite the bowling alley in front of the town's Old West bank, livery stables, and saloon facades. In presenting his productions, Ernie researches the garb and guns of the Old Western fighters as meticulously as a remake of the *Titanic*.

Getting to be friends with Ernie and Carole was one of the smartest things we ever did. Ernie is a consummate actor who would be superbly cast as Grumpy if someone had the good sense to remake *Snow White*. In his one movie role, he totally carried *The Howling 9*, which may be the worst movie ever filmed in Pioneertown.

Their living room–cum-office is the center of life in Pioneertown, a source of all information and knowledge. The coffeepot is always hot, and the citizenry are always dropping in for a chat, a gossip, and a piece of pie.

"Tony will be leaving any day now," Carole alerts us, as she ladles out great plates of freshly baked enchiladas.

"How do you know?" we inquire.

"I've been watching the Wisconsin weather forecast, and the ground is expected to thaw this week. As soon as it does, he'll be heading back up there."

Tony's leaving is both good news and bad. It means that our weather is warming up, but the loss of Tony is a blow. Tony, as could be expected of a man who spends his life in a furious struggle to redefine nature, is politically conservative, and thus we disagree on almost everything. But he is pretty much the only person out here who closely reads the *LA Times*. For all its sins (employing the worst cartoonist in Christendom), the *LA Times* is a pretty good rag. Though not a journal of record and without the pretensions of *The New York Times*, it does go far and wide in covering the world and is, to my mind, a better paper than its east coast adversary. While reviling Liberal opinion Tony is at least familiar with it. And he cans the Republicans as much as the Democrats and the pro-Democrat organs. Thus conversation with Tony is as lively as one can hope for, and his disappearances are an annual blow to those of us who like a vexing conversation on national and foreign matters.

Tony does, however, disappear when the north thaws. How he does it is usually a mystery. One day he is simply gone, and will not be seen or heard from again until the cold returns. He does not say goodbye. Usually, he has bought a truck in the course of his endeavors, an old one that doesn't have to be smogged, and he'll drive it to Wisconsin, work it like he works himself, and sell it for twice what he paid for it. Powerful old rust-free trucks are valuable up by the Great Lakes.

Through the winter, Tony had shown Boo how to collect the yellow sap from the huge pine trees that grace our land. They would return from an afternoon hike with great hunks of the sticky gum to burn on top of the fire — scenting the whole house with brain-blasting pine fragrance. Now, with the arrival of spring and the departure of her hiking partner, she has set up a primitive camp beneath one of the largest juniper trees in the Hidden Valley. This gnarly old twisted giant — some say it is over two thousand years old — gives off the sweetest pine scent, and is the true smell of promised warmth to come. It is also a perfect blind — the valley's premier spot to sit and watch and not be watched — staring up at the biggest golden boulders for miles around, some one hundred feet high. Here is the exclusive penthouse for the king of the skies — the golden eagle. With a seven-foot wing span, it's hard to miss him, but somehow Boo has managed each time.

Before Tony left, we were thumping along Pipes Canyon Road in my 1982 Ford 150 truck — which, having been purchased from Adam, was in a sorry state. At least the exterior was, as Adam, when he got mad, was prone to attacking his vehicles. I have never known him to hit a person. The window on the passenger side was missing, and I slowed to study what appeared to be roadkill. The golden eagle had beaten us to the scene but, startled by our arrival, decided to take off. However, it was caught between the truck and the graded dirt at the side of the road, and had difficulty getting airborne. For a few hundred yards he flew beside us, his wingtips in the truck, flapping by Tony's face. We could see the detail of the golden feathers as we stared speechlessly until the great bird attained sufficient velocity to rise above us and make its way to a nearby Joshua tree, where it landed, eyeing us and the carrion. We left it to its meal.

Pappy was part Indian, and his animal spirit was the golden eagle. The night he died, it sailed above his house. And it reappeared the day Harriet, his widow, remarried, circling high above the guests to give its blessing, all agreed, to the newlyweds.

The saloon is still called Pappy and Harriet's. On the walls hang paintings of Pappy—half man, half eagle—and on the bar sits a large bust of the deceased proprietor, staring out at the ageing weekend cowboys and their rhinestoned gals, dancing a slow quickstep to the band. The bar rolls up at midnight these days. When Pappy was alive, the music went all night. Pappy loved to dance.

With the first real warmth, the first cactus bloom. The brilliant vermilion flower is so improbable even it looks surprised to be showing itself off so shamelessly amongst its plain, prickly neighbors, like the first girl in the street to swish through her front door in a gaudy sundress after a long winter's chill. The flower almost looks artificial, like the finest paper.

The centerpiece of the rock garden that in turn is the center of the driveway is a beautiful ponderosa pine that stands right before the house. It was planted by Saundra Edwards, and nurtured by the bathwater she would carry out to it after washing the children, thirty years ago. Beneath it, a dozen different types of cactus flourish, their blooms competing with one another for brightness, wooing the bees that flit from one to the next like a fat man at the buffet brunch bar. Suddenly, everything is flowering, even the otherwise charmless cholla. No sooner have the blooms died on one variety than another, even more stunning, appears — the claret cup hedgehog, purple sage, apricot desert mallow, deep blue chia, rich red chuparosa or sucking rose, pale-pink desert willow, yellow marigold, and the vivid red Indian paintbrush, which has inspired Boo to match the color on our dining room walls regardless of my protests and the horrified looks of the locals. The desert floor, barren for the rest of the year, shape-shifts into a great woven tapestry of tiny "belly flowers" so small that the best way to appreciate them is from flat on your stomach.

The Joshua trees are also in bloom in the spring with great clusters of creamy flowers crowning their spiky heads. The Indians used the trees for making sleeping mats, and they wove sandals from the fiber. In the Apple Valley museum is a one-thousand-year-old sandal found in a pack rat's nest.

They pounded the tree's roots for soap. Yucca and Joshua trees provided everything, from spikes for needles to strong drink from the fermented blossoms. Moccasins and sandals made from yucca leaves were wrapped with juniper bark.

The trees were once called "the cowboy's friend", as they would burn even when wet. No one burns or touches them these days. Being caught cutting one means serving time.

In the late 1800s they were cut down for pulp for newspapers on the east coast and Britain. This was a complete failure, as the crated pulp overheated and spoiled.

During World War I — being light and sturdy — they were used to make artificial limbs, and were even turned into Panama hats. The Joshua tree forests disappeared from much of the Southwest, and the High Desert is one of the few places they still flourish.

In their place grew tumbleweed, a curse imported from Russia (its seeds mixed in with imported flax) after the Civil War. Pioneertown was named after Roy Rogers' band "Sons of the Pioneers", who recorded the hit that still gets older Americans misty-eyed — "Tumbling Tumbleweeds." But the fact is that the early cowboys would never have seen a tumbleweed, which is just a weed, a thistle, and a destructive one at that.

It first appeared in the Dakotas not long after the Civil War, and covered a third of the nation and much of Canada within a decade. This nasty plant breaks from the main root and tumbles where it will, releasing as many as fifty thousand seeds in a good tumble. The cowboys never happily "tumbled along with the tumbling tumbleweed", as the dirge goes, as the much-loved plant ruins pasture. As it's not native, it has no natural enemies, and today Cal Trans spends millions each year trying to control the thistles along the roads. They are dangerous to drivers and a fire hazard. They don't so much burn as explode, and they tend to bunch up. They block drains and waterways, and contaminate fields with a virus.

In late spring, Sean moved into the guesthouse, or poolroom, or both. The deal was a makeshift matter that vaguely involved a reciprocal arrangement whereby we would provide him with a dwelling, and he would work and not pay rent.

Sean, when we met him, was a lay preacher at the Pioneertown Church, a sect of a larger sect, or a moonbeam from a greater lunacy — the Baptists. He was recovering from a ferocious addiction to methamphetamine, which he had overcome through devotion to hard liquor — in the main, tequila — and the study of the Bible. These two loves were equaled only by his attachment to guns.

We had first visited him at his small trailer at the other end of Pipes Canyon in the mountain foothills, for Boo to take some lessons as a shootist. Sean, with a .22 six-shooter low on his thigh, was on his bed studying the Old Testament. He put down the Bible, took a swig of tequila, and joined us outside — there being not enough room for us to join him inside. By way of instruction, he drew his gun and fanned from his hip at an old can some fifty feet from the trailer. The can flew into the air, landing a few feet away. He fanned the gun again, and the can flew once more into the air. After six fast shots, the thing was riddled with holes, and Sean reloaded and explained he was using .22 magnums.

"They have that much more punch," he added, showing us the extra length and therefore powder of the bullet. I raised the gun, took careful aim, and missed. I walked over and set the can standing, fired again, and missed again. My fourth shot came close enough to spray dirt onto the can, knocking it over. Boo did a little better, knocking over the can a couple of times.

"Handy if we ever get attacked by a beer can," she reflected.

Sean enthused, pointing out that if the can was a heart we would have gone close enough to slow an assailant down, but I reflected that a target that was shooting back and moving things could get bloody — for us.

"Then get a shotgun," he advised.

Sean could not find suitable work, and Tony had gone back to Wisconsin. Sean might not have been as strong as Tony, but he had a tractor, and even Tony wasn't as powerful as a John Deere. We set about doing some landscaping.

Together, we scoured the land for suitable rocks with which to construct a grand stairway that would lead from the house to the Hidden Valley. Sean wanted something definitive, something he could photograph as evidence of his abilities. Something to show off.

We collected about thirty good-sized flat stones — some weighed half a ton — but Sean figured we needed a base rock that would serve as the first step in the stairway on which the big steps could sit. He located the appropriate rock, which was shaped rather like a whale. It weighed as much as a decent-sized whale — well over a ton. We managed to wrap heavy chains around it, and these we attached to the backhoe. Sean lifted it high into the air and backed out through deep sand towards the house.

Sean was pretty good with his tractor, but had never been taught the finer points of tractor work, and the tractor started to spin in the sand. I was standing by, nervously aware that tractors were dangerous machines, all the more so in sand with a heavy object high above. Then Sean completely lost control. The whale rock was spinning, the tractor threatening to roll over. Somehow, I caught Sean's eye for a fleeting moment. He was terrified. He couldn't jump, as the tractor or the rock or both might land on him and crush him. I was helpless, and could only watch. For a few seconds, Sean's fate was in the hands of the God he talked so much about. Or in his own. Only one back wheel of the tractor was on terra not very firma.

With the tractor, the backhoe, and the whale rock combined, Sean had lost control of maybe five tons of metal and granite. He had to alter the balance and bring the wheels back to earth to stop it all turning over on top of him. Relinquishing control of the steering wheel he threw himself across the tractor hoping his weight (some 180 lbs.) might turn the tide.

Doubtful, it stood for a few seconds. But Sean's redistribution of weight finally brought the tractor back to earth, and he jumped off and ran. The whale rock was still spinning in the air, but the tractor was upright and Sean was saved. Both of us were shaking — Sean more than I — and we took the opportunity to seek out his tequila bottle, where we found comfort.

I told him that we were trying to do too much with not enough experience, but Sean knew what he had done wrong and wasn't about to repeat the mistake. He got back on the tractor, lowered the whale rock to a few feet off the ground, and slowly backed up through the treacherous sand and onto the hard dirt roadway.

Soon the whale rock was lying in place — and in a few days the stairway, comprising twenty huge rocks, rested on its massive shoulders and provided easy access to the Hidden Valley. The effect, Boo remarked, was of a giant's causeway. But Sean and I dubbed it "The Stairway to Heaven".

That afternoon, Sean went off alone, no doubt to contemplate his deliverance from death's clutches. He wandered down to the churned-up sand and inspected the mess he had made of the land. Something glittered in the decomposed granite. He leant down and picked up an arrowhead, which he brought to the house. It was a particularly pretty thing chipped from a hard blue stone and carrying a funny glazed look.

In the course of determining something about the people who had been on this land before us, I had got to know Jim Brock, an archeologist who lived in Pioneertown but worked in the Coachella Valley.

The gated cities of the valley are spewing out towards the Colorado River as the developers blithely build over the remains of the people who came before. People like Jim are employed to inspect areas and give the development a green light.

Jim, I had discovered, didn't take to that form of archeology and hence was not as often called upon by the developers, who preferred more compliant "experts". This enabled Jim to spend some free time helping the other experts hold up the bar at The Palace. Sean and I, somewhat excited, headed off to find him. The setting of Boulder House, with a clearing surrounded by high rocks on all sides, was perfect for an Indian village. Bill's son had found a clay pot with seeds still inside one of the caves. The prospect of uncovering a village had us most excited.

Jim looked long and hard at the arrowhead, and asked if he could borrow it. Sean and I agreed. I said it was Sean's as he'd found it, and he said it was mine as he'd found it on my property. We argued, and Jim went on his way.

A few days later, Jim entered the bar with the arrowhead. Now it was enclosed in plastic and tagged. It looked rather official in the little bag.

Jim was a taciturn man, and got straight to the point "First," he said, "it's not an arrowhead. It's a spearhead."

I ordered Jim a beer, and he, having jogged down to The Palace, accepted enthusiastically. Jim is a weighty man both physically and intellectually. He can be irritating, as he tends to keep his knowledge to himself. As a journalist, I expect people like Jim, once asked, to spill their guts and tell me everything they have learnt. But Jim is a measured man—almost aloof.

Today Jim was, for once, borderline excited. The glazed look, he informed a bunch of people who had gathered around the spearhead, was created by the last ice age, dating the piece to between five thousand and nine thousand years of age. Thus Jim's excitement.

"This means that man was here long before we thought," he said, adding that this was not only his opinion but that of other authorities he had consulted.

Its previous owner (Sean and I were still arguing who should keep it) was, Jim explained, probably Pinto Man. Pinto Man was the Southwest's earliest human inhabitant. The spear, Jim informed us, was of the kind attached to a throwing device, in which it rested, giving the projectile greater accuracy and distance. The Australian Aborigine employs an identical method of enhancing the efficacy of the spear. They call it a Woomera. In fact, a missile base in the midst of an Australian desert is called the Woomera Rocket Range. Australians, like Americans, enjoy paying tribute to their indigenous people by naming things after them. It's one way of showing how much we care.

The spearhead lies locked in the safe with the labels from the museum that Jim took it to. Soon we will take it to some other museum, or perhaps present it to one of the local Indian casinos, or just continue to get it out and show it to people.

24

The finding of the spearhead sharpened Boo's interest in those who came before us — she did, after all, have a master's degree in anthropology — and I left her to tramp the land with Jim Brock, hopefully to discover other spearheads and perhaps the remains of a prehistoric village.

The past, the world that came before us, might best be summed up by an old-timer who remarked, "Old history we ain't got so much of at all." Much of what we have is a mess of contradictions left by explorers, historians, archaeologists, and anthropologists, and the equally unreliable histories of the white settlers. Mostly overlooked are the oral histories of the remaining Indians both local and afar.

But we know that the blood and tears of the native people flowed in the San Bernardino Mountains that confront Boulder House to the west, following the arrival of the Spanish and the Cross in the late 1700s. If there was less blood it was simply because there were fewer Indians, but not as few as some histories might have us believe.

The people who once walked this land are known as the Serrano and the Chemehuevi Indians — branches of the Shoshoneans who lived more to the east. Through the fog of times gone by it is apparent that they were better suited to the land than us — their only great fear being the grizzly bear, which was fear enough.

The Bear Shamans exploited the acute presence of the grizzly to maintain control of their people for a thousand or so years. Grizzlies grizzled all around, and created an eternal horror to a people who lived in cat-tail tulle huts, which the bears found to be a potential source of good food. One can imagine the terrified woman nursing her kid while a determined bear snorted, screamed, and growled outside the flimsy dwelling.

One of our nearest towns is Big Bear. It was aptly named, for it was once the state seat of the Big Bear. If popular elections were held three hundred years ago, the grizzly would have won — claws down — for here was once the largest concentration of grizzly bears in North America.

The Bear Shamans kept their power by exploiting the terror of the grizzly at night and offering protection; but with the arrival of the Spanish, the power that underpinned the old way was destroyed. The emergence of young natives as *vaqueros*, horsemen of sublime skill riding mounts from Mexico, hit ancient tradition hard. These horsemen learnt a new sport, perhaps California's first — that of bear roping. The great creatures known to the purists as *Ursus arctos horribilis* could be easily roped and strangled. Soon the bears were gone, and with them the power of the Bear Shamans.

Those who could (the young men) escaped on the Mexican horses and disappeared into "Greater Mexico". The power of the shaman was erased in the colorless dust under the hooves of those horses.

Meantime the Indians were put to work in the concentration camps that the Mexican Spanish were building and calling missions. Today, civilized tourists visit the missions and marvel at the beautiful simplicity, speaking in hushed and sacred tones, admiring the polished tecate tiles and the massive wood beams. This is a little like visiting Dachau or Treblinka, and ogling in reverence and respect.

The mission system was Mediterranean — European-style inquisitorial concentration camps, state garrisons that imprisoned the local population, who were used as slaves and worked to death. The garrisons were built as part of California's first freeway system — "El Camino Real" — the King's Highway. The missions were a chain of death camps. In all, it was a form of ethnic cleansing.

That was the fate of the Indian tribes that came and went from the High Desert. It has been given short shrift by history, but so has the fate of Californian Indians in general, even though until the white man made his presence felt they comprised nearly one-third of all the people of North America.

Boo was furious to find no evidence of a village anywhere on the land, and was ready to slap Jim when he announced that the spearhead was probably an "isolate" — a one-off — possibly even carried in the body of a deer that was shot somewhere else but made it up here, to later die. Most likely, she grudgingly had to accept, the Indians had no permanent address up around Boulder House, but used it as a transit camp three hundred years ago, on their way from the lower desert to Big Bear when fleeing the summer's brutal heat. The area is strewn with caves, some with blackened walls, which may be evidence of their fires.

They moved often, these travelers, following the path of the water and the weather, migrating to the pine forest in the summer and wintering in the desert in much the same fashion as elderly and wealthy retired Americans do today. Their camps were guarded in their absence by "spirit sticks", as they had no Sheriff's Department. Water was more prevalent in those days, and it is not difficult to imagine the valley that lies before me as once approaching lush.

Today, there is plenty of food that can be taken from the land, as the natural food sources haven't been touched by humans in one hundred and fifty years. An Indian woman, returning to Boulder House today, would find abundance. If the going gets really, really tough, Boo and I and maybe Sailor could survive, if we knew how, on history's surplus. For food was found almost everywhere.

Our predecessors would have enjoyed a rich and varied diet in a good season, with plenty of game — ground squirrels, gray fox, bobcats, bighorn sheep, deer, bear, chipmunks, mice, kangaroo rats, and packrats. Meat was boiled in cooking pots, or broiled over hot coals. Ground meal could be made from the seeds and beans of many plants — acorns, catsclaw, mesquite, and pinyon pounded in rounded stone metates to make a kind of flour. We recently discovered one such metate — a lovely stone with a hollowed indent, and decorated with simple pictographs — wedged between a row of other rocks in our cactus garden. Bill hadn't bothered to mention it.

Bows and arrows were manufactured from the manzanita and desert willow. Arrowheads — much smaller than those of Plains or Eastern Indians — were made from quartz, obsidian, jasper, and many other readily available rocks that the area is blessed with. Small animals were hunted with stones — the Indians were expert stone-throwers—or pulled from their burrows with a specially crafted crooked stick.

In spring, the berries and cactus fruits were eaten for nourishment and moisture. The blossoms of the cactus flowers were roasted, and roots also served as medicine.

Dried seeds were stored in pots with tight lids to keep out the rodents and the damp. When the people moved camp, they hid them for later use. Such a pot was found by Bill Lavender's son in a cave a few hundred yards from where I write. It is hard not to think of what happened to the people who left it there, expecting to return.

The Chemehuevi went naked except for sandals, though the women wore a very fetching sack dress, and in the winters all donned blankets made from rabbit fur.

Drugs were everywhere. Booze, speed, and acid were on hand. The booze they made from distilling all manner of cactus flowers, and the speed they took from the "squaw grass" or "Mormon Tea" that grows all around. It is a light high, but a pleasant one, and tasty if prepared properly—which is not hard.

The acid menu is, if Tony is to be believed, decidedly diverse. The old favorite is Jimsonweed or the Devil's Trumpet, a potent hallucinogen that can cause madness and death. It was called Sacred Datura by the Indians, and utilized in religious ceremonies by the shamans, who would go into incredible trances, see things, make predictions, and turn into animals and the like. Much planning for the future was conceived under the spell of the weed. Presumably, they knew what they were doing. Today, hospitals across the country treat the unwary and the foolish who have dabbled with this deadliest of the deadly nightshade family. Whether snorted, smoked, or drunk as tea, the super-powerful hallucinogen "will render the taker blind as a bat, mad as a hatter, hot as a hare, dry as a bone, the bowel and bladder lose their tone, and the heart runs alone", according to a national poison center's mnemonic for the clinical effects of typical poisoning.

History is full of references to this mind-altering weed. Shakespeare got good mileage out of it in *Anthony and Cleopatra*, *Romeo and Juliet*, and *Hamlet*. It also appears in Homer's *Odyssey*. One does not need to travel far to encounter Jimsonweed around Boulder House. It grows along all the local roadsides, and is a very fetching sight with its large white trumpet flowers. So far, however, we haven't been tempted to pick any for afternoon tea.

San Pedro cactus is another potent plant that can be found in our garden. The number of spines measures its strength — the maximum being nine. A drink made from an inch cut from a San Pedro boiled with water can reduce the unwary to the mental condition of a rabid dog for three days. Tony once remarked on the cactus's qualities to a local who determined to get high, and proceeded to make a batch despite Tony's protestations.

"He drank half a cupful," Tony recalls, "and then he threw it all up. But it was still powerful enough to have him begging to come down days later."

Tony is not sure to this day if the chap ever did make it back to normal, but the lesson has not been lost on others.

With the knowledge of these drugs and the fear of the grizzly bear, the shaman had some powerful tools indeed.

Mescaline can be purchased in some cactus outlets managed by people who have no idea what they are selling. Fortunately, the great majority of those buying these plants are equally ignorant. One psychedelic that Tony pointed out to me while exploring a cactus shop comes laced with arsenic. The trick is to remove the stuff before eating or making a brew. Tony's knowledge about how that is actually done is limited, so we passed. Don Juan need not worry about his day job.

Across Pipes Canyon Road at the end of Roadrunner Rut are the scant remains of what is probably a Chemehuevi village. Brock speaks enthusiastically of the site, even though the arrowheads and pottery have been looted. For some of the finest rock painting in the entire desert still exists there, along with a smooth chute that Indian children would use as a slide. Rodney recalls playing in the ruins of the old village as a boy almost fifty years ago. Those days, he says, there were pottery and weapons scattered about.

The Serranos of what we now know as Big Bear dressed in the skins of deer, rabbit, beaver, and otter, and wore buckskin leggings and intricate fiber sandals.

Tattooing was universal in this most primitive of societies, as it remains in ours. The main weapon, a five-foot bow, was manufactured from ash, mesquite, or desert willow, and was—depending on the source—effective against firearms at either fifty feet or fifty yards. Trade was brisk, and the desert Indian men could travel forty miles a day on foot, sometimes through one of the hottest and harshest terrains on earth. The Serrano were also devoted to a form of football, utilizing a round stone.

The local Indian lands were first explored by the white man when the Spanish decided to expand God's universe to include these unfortunates. On 20 May 1810, the Spanish found good water and land at what we now call San Bernardino. This happened to be the birthday of an Italian saint (Bernadine), which occurred in the year of Our Lord 1320. The name was translated into Spanish, and as many natives as could be found were rounded up. A rancho,

Rancho San Bernardino, was completed in 1811, and immediately a series of earthquakes shook the grounds of the Indians. The Serrano considered this some sort of warning from their gods. They promptly burnt the rancho and drove the padres back to the San Gabriel mission whence they had come. But the Catholics returned — this time not to build a rancho, but another mission.

The mission was built, and promptly attacked and destroyed by the would-be victims of the cross, and once again the enemies of promise fled. Some people just don't know when they aren't wanted. The Catholics returned to build a large mission surrounded by a larger adobe wall, which was never breached.

Finally, the Serrano came to kneel at Christ's feet, even interpreting the Twenty-third Psalm with a sadness that is palpable.

"The Great Father above a Shepherd Chief is. I am his and with Him I want not. He throws me out a rope ..."

Meanwhile, to add to Indian confusion with the white man's religion, the Mormons arrived in March 1851, and promptly tore down the forests, further destroying the habitat. They built communities, but left them as quickly as they had been created. They were "recalled" to Salt Lake City, and California remains largely rid of them to this day.

The various descriptions of the inhabitants of this region, chiefly the Serranos, are bewilderingly contradictory. Captain John C. Frémont, who, to the fury of those who knew the man well, is credited by many as the man who opened up the West, in 1844 wrote of the local Indians, "humanity here appeared in its lowest form, and in its most elementary state". But those who have closely studied the history of the West might say the same of Frémont. The great explorer Joseph P. Walker was more withering in his description of Frémont than Frémont was of the Indians. Walker described Frémont as "the most complete coward I ever knew".

Frémont's unsparingly hostile commentary on most of the Californian Aboriginal people must have delighted his benefactors in Washington, principally president James K. Polk and Missouri senator Thomas Hart Benton. Polk and Benton, both barkers for Manifest Destiny, were delighted to learn that the natives were subhuman — it being easier to dispose of a people once it is established that they are not people at all. That Frémont was a coward, a crook, and a liar did not deter following generations from naming schools, cities, and highways after him. He died in obscurity but was never properly disgraced, except by Joseph Walker. While Frémont had nothing but contempt for the Indians, Walker managed up to eight Indian wives, and for much of his life lived with the native people more often than he did with his own countrymen.

While Frémont described the local Indians as the most wretched of people, early settlers described them as being well fed, even fat and rugged; in fact, the name Guachamas, a subgroup of the Serrano, meant "plenty to eat".

By the time California was admitted to the Union, as a free state, though with the avowed policy of exterminating the Indians, there weren't many left, and those who remained were reduced to the state that Frémont claimed to have found them in — wretched and miserable.

The remnants or fragments of the people then came under the benign influences of the US Government's Bureau of Indian Affairs. The BIA had the Catholic Church create "Indian Schools" in the 1880s to "remove Indian children from the influence of their native cultural and religious beliefs, and teach them the way of the majority culture. The children were forbidden to speak their native languages and were severely punished when they did."

Genocide of this kind is not a matter of public scrutiny when it comes to the hapless but friendly Serrano. The native children were undoubtedly taught to labor in the boiling sun for the new white landowners, and soon the schools were known as "industrial schools."

The desert windstorms and the flash floods are as cruel to the remnants of those who came before us as the looters. But the worst offenders are the bulldozers of the developers. Jim Brock, the local archeologist, laments that many of his colleagues are ignorant of what lies beneath the paths of huge machines that are forever extending the domain of rich retirees, especially in the Low Desert. Typical is the brand-new city of La Quinta, a perfectly manicured place of gated estates, endless golf courses, and the latest imported cars. Here a new peon class of illegal immigrants can be seen through the broiling heat clipping the grass by the footpaths (which never host the feet of the rich), or driving their dilapidated trucks and jalopies around the estates. These peons live in their cardboard and corrugated shanties, a few miles from the elegant playing fields of the Old Rich. They are mostly hidden in the reeds by the stinking waterways, thick with sewage and pesticides. They have come hundreds, even thousands, of miles, to cross a border some fifty miles away, to live and toil amongst the fragments, the shards, of the forgotten people.

But the developers of the new cities have their tame archeologists who are, according to Brock, either too stupid or too keen to keep their clients happy to discover what lies below.

The best known of all local Indians was Willie Boy, a Paiute Indian whose story was turned into the Hollywood movie *Tell Them Willie Boy Was Here*. Robert Blake played Willie Boy, and Robert Redford starred as the kindly hunter of the young man who had the misfortune to get caught up in the ways of the white man's politics in 1909.

Willie Boy was rejected as the suitor for Isoleta, the daughter of a local Indian, Mike Boniface, who banned the union despite their love for each other. The two men fought, and Boniface died from a bullet—probably from his own gun. Taking Isoleta along, Willie Boy eluded a mounted posse, which in the film is led by Robert Redford, outdistancing them on foot. Unhappily, president Harding was campaigning at San Bernardino at the time, and was accompanied by the press corps who, as horrified as modern crews are when forced to Crawford Texas to cover the antics of the modern president, stumbled upon a real story.

Willie Boy and Isoleta headed into the boundaries of Pipes Canyon believing that no white man would bother pursuing them. The death of an Indian was scarcely worth reporting. Unfortunately for the two young lovers, the Washington press corps, bored beyond comprehension by Harding's set speeches and finding themselves in a Wild West fantasy land, jumped upon the death of Boniface and beat the story up with a very large stick. Harding, realizing the coverage far exceeded his stump speeches, found a bandwagon he could not resist jumping upon, and turned the incident into a frontier uprising. The Hollywood mythological manifestation of these events had Robert Redford leading a brave posse against the killer. In reality, men who would never have got out of bed to avenge a slain Indian or consider crisscrossing the desert for a week in pursuit of some obscure Paiute and his girl sprung into action.

Willie Boy was turned into a national political cause, and the media treated his run across the desert as a new Indian war. Getting poor Willie Boy became a matter of national security, and president Harding could not resist expressing concern over the danger that a barefoot kid, down to his last few bullets, posed to the southwest. After that, the story gets a little hazy. Popular history has it that Willie Boy killed his girl rather than surrender her. A less popular tale, the Indian version, has it that the posse killed Isoleta.

Either way, Willie Boy and Isoleta, ignorant of the political-media event that attended their desire to be united, would never know that their demise was the result of just another Washington beat-up.

After Isoleta's death, Willie Boy continued down Pipes Canyon—close to where I sit writing—and across to Devil's Garden in the Morongo Valley. There he finished his life with his last bullet. As Ed Edge, the local authority on wells, reflected over a beer nearly one hundred years after the incident, "It was all political. Why else would they have gone to any trouble over an Indian that killed another Indian?"

Local shame at being forced to hunt down a kid and his girlfriend was mitigated by the public clamor, and no one stopped to wonder how the boy was able to humiliate a well-mounted posse, killing their horses at whim, wounding a sheriff he could have killed, and then taking his own life when the game was no longer worth the candle.

The Indians burnt Willie Boy's remains where the body fell, in the Devil's Garden. Isoleta was buried on the reservation. The Indian women were allegedly interrupted in their task by voices from the grave of Boniface. They fled, and their task was completed by white men. Or so the story goes. Some suggest that, because she was riddled with the white man's bullets, they took over proceedings to ensure the truth was never known.

With Willie Boy's death, resistance to the white man's ways ended — at least in this part of America.

The remaining Indians have settled on the Morongo Indian reservation at Banning or Mission Creek, where their descendants can be found enjoying the profits from the ever-growing casino industry. Indeed the clannish remnants of the tribes are amongst the richest people in the US. One member of the Agua Caliente tribe (he is one-quarter Indian) used to be one of the hardest workers in the High Desert. Today, he rakes in $60,000 from the casino without lifting a hand. The Cahuilla, who once roamed the lower desert, own most of Palm Springs — the white man, not realizing its value, forgot to steal it from them. Today, the tribes play by the new rules, contributing to the war chests of Republicans and Democrats alike. Californian Governor Gray Davis has just allocated $10 million for a freeway off-ramp just down the road on Highway 10. It will make access to the Morongo Indian Casino less arduous. Perhaps it will help ease the white man's burden — the off-ramp, that is. As more (and bigger) casinos sprout in the wilderness, the wealth and power of the remnants of the Aboriginal population will grow. Money doesn't talk — it swears.

25

The coming of spring coincided with the collective realization that some work had to be done soon, as summer's hounds were on its traces, and labor would be as hard to find in the heat as it was only a few weeks before in the freeze. Work — the bane of the drinking classes — of all kinds was available. Trees needed to be trimmed. Serious repairs to roofs that had been patched throughout the rains cried out for attention. Winter winds had ushered forth a half-inch of dust that would soon turn to mud and then algae on the pool's bottom. The poolroom was in a sorry state, with water having cascaded through the roof and ruined what should have been a pretty one-bedroom apartment. Instead it was a sodden, mildewed threat to the safety of all but the fast-growing rodent population.

All creatures great and small and just plain fat suddenly materialized with the new season. Quail in great numbers appeared from the brush they had retreated to for the winter to get on with the warm-weather business of making more quail. They arrived in a great rush, racing back and forth in pairs with their red headdresses bobbing nervously, like two gossip columnists, horrified to find themselves in the same hat, chasing the same scandal. They nested in the bushes and up amongst the rocks, blasé in the knowledge that they were not likely to get shot by these strange new people in the big nest on their land. At first they all fled squawking when Sailor made a nosedive at their bushes. But they needn't have bothered themselves, for this is one bird dog who wouldn't thank you for a bird. Not when the whole place was suddenly, magically, crawling with something far more interesting — lizards. Sailor will happily spend all day trying to dry-gulch a lizard, and entire afternoons were now given to Mexican standoffs in the baking sun.

The quail, like its namesake, the former vice-president, is not the smartest of all God's creations. If you're short on dinner, we were informed by our neighbors, you need only put honey in the bottom of a plastic cup and wait for a quail to stick his head in. With the cup covering his eyes he will think it's night and go to sleep, and you can bag him. This task has not been successfully completed by the author.

Spring is referred to as "the season" by those few locals who are engaged in activity related to tourism — the only industry that keeps the town afloat. The prospect of the heat to come made the winter more bearable, but spring, when it finally arrived, was unmercifully short. Someone upstairs turned a knob, and the world and the creatures that inhabit it changed almost overnight.

Our first spring in the desert was heralded by a tiny cheeping noise that appeared to come from under the big four-poster bed. Being hard of hearing, my first thought was that Boo had mislaid the last of her marbles as she maintained she could hear what she thought were birds — birds under the bed. But after a few days, even I could detect some small voices, and they did appear to be coming from under the bed. The bed is so big that even if it wasn't bolted to the wall it would still be too heavy to move, so there was no way to determine what might be happening. And so it was that after the fifth day of chirping, a rodent the size of a baby's thumb emerged and made its way drunkenly over the tecate tiles. It was hairless and had only a few of the characteristics of the kangaroo rat it might have grown up to be. Boo mothered it in a box filled with cotton wool and, as we wondered what to do with a creature that was more fetus than animal, another little pink object squirreled its way through a tiny crack between the bed's support and the tiles. Then came another and another, until Boo had five babies wriggling through her cotton wool.

"Yep. Looks like you got yourself some baby pack rats," the lady at the High Desert Museum assured Boo. "But they probably won't make it without their mother if they're that young."

Undeterred, Boo hurried home with a can of baby formula and a miniature feeding bottle, and for the next week fed the little creatures in the shoebox. They thrived and grew. In two weeks they were recognizably rats.

Sean was amazed that anyone would go to such lengths to save vermin. He had once seen a pack rat pushing a potato up a hill, as he sat fulfilling his ablutions. As he was carrying a .45 at the time — Sean liked to take small arms to his outdoor toilet, usually to deal with snakes — he shot it stone-cold dead.

But the woman at the feedlot on Old Woman Springs Road wasn't at all surprised, and assured us that she was capable of taking over and raising our small shoebox family to an age where they could be released into their natural location — the desert.

Meanwhile, their relatives — the pack rats and the mice — continued in their merry vein. Though we were hardly being plagued, there was every indication that we would soon be facing something out of Camus—albeit with hantavirus. Having once made a documentary on health care, Boo had become amazingly aware of that blight in northern Arizona, not much further away than LA. It is a disease that is often fatal, and involves a horrible death. And it could be in our house. I was constantly working around the house and thereby disturbing rats' nests with attendant droppings—the agent that spreads the virus. It was a clear and apparent danger.

Sailor watched the rodents' frolics with interest and then adopted an almost fatherly attitude to them—even allowing them to eat his food. Little bits of dog kibble were found squirreled all around the house. Even in Boo's lingerie drawer.

Upstairs, things were even grimmer. There, a very large rat, a rat the size of a small kangaroo, had moved in and had taken to roaming freely while obviously preparing a nest.

The subject of the eradication of these pests is one of considerable debate. John Edwards is a great believer, as are others, in the cement solution. This solution is, in fact, a solution of cement and water. For reasons only the rodents can explain, they are fond of cement. But the salt in the cement makes them thirsty. Put out a bowl of cement and a bowl of water, and our little friends will lick the cement, head for the water, and concrete their innards to their other innards and die. No poison. No danger to the dogs.

Boo wouldn't hear of such cruelty. There would be no slow, agonizing deaths around here. But after much screaming and arguing, she was prepared to compromise.

I was permitted to place traps on the ridge of rock in the den where the rats would perch while watching *The Money*

Hour. Within days, I had dubbed that small piece of planet the "Highway to Hell."

On the first night, I trapped two, and thinking that all my problems would soon be over, I gave the beasts a funeral. That is, I buried them at a decent depth so they wouldn't be cannibalized by other rodents. As I repaired the shovel to the garage, I wondered about the burial policy. The land is hard, and there are only a few places where one can stick a shovel more than a few inches into the ground. Most of those spots are near the house. There are some soft spots down in the Hidden Valley, but that's a long place to walk to bury a rat.

Nevertheless, I returned to the house with some sense of achievement. Perhaps I had wiped out a good percentage of them. Perhaps they would move somewhere else. The next morning, I had three in my traps. The policy of repatriation in the desert, then burial in same, degenerated into a quick trip to the toilet and from there to the septic. How easily we are brutalized.

I was getting pretty skilled at dealing with these pests, but they — we were soon to learn — were getting the hang of mouse traps. The kill rate dropped off. The rats were back, more brazen than ever. The big upstairs rat, though dubbed "King Rat", was, we suspected, a queen. These suspicions grew with the sound of tiny mousey cries amidst his complex. King Rat, in the meantime, had taken to visiting guests that might be slumbering in the den. There were reports of him/her standing a foot high with another foot for his tail, watching Fox Sports.

All through this, Boo had been advocating the deployment of a cat. I had fought this escalation on the grounds of collateral damage. Cats eat birds, and I felt that allowing a cat would be a betrayal of my love of birds.

We fought about it on a daily basis. Boo dragged everyone who came into the house into the argument. Lil Debbie agreed that I was being stupid, and strongly supported the cat solution. So did Ed Gibson, who took a cavalier approach to his own black cat's bird-catching. Ed also liked to point out that the rats would not only eat their way through the electrical cable and the phone lines, but had been known to consume the very foundations of houses, which eventually collapsed. Finally, Crinkly Jim, Lil Debbie's new boyfriend, pointed out that American birds are smarter than Australian birds. They have evolved with natural predators, while their Australian cousins have not. Until the introduction of domestic cats, the Australian birds were predator-free and thus utterly clueless about the murderous future in store. Today, feral Australian cats have grown to be twice the size of the lovable household kitty, and are capable of killing thirteen birds a day — or, more often, a night.

At that time, Carole had rescued an animal known as Inky on the very good grounds that it was as black as the future. Even its white bits were black. Boo took him, sight unseen, and I personally undertook the formal duty of releasing Inky from his cat box in the children's room at the top of the stairs. As we have no children and the cat was small, this seemed to be the appropriate place. It was well away from the path of the dogs, and the bed was the only one made up.

Inky — who soon adopted other titles, including Black Death — inspected the small room and found it wanting. He disappeared and was not seen for days. But his handiwork was soon in evidence.

The rains seemed to have stopped, and I deemed it wise to patch up some spots in the rock bedroom where water had made its way through the skylight. The job was a small one, so I did it standing on the bed with the trowel above my head. I wiped the mud off in the last crack and started to exit the bedroom through a small stairway. There below me lay King Rat — or at least some of him. His head was missing entirely, as was much of his torso, some of which I found in a pile of vomit not far away. But this was a dead rat. His kidney had been torn, intact, from his body and thrown a few feet away. The rest of him lay, rather formally, on a mat where he had been deposited. Inky was nowhere to be seen. The rat was so big that at first I thought it was an eagle. Programmed to assume that cats kill birds, it took me a second to remember they also kill rats. I was about to scream to Boo "This mother has killed the golden eagle!" when it became apparent that this was the remains of a rodent. If nothing else, the tail was a giveaway. Few birds have long bald tails, in my experience, and this creature had one like a big red kangaroo.

He was too big to flush down any toilet, so at least he had the honor of burial amongst his peers.

Inky — now also known as The Black Flash and Zorro — was, in absentia (since leaving the children's room he had not been sighted), a household hero. Days passed. The killer showed signs of his presence, but not of himself. He was eating and drinking and using his little cat tray as a bathroom. Like the Viet Cong, he wore black and controlled the night. Five days and nights passed without a sighting, but on the sixth, Boo found two decent-sized rodents (nothing like King Rat, but enough to give most a scare) laid out on the same mat. Again, their bodies ran in line with the weave of the rug. When I inspected them, I ruminated that Killer might start doing them up in body bags.

It was almost a week before he made another public appearance. Green eyes could be seen staring from high in the rock room, a place where the room ceases to be a room and becomes a maze of small caves. There he was—above us in his lair—inspecting us. Soon he was down and about, attacking Sailor and walking over the computer keyboard in mid-sentence. Arrogant as the rat he had brought down.

The rats had gone into retreat and borderline capitulation. Victory, as the old rattraps were branded before the Taiwanese took over the mousing game, was ours.

Everything was mating, and Lil Debbie was no exception. The first time we met Crinkly Jim, Boo was very taken with his intelligent disposition and wry humor. I was impressed by the fact he held a construction license and knew more about building than I would if I had tried.

Jim's late wife had been one of Ken Kesey's original Merry Pranksters, and Jim was keeping the tradition alive. For years, he drove around with a stuffed killer Doberman in his car. Like so many locals, he was always laughing at life's quirks. His face was a mass of lines etched deep. He might have been called Wrinkly Jim, but Crinkly stuck. He didn't mind the title; he didn't mind much at all. His laugh was a series of coughing sounds that were actually chuckles which the years of cigarettes had distorted.

Jim had moved in with Lil Debbie, and I called in to visit them on my way home from town. The two had been drinking since they woke—about 11.00 (a.m.). I sat studying the sun's pale path. Lil Debbie had a clock that emphatically stated that we had reached five in the afternoon. But the clock, a nice one, had been telling that same story whenever I had bothered to look at it. Lil Debbie liked the clock—but not because it told the time. It was an old thing, and she could have wound it, but Debbie didn't keep clocks that keep time. The sun suggested fourish. Soon the clock would be right. The sunlight washed the room in its thin afternoon colors as the sun inched towards the peak of Mount Gorgonio. Mostly, the room, indeed the entire house, was covered in pictures and images of John Lennon. They were cleverly arranged. Pictures that Lil Debbie's hero would admire. She'd spent much of her life trying to do John Lennon right, and she hadn't done a bad job. Lennon stared out from every point like Mary in a Catholic church. Debbie fixed another screwdriver. One wall was a collection of blue bottles. They shone, and Debbie shone. She had recently showered, and the blue light spun into her curly damp hair as she stood smiling, always smiling, above me. A pixie, I thought.

Jim was drinking a huge bottle of cheap Magnum beer — the type often criticized for being heavily promoted in black communities. It is laced with raw alcohol, and he was taking it as a chaser to gin. He offered me some, and I asked Lil Debbie for a glass.

"Shit, she'll have to wash it," Jim remonstrated.

Lil Debbie brought me a glass as Jim explained why Magnum was the best beer, and how I should get acquainted with it. I took a sip.

"Sorry," I said, putting down perhaps the only beer I have rejected in my life. "That stuff will kill you."

Jim then announced that although his liver, spleen, kidneys, et cetera had been pronounced DOA at every hospital he had visited in years, "That was all shit."

"I'll live for years," he added confidently as the phone rang.

Lil Debbie answered, and it was Loma Linda Hospital asking that he come in for some tests.

Dates for the tests were discussed. The first was out of the question because of a party on the preceding twenty-eighth.

Jim insisted that tests were a waste of time for at least a week after the party, and then remembered that he had another party coming up about then.

"Let's make it the seventh," he suggested.

The hospital secretary seemed to think that all this was a good idea, and agreed on the date. Jim hung up the phone and winced. His elbow had hit the tabletop right where a benign tumor had been removed a few days before. Jim rolled up his sleeve and displayed a large bandaged elbow. He thrust it at me from a few feet across the table, and wondered if it was bleeding.

There was blood, but it wasn't dripping.

"No, looks all right. What happened?" I asked.

"They took this tumor out. It was bigger than a golf ball. I was going to bring it back and dice it for the chili."

"Pity to waste it," Debbie added. "We could at least have fed it to the dogs."

"And it was benign." I added, hoping I was entering into the spirit of things.

"Of course it was benign," said Jim pouring himself a half-glass of gin.

The doctors had told Jim he had about one hundred days to live, which was good news for him as it assured him continued access to social security. The government didn't mind handing out a few hundred bucks a month to people who were soon to relieve themselves from the welfare rolls, and they were happy to also provide free pharmaceuticals.

"There's good money in dying," Jim rejoined. "Thousand bucks a month."

But while the doctors had told him his liver had virtually ceased to function, and Jim had assumed a yellow countenance, he was confident that he could build Debbie a house and live with her for many a year. Debbie seemed to agree that there was life in Crinkly Jim yet—but whether it would be with her was another matter.

Lil Debbie was simultaneously being wooed by George, a retired bar-owner from Long Beach whose financial prospects were better than Jim's, though his prognosis was similar. George was due at the hospital to have half a lung removed the next week, the same day his estranged wife would enter another hospital for some complicated surgery. If the wife died, George had the house, and prices in Long Beach were looking decidedly sunny. George was as tough as Jim, but perhaps more determined. Determined, that is, to outlive his hated wife, take possession of her house, sell it, and buy Lil Debbie *her* house.

A few weeks later, I was standing outside the bowling alley on Mane Street when George drove by puffing on a cigarette. He was looking pretty happy with himself.

"I thought you were in hospital," I inquired.

"I was," George replied with a remarkably impish look for a man in his late sixties who was supposed to be at death's door.

"Have been, and I'm out. They threw me out right after the operation, which was fine by me 'cause they wouldn't let me smoke."

"How are you doing?" was my obvious question.

"Well, it hurts a bit."

George pulled up his shirt, revealing a massive fresh wound.

"Shouldn't it be dressed?" I wondered.

"Nope, the air's the best thing for it, I figure. It don't smell, do it?"

It didn't.

"And how's the wife?"

I then realized why George was in such fine spirits.

"She died under the knife," he said with a naughty smile.

"Well," I ventured, "there's two pieces of luck.'

"They sure was," said George putting his truck into gear and cruising off with a conspiratorial smile.

26

Breathing like a hound down spring's throat came summer—the real challenge of the Mojave Desert. In the minds of those who cannot learn to love it, the Mojave is synonymous with the most unpleasant extremes. Extremes of heat and extremes of violence. As we live in the High Desert, we can kid ourselves for much of the year that we are not actually in the desert. But when summer arrives, the lie is exposed.

"The season" ends because city folk stay in their cities, and locals try to stay out of the sun's daunting rays.

There can be no pride in surviving autumn, winter, or the spring. That's the easy bit. For three months a year—three months that feel like three years—mad dogs and Englishmen try to stay in shade or indoors until indoors is hotter than outdoors.

"Wait till the summer comes," we were cautioned time after time.

"We don't mind the heat," we would reply. "We're used to it."

"Yeah, I guess Australia's pretty hot, but it's nothing like this. You'll see."

Weather has a way of directing human behavior in a fashion

that city dwellers are scarcely aware of. It might reach 110 degrees in LA and even more in The Valley, but for the most part this heat is experienced as an inconvenience rather than a daily (and nightly) reality. August, we were gleefully informed, is like a bad LSD trip made worse by the belief that the heat will never end. August is the cruellest month. September might be as hot, but there is in the air a suggestion that the heat has done its best, a whiff of relief.

As the temperature rose, the house, being built into the rock, remained cool, but I knew it was time to master the workings of the swamp coolers that Bill Lavender had positioned at strategic parts of the building. Bill had explained the subject back around Christmas, which seemed a lifetime away. I knew they functioned or were supposed to function in the same way as an air conditioner, except that they used virtually no power and little water, and did not damage the ozone layer by releasing freon. They work by spraying a trickle of water onto porous beds of Aspen paper, which make up the cooler's walls, and using a tiny engine to spin a large fan that blows the water-cooled air through a series of ducts and into the house. The result was an amazingly effective and environmentally benign cooling system that soon had to be turned off as the house became as cold as it was in the frosty days we had hoped were behind us.

While I fiddled with such, Boo was getting herself into a state over the emergence of a new threat — rattlesnakes.

"The rattlesnakes have woken up and they're hungry" rattled the headline from *The Desert Sun*. It was the moment Boo had been dreading. The manager of the city dump, the article went on, had already killed three big rattlers in a week. Peter, a refugee from the old commie days of Czechoslovakia, did not remember them appearing this early before. Peter had escaped the brutal forces of that state by crawling through a forest and swimming a river, and became an accomplished snake man after finding his way to the free world twenty-five years ago. Peter had given up on keeping rattlesnakes.

The article explained this early arrival phenomenon. It was global warming. Or El Niño, followed by La Niña. Take your pick. The rains had caused the vegetation to go berserk. Everything was shooting up like a drugstore cowboy, and the rodents were having a field day. Jack rabbits bounded across the scrub, dodging their cotton-tailed cousins like cars on a freeway. Chipmunks, mice, and pack rats threw parties, and the rattlesnakes waited for their chance to gatecrash. They also come down from the rocks looking for water, and it was not unusual to find them curled up near the tap. An old man had recently bent down to uncoil his garden hose where a Green Mojave—the most deadly of all the rattlers—was curled up enjoying the heat of the warm plastic, perfectly camouflaged. By the time he got to the doctor, the finger that had taken the hit was completely black and had to be amputated.

It's not that Boo is fond of black widow spiders or scorpions, but she is quite happy to leave them alone as long as they watch their manners. But snakes are a whole different game. They terrify her, even though most are not only harmless but practically a man's best friend. Take the Rosy Boa. It is a smaller member of the boa-constrictor family, and has a reddish hue that is best described as "rosy". It has no venom. It doesn't even bite. But not only will it gobble up mice after crushing them, it will do the same to a rattlesnake, though I am not quite sure how. It is a snake you can give children to play with, as it seems to delight in slithering around one's body—no doubt enjoying the warmth. After encountering one in the laundry one morning and admiring its beauty, Boo was placated on the question of the boa family, and even warmed to the idea of their being present. But her nerves began to fray when Boulder House was described as "rattlesnake heaven", and especially when the rattlers started coming to the front door.

The locals, as always, were delighted to offer city folk advice, but, as always, the advice was contradictory and not altogether reassuring.

Always watch where you put your feet—and hands. Always carry a stick. Always carry a flashlight. They're nocturnal. Always keep your dog locked up. Talk to them. Tell them you like them. Get a mongoose. Forget the mongoose—the dog will eat it. Get an outdoor cat. Forget the cat—the coyotes will get it unless the owls get there first. Get rid of all the vegetation around your house.

Get rid of the dog's water bowl. Shoot the sons of bitches.

Get a goose. Geese love snakes. The geese appealed to Boo until someone pointed out that they also love water. Our swimming pool would have a nice coating of slimy goose shit within a week.

All agreed that baby rattlers are the most likely to inflict bites that could be mortal, and most dangerous of all is the Mojave Green. Apparently, it attacks both the heart and the nervous system. The little ones are worse, as nature endows them with ample venom to help them on their path to adulthood. But nature omits to inform them that a quick bite will usually deter its enemies. Sinking its entire store of venom into a large animal (for instance, a human) is a waste of good venom, as an eight-inch rattlesnake has no chance of consuming even the smallest of children.

In the end, we settled on a kind of peaceful coexistence on the property with Mutual Assured Destruction agreed upon in the immediate perimeter of Boulder House.

I had no fear of rattlesnakes, having dealt with their far more deadly Australian cousins as a kid in the Australian bush. Within the first week of summer I found it necessary to kill two, but only because they were virtually entering the house — one had crossed the porch — and I feared for Sailor and Boo. These were an average-sized couple clearly mating somewhere very close to the house. Having watched our beloved Harry (our first springer) decline following a snakebite, I reluctantly put a spade through their necks, and carefully buried the heads. One thing not common to the Aussie snakes, to my knowledge, is the fact that the rattler can kill when it is already dead. It is essential to bury the head, as its muscles continue to contract after it has been chopped off; if the creature manages to sink his fangs into man, woman, or dog, it will pump all its venom into the victim. I guess it's things like this that cause people to fear snakes more than any other of nature's more unfriendly creations.

But if the snakes stay out of the house I maintain a live-and-let-live approach, as when an Australian friend, Woodley, stumbled on a huge western rattler a few days later.

Big Foot Woodley had just arrived from Australia, bringing an inflatable, floating bar, and while I was attending to the pool he had wandered off a few hundred yards to a ridge, where he came face to face with the biggest and loudest rattler I have ever seen. I saw him waving frantically from the ridge — not a difficult task, as he is almost seven feet tall and has arms the length of a standard pool table. I grabbed a spade and went to inspect the reptile. Sailor had already bounded over to check things out.

A big rattler is one of nature's finest sights, and one can imagine why Eve got off on snakes when looking at this coiled mass of gold and brown — its flecked scales perfectly woven for what might have been five feet. Sailor walked past it, inches away, and its rattle rattled and my blood ran cold.

The snake was backed up against a boulder, and I raised the spade to end its life. Sailor, oblivious to the danger, had wandered a short distance to launch an assault on a small shrub, which presumably harbored a lizard. Sailor has not the faintest interest in snakes, or, for that matter, birds, quail, or any prey that should concern a bird dog. Lizards and tennis balls had continued as his dual obsessions, although as the weather warmed he would take an interest in flies, spending hours vainly snapping at them. Like the lizards, the flies always escaped, but this in no way reduced his determination to rid Boulder House of these pests. He disliked ants, another of the plagues of summer, but gave up the habit after being bitten on the nose by an angered ant — a development that was to cause me to have to rush him to hospital, at 1.00 a.m. — a return trip of some one hundred and forty miles.

I was well into *The Ruthless Gun* and enjoying a cold beer out in the courtyard when Boo burst in to announce that Sailor's face was swelling and that he was beginning to resemble Bob Hope.

"You're imagining it," I replied, but she insisted, and after half an hour I had to admit that he was getting a queer look around the head.

"A snake must have got him," Boo shouted. "We have to get him to the vet. Now!"

Sailor might have been aware of his swollen nose, but concentrated on enjoying the journey — an hour and a half of it — roaming the back seat and barking furiously at the cars that were travelling at that late hour. The nurse refused to even allow him to see the vet, and examined him in the outer office. She was good-natured about it, but insisted the vet was far too busy to deal with what she thought "might be an ant bite". The springer pranced happily around the office catching up with the latest smells, while Boo argued that he had probably been snake bit — and was likely to pass away at any moment. I stood glumly by the door as the kindly woman explained the difference between a snake and an ant bite until a distraught woman burst into the emergency clinic with a small mutt that seemed to be bleeding from every part of its body. It was hard to tell what sort of a dog she carried in her bloody, tear-drenched arms. She shrieked hysterically about a pack of coyotes that had savaged "her baby", and even Boo forgot the faint swelling of Sailor's nose.

But that was to come. Here I stood, spade on high, ready to sever the neck of this fabulous great western rattlesnake. The serpent looked up at me, and it was clear from his look that his time had come. He could strike — and probably was about to — but it wouldn't help his cause. He knew he was a goner, and it seemed sad to end the life of so magnificent a creature. But Woodley was watching, and I knew — as did the snake — that it must die. Then I thought of Sailor, whom the snake could so easily have killed, and slowly lowered the spade and stepped back. The rattler silenced his rattle. We watched one another for some time, the snake eyeing me balefully, and me returning the stare with one of admiration. The creature showed less fear than I felt. Finally, we left the monster on his sunny perch, and returned to the pool, Sailor springing happily beside us.

27

I lay in bed listening to the sound of a car winding its way along Coyote Road. It's such an unusual sound out here that, on those rare occasions that I venture into LA, I keep looking up every time I hear a car's engine, wondering if it's coming to visit me. But on this not-yet-hot morning it clearly was.

I staggered out to greet these God-early visitors, and was met by Bob Dix and a man I had never seen before. He had hair down to his waist and a sharp nose below his headband. This was Iron Horse, an extremely skilled drum-maker whom Bob introduced as "being from Arizona and a friend of Crazy Fox".

Bob Dix, the oldest regular member of the travelling circus that Adam surrounds himself with, is a refugee from the world of the rich. For Bob, the wheel of life has turned a full circle, for his father, Richard Dix, was a Western star bigger than Roy Rogers and Gene Autry, who were instrumental in Pioneertown coming into being. Richard's heyday was the silent movies era, though he successfully made the transition to the talkies. Bob, as a child, would come out to Pioneertown when his father was a handsome household name. Bob inherited his father's looks, but although he grew up in Hollywood with the kids of the other stars and made it into a dozen or so movies, he never attained his father's fame. He is most happy telling tales of hanging out in the bars of Beverly Hills at a time when heavy drinking was not restricted to such places as Pioneertown. His stories involve much innocuous name-dropping. It's difficult for them not to, as he hung out with the stars and acted with them, and has no choice when recounting his tales but to mention Rogers and Autry, Roger Moore, Bob Redford, and inevitably John Wayne as inhabitants of the world he moved in, mates and accomplices in great feats of drinking and partying.

Now he is back in the Wild West, living in Adam's tiny cottage, a place where the party never stops. His wheel has turned, and I expect he will serve out his days in Pioneertown, and I hope they are long.

Bob had told Iron Horse of the unusual rock formations on our property, and Iron Horse wished to play his drums amongst the rocks. And play them he did.

The drums took Iron Horse about a year to make, and his connection with Crazy Fox was based partly, I learnt, on the latter's abilities with the various skins required for various sounds. Crazy Fox, as a reader may have gleaned, is an Indian (of the Native American persuasion), and being so can take animals—for food and/or spiritual reasons—and is blessed with a particular skill when it comes to the drying and tanning of same.

Iron Horse, also an Indian, concentrates on the wooden bowls that make the drum of the drum and the tension of the skin. At least that was what I gathered in the time it took for the drums to be removed from the truck and placed in a triangle below the great rocks of the Hidden Valley. The largest drum stood about four feet high and four foot wide—at the top. All three drums and even the drumsticks were new. The product of a year's work was about to be tested.

Iron Horse took a position amidst the drums, raised the long drumsticks—their leather-clad balls the size of my fist—and put an end to conversation.

Iron Horse had not come to play for me—he had not previously known of my existence, but I was damned happy he had come. The Hidden Valley filled with sounds it might have heard one hundred or one thousand years ago, but sure hadn't heard for a while. The music cascaded off the rocks and then seemed to flow down the valley, following the old watercourse, and across the flatlands below. There was no pause, beat, or let-up in the sound, which was more like a melodic rumble. After ten minutes or so, Iron Horse was satisfied. The drums were good. We shook hands and agreed to meet up again soon at one of the local drumming circles.

While the Hounds of Spring cause Tony to disappear to Wisconsin's cooler climes, they also drive Frances and John away from their idyll in San Felipe to summer in Pipes Canyon. It says something about how hot it gets in the Gulf of Cortez that anyone even vaguely in their right mind would rather summer in the High Desert. Even Tony has the good sense to flee, and Tony will toil for sixteen hours a day and complain about being overpaid. I suspect that John and Frances return to feed their coyotes, who by the summer have eaten most of the spring quail and the slower rabbits. They then take to hanging about the cottage that comprises one of the confusing number of homes that these two old outlaws occupy. Their Pipes Canyon home sits a mile from where I sit, and in the summertime the coyotes prance outside amongst the rocks and low brush, awaiting the feast to be bestowed on them by their septuagenarian hosts.

The coyotes, being democrats at heart, have taken to picking up their bowls and carrying them off to share their good fortune with the rest of the pack, an activity that causes John and Frances some irritation. They do not object to this habit, being democrats themselves, but the loss each evening of half-a-dozen food bowls taxes their patience and their pockets. I personally don't approve of feeding wild animals at all, as we don't need a pack of coyotes baying around the house here on Coyote Road and eating not just their own dinner but the dog's. I doubt they could catch Inky the Cat.

But John and Frances have no dogs — except for the coyotes, who have, over the years, become as tame as our dogs — which means that they have reached a level of maturity required for a position at the White House. They are definitely not safe with children or nervous adults.

On a balmy (read boiling hot) summer night, one can sit on John and Frances's porch and watch the coyotes come within spitting distance to consume whatever delicacy has been prepared for them. Their democratic impulse — to remove the bowls holus bolus — has forced John to nail the dishes into the very rocks. All this provides guests with a relaxed situation from which to intimately observe the animals.

Often, as we reflect on the nature of these shy beasts, the silence is interrupted by the sound of drums. A principal rite of summer is the drumming parties hosted by Adam Edwards. And what a host Adam is. He builds a huge fire pit, brings in as much Bud as his varying fortunes allow, and invites myriad girls from LA to entice as many of his mates as possible to dance around flames that frequently shoot, flicker, and spark twenty feet into the air. The music is provided by the vast assortment of freaks who frequent the mountains, the high plains, and the lower desert.

Iron Horse is but one of the attractions at Adam's drum nights. In fact, drums, though common, are augmented by almost every musical instrument in existence—from the first, second, and third worlds—and it might be said that what is achieved is not so much music as something approaching a frenzy. A very loud one at that. This, combined with the leaping flames and leaping individuals, attracts the attention of the few hundred souls who can hear and see the show. That is, those within a few miles' radius. As many are in attendance, this raises few problems.

At Boulder House, we can't see Adam's place, but have no difficulty hearing the corroborees across seven miles of yucca forest.

The first night that Boo and I attended, Adam, in an experimental mood, picked up a bale of hay—meant for Smokey the horse, whom he was minding—and hurled it into the fiery furnace. The effect startled even Adam, as the hay, which had dried in the summer sun and was probably close to spontaneous combustion, exploded. Those sitting or dancing or playing their instruments were showered in burning vegetation, and, as many of them were semi- or totally naked, were rather inconvenienced. But Adam soon realized that no one had been gravely burnt, and assumed his merry mood. I don't believe he has repeated the trick.

Those who were seated at this pagan performance were incongruously sitting on old church pews that Adam had liberated at some stage of his illustrious career.

Adam's drum parties, at their best, are strange, indeed wondrous, sights. If one walks away into the yuccas to where the fire's light no longer obstructs the stars, the scene is heathen: up to sixty people, aged from six to sixty-five, lost in a mesmerizing mixture of an improvised interplay of instruments and dance around the bonfire. It is a beacon of brilliance in a world where the only other light comes from the moon and the stars.

28

Mike Bristow and I were having a beer one DILLIGAF afternoon when Ed Gibson arrived. I was about to leave, and Ed suggested I keep a watch out for a horseman with a packhorse on Pipes Canyon Road.

"The horses look about shot," Ed said with faint disgust. Ed has, with the advance of years, been forced to give up riding, and he took a dim view of those who didn't treat nags as they should. Ed took a dim view of a lot of things. In Ed's opinion, things rarely went right, if at all. Ed would not be the right man to found an optimists' club. He has a pessimistic view of most things, and can be judgmental.

I had pretty much forgotten his comment when I hit Pipes, but was startled to see a wildly dressed individual astride a spent creature, which trudged through the simmering heat that rose from the asphalt. The packhorse looked in no better shape.

I stopped the car and inspected the scene.

"Those horses are in poor condition," I remarked, noticing that the rider was wearing red, white, and blue attire, complete with stars and bars.

"They need water," the rider replied. I agreed.

"Do you have any?" the rider wondered.

"I carry water, but not enough for two horses," I replied, considering any person expecting the driver of a sedan to have water enough for two horses to be one kangaroo short of a paddock.

"I'm Captain America," the rider volunteered.

I nodded. He'd need to be.

"Where do you expect to find some?" I asked.

"Well," Captain America said, "there is water at Big Bear. Do you know where it's at?"

The road to Big Bear doesn't even warrant a name, and is little more than a watercourse that winds seventeen miles while climbing five thousand feet through the San Bernardino Mountains. I had once taken it to prove something to myself, and figured I just made it through. That, in the Ford 150 with wheels almost my height.

Captain America was going to attempt it in the mid-afternoon, with the sun starting to make its point, and I didn't like the chances of those horses making it alive—especially as Captain America didn't know where the road started. In fact, I doubted Captain America would make it alive, but my concern was for the horses—not for the fool upon them.

"You will have to bring them to my place. It's back a piece. About half a mile. I expect they can make it that far."

My contempt seemed lost on Captain America. About an hour later, he led the weary beasts into the Boulder House compound. They were in terrible shape. He watched as I led them to a water trough and hosed them down.

"See that mountain range," I said, pointing to the Little San Bernardino range about three miles off.

Captain America nodded.

"See the mountain range beyond that? See the one beyond that? Big Bear is on the other side of the third range."

Even Captain America figured his plan to ride so far might be ill considered.

"Can I stay here the night?" he asked.

The lead horse, having consumed an amount that would have filled a small swimming pool, had finished drinking. It moved around the saddle horse and started nosing at one of the packs. The pack burst open, and half a bale of hay landed at their and our feet. The packhorse kept drinking while his mate commenced dinner.

When the nags had drunk their fill and eaten what hay there was, I tethered them by the front door of Boulder House, and gave Captain America some food, telling him there was an outside bed down by the pool. We had plenty of beds inside, but I wasn't in the mood to have in the house some clown who'd been determined to drive his horses to death.

That night, the moon was full and bright. I went upstairs and tried to write, but the brilliant light formed incredible patterns on the rocks and on the yuccas, and I kept stopping work and eyeing the moon's handiwork. It seemed stupid to be bent over a computer keyboard when a dazzling world stretched before me. Such sights had brought us to the desert, so I took them in. My eyes ranged from the rock crops before the house, then to the ridge where the Ten Years Ago Tree stood stark as stark can be, all twisted in death but without the sense to fall over, to the plain below and then the mountain ranges beyond.

It was late. I watched for so long that the computer screen went blank. *That's better*, I thought. The room was in complete darkness, save for the rays of the moon.

I had forgotten the horses tethered below me. I couldn't see them because of a balcony that lies in front of the computer room. A window at the side of the office complements the one directly in front of me—the one that comprises my view. The view to the side is blocked by a tall pine. The balcony runs all the way around past the kids' room.

The wind must have moved around, because I caught a smell from the horses and thought of taking a ride. Fuck Captain America. Then came a soft but heavy (if that is possible) thump to my right. I looked at the window, puzzled. A lion was looking around below. Looking at the horses. From there, it could see them. But I didn't think of that at the time. The window was open, and a lion was a few feet from me.

A calmer man, a *National Geographic* type, might have taken the opportunity to study the cougar, as the local lions are also called. It was, after all, only a few feet from me, and all that separated us was a thin, fraying flyscreen.

"What in the fuck!" I cried, jumping up and staring at the lion, which, in turn, took one look at me and jumped himself. Jumped head over heels, did a back flip, and was gone.

Trembling with excitement and some fear, I rushed down to tell Boo. She was sleeping, but I shook her awake. She was a little peeved. I seemed to have all the luck in sighting animals. The western Rattlesnake, the golden eagle, and now The Lion. Bill Lavender had seen the—or a—lion some ten years ago, but it was a way off, on the ridge.

We discussed this remarkable occurrence. That a lion could come so close to the house was unthinkable. Lions stay clear of humans and their habitats—unless one threatens their food source. Lions do not go looking for humans. Sure, there have been people—kids and women—taken in recent years, but the consensus of the park rangers was that these people had inadvertently come close to where the lion had hidden its next meal. The lion's den, as it were. Some years back, a woman practicing for the Olympiad cross-country skiing had been killed to the north, and another woman was taken to the southwest, in the mountains behind San Diego.

Boo and I had studied a stuffed cougar taken in the Sierra Nevadas. We once found ourselves at the back of nowhere somewhere off the greatest of California's highways—the 395. In a valley surrounded by granite bastions that soared two thousand feet above us, we came upon an old lodge that seemed deserted and, as usual, we decided to explore. The doors of the barn were ajar, and we slipped in to find two Latino workers busying themselves preparing various animals for display. Had the workers been Anglo they probably would have objected to a couple of strangers treating this outpost as their own, but instead we were treated as though we owned the place and our arrival had been expected. Through Boo's mangled Spanish we learnt that the two were Northern Californian Mexicans. One was old, very old. He was in charge of a young man, his grandson, and was overseeing the stuffing of a golden eagle.

Throughout the barn, various animals were in various stages of being stuffed in preparation for being displayed at the main house, which stood a few hundred yards away overlooking a vigorous stream. The animal that caught the eye—indeed gave us a momentary shock—was the lion. For a second, we thought it was alive, so close to perfection had the animal been presented. As it was rearing, it appeared about to attack. It was long dead, but perfectly stuffed. I thought of Lenin and Pizarro, the only humans I remembered being stuffed. Boo had seen the latter while in Peru, and was delighted to find the stuffing coming out of the tiny figure's rear end. But he had at least been resting up in Lima's National Museum for almost five hundred years, while poor old Lenin had stuffing coming out of his ass after sixty years.

We stood there staring at the immaculately stuffed lion, and I thought of Lenin. If he had been better stuffed, perhaps the Soviet Union might have lasted another twenty years. After all, the failure to adequately stuff the founder of the great Soviet Empire suggested the empire would last about as long as the old stuffed coot. Which is precisely what happened. Entombed and disintegrating in the dead center of Red Square, he can hardly have inspired the populace. If you can't get Lenin properly stuffed, you can forget about Afghanistan. If this old Northern California Mexican had stuffed Lenin — and he looked old enough to have been around at the time — the worker's paradise might have turned out to be just that.

Boo, ignoring my digression to these arcane matters, asked the old gentleman (the master stuffer) if she could pat the mountain lion. Boo asked in Spanish, but the old man replied in appreciative English that she could. We both did. The animal was hard, and the golden hair was coarse. It was no African lion by any standards, but still a big and scary beast. Its fangs were particularly pronounced. The old man said the beast had weighed one hundred and sixty pounds.

"About my weight," I observed.

That night we made it to Lone Pine, where we visited Nels, a man who knows the wild better than most. Nels had plenty of time to reflect on mountain lions, as he moved cattle from the mountains to the low pastures in the fall and back up to the alpine climes in spring. He'd lost stock to lions, and no cowboy or his boss is happy when $600 plus goes to sate a cougar's blood lust. They are also hard to track, unless there is snow, and more dangerous than a bear, according to Nels.

"You should remember their strength is pound for pound about eight times that of yours," Nels remarked.

I pondered the figures. Their real fighting weight is nearly 1,600 pounds. They usually have the added advantage of height. All the people taken, to my knowledge, were jumped from an overhanging limb on a trail, hence their name "ghost cat". You don't know it's there until it is upon you. The cougar's ancestor, the saber-toothed tiger, which once roamed the High Desert, would spring on the back of its prey—a woolly mammoth being a favorite dish—and plunge its sabers into the victim's veins. It would ride the thrashing giant while draining its blood through vampire-like holes in its foot-long teeth. Some described the forbears of the wild animal that had paid us a visit that summer night as being "the greatest fighting machine nature has ever invented".

Perhaps. I'd like to see a saber-tooth take out a big croc.

"Why," I asked Nels, "if they are so powerful, don't the cougars take men?"

"They will if they have to," he replied. "But maybe they don't know that we are weaklings compared to them."

But why, I wondered to Boo on the night I prematurely scared off our lion, would it come near enough to almost enter a large human dwelling?

"The horses," Boo suggested.

Indeed, we had forgotten about the horses. They had been pushed almost to death. A lion, roaming far and wide, would no doubt pick up the scent, and calculate that the animals were in bad shape. From the balcony, it could have pitched itself onto one of the horse's backs and do what grandfather did to the woolly mammoths.

"You'd better go and warn Captain America," Boo said, and I set off in the dark for the pool some fifty yards from the main house. It was a little unnerving, and I swung the torch around hoping I didn't pick up on a huge set of eyes. But Captain America was sleeping in the open air, and there was a slim chance the lion would have a go at him. Which would suit me fine, as I might be able to claim the horses. Captain America didn't strike me as having a large family, if any family at all.

I woke him, informing him that a cougar was on the prowl and might be interested in his horses. But he wasn't concerned. He muttered something about how he'd be fine, and returned to his slumbers.

I returned to the house, wondering if I could kill him and make it look like the lion did it. I doubted I could.

I raised the matter of big cats with the DILLIGAF sergeant at arms, Mike Bristow the following Friday at The Palace. We were sitting out in what would be a beer garden had there been anything green growing in it, and I told Mike about the incident.

"I had a cougar as a pet for twelve years," Mike replied.

Why, I inquired, had he spent twelve years with a mountain lion in the house? He rather disarmingly said that at the time mountain lion cubs were cheaper than cheetahs. He added that an unpleasant experience with an African lion had convinced him that he might be biting off more than he could chew. Mike didn't get bit, but the African lion (which also enjoyed a career in the porn industry — I did not determine in what capacity) gave the owner a nasty nip after giving Mike and his wife, Mel, a few unpleasant moments. Mike's description of the roar of the beast as it prepared to attack as "reverberating inside my brain" put me off the idea of having an African lion around Boulder House for good.

"We thought about bobcat kittens, but the bobs have an attitude problem," Mike added.

"I bought the cougar off an animal trainer. He had half-a-dozen cougars, two bobs, and some bears. One of the cougars was related to the first Ford Lincoln Mercury Cougar. The sound they make isn't like the sound in the ads."

Mike described the mountain lion's roar as "a sort of a purr", which presumably did not reverberate around his brain.

"The guy had a box with two bobs and two cougar kittens, and I just put my hand in, and the cougar ran up my arm.

"I paid $750 for her, bottle-fed her till weaned, and then started her on the same stuff the LA Zoo used — shredded horse meat. I'd buy it in fifty-pound lots. Fully grown, she'd eat two and a half pounds per week. She loved dogs, and would drag a neighbor's dog to the ground and then start licking its ears. She just wanted to clean them.

"I taught her to fight. At eleven weeks, my body looked like a railroad map."

As a tray of beers arrived, Mel remarked that the big cat's licking was a problem. "It was rough, like sandpaper. It would take layers of your skin off," she said.

"Like a rasp," Mike added.

"What happened to it?" I wondered.

"We had it for twelve years," Mike said, "but they wouldn't let us keep it when we moved to San Bernardino County, so we put her on the Kitty Underground."

"The Kitty Underground?"

"When you own a lion, you get to know a lot of people with big cats. You also get to know your neighbors pretty well."

Mel remarked that the main thing in having a lion is "never show fear".

"She'd pick up on it, and she'd bite. My cousin got bit on the leg. He passed out."

At that moment, a huge horse I mistakenly took for a Clydesdale was brought into a corral that ended a few yards from where we sat. It turned out to be a Belgian, and it proceeded to roll in the dust, sending up clouds. The breeze deposited the dust on the assembled DILLIGAF members, who happily watched the spectacle. When the dust settled and the draught horse regained his huge hooves, someone was talking about his great-great-uncle who apparently invented the telephone on 3 May 1884. Unfortunately, the man omitted to apply for a patent, and someone called Bell stole the show.

A few days later, I ran into Horseshoe Freddie at the Joshua Tree Saloon. Horseshoe Freddie is the best and most respected of the remaining horsemen in these parts. He was raised on a ranch in Colorado and had come out to the High Desert in 1949, when there was a sizable cattle industry. The cattle have been mostly phased out, but Freddie has retained a horseman's life, and his nag can find its way home from The Club to Joshua Tree even if Freddie is asleep. That's a good seven miles over rough country. Freddie is a good-enough horseman to sleep astride his horse and still stay in the saddle. Naturally, he knew a little about Captain

America, and nothing he had to say was good. He recounted that Captain America had ridden a horse to Palm Springs during a recent summer.

"You can't do that to a horse," Freddie opined. The horse seemed to agree, as it passed away down in the boiling desert.

29

Down in the lower desert, the temperature can hit 180, a figure that excludes human life. It takes a lot to fry the human brain, but fry it will.

I sat having a beer with Dave in the Wine and Roses bar overlooking Yucca Valley's little airport. Dave is a safety officer on a large building site in the Low Desert, and has been dealing with the problem of heat a lot of late. In the past, construction would cease in the baking summer months, but now too much money is at stake as the gated communities spread like a disease across the desert. The builders know the vagaries of the economy. They have seen floods of money dry up before, and the half-million-dollar houses have to be built and sold with a weather eye not to the weather but the economy. The faster these tract houses for the rich can be sold, the surer they are of abundant profit.

Dave has to walk the line between meeting the demands of profit and not killing his work crews, who are usually from south of the border. He arrived on one site recently, driving through clouds that rose six hundred feet from a burning orange-packing factory, to find one of the workers unconscious. Within minutes, two other men had fallen to heat stroke, and Dave, equipped with saline drips and the like, closed the site and ministered to the fallen. They recovered, but in future they will have to be watched closely. According to Dave and anyone else in the know, the brain fries faster once it has first fried. Just as cold water boils slowly the first time but faster the second, the human brain, once mushed, mushes more easily after each mushing. Apart from brain damage there is the risk of death, and a death on a job site will lead to a law suit, and a law suit will gobble up the profits of half-a-dozen half-million-dollar houses. So Dave has a narrow row to hoe.

Later, as I sat writing, the heat caused me to open the front window. I leaned from the laptop, slid the glass, and watched as a horned toad gracefully sailed into the living room. He sat on the carpet for some time, ignored by the dog. I captured him, with great ease, in a Trader Joe's meringue bucket. The toad was gray, about the size of a woman's fist, and, in common with other horned toads, had horns. They weren't dangerous, and I stood reading the calorie count on the meringues as the thing expressed lethargic resistance. It hopped about a few times as I carried it outside, depositing it near the dog's huge water bowl, and wandered back inside. I was about to deposit the meringue top in the trash when I noticed that the toad was still in it, clinging on — no doubt enjoying the remnants of sugar, flour, and vanilla. I returned him to the water trough and went off to mix a drink. A thought came to mind halfway through the process, and I returned to the laptop. Remembering my drink, I wandered back to the kitchen and was about to take a sip when I detected a scorpion struggling in the icy pina colada. The local scorps are not to be taken internally. I scooped the creature from my drink, crushed it, and returned to the battle station.

Dan Dan, who works in the Low Desert, deals with scorpions and other terrors of the desert as part of daily life. His work, installing music and security systems in the tract palaces, finds him often in attics where the heat can reach 160 or even 170 degrees. The attics are also the homes of the black widow and recluse spiders — huge nests of them, sometimes a score of nests to an attic. Into them he goes, clad in a sort of homemade space suit, his face masked, his gloves and boots taped at the ankles and the wrists so the spiders can't get at him. With each step, a mini mushroom cloud of fine desert dust erupts from his feet and covers him in layer after layer. Just how hot it gets inside the suit is anyone's guess, but when Dan climbs from the attic he actually makes a squishing noise as his sweat slurps about the suit.

Worse are the date-drying warehouses. Only a few miles from the grand tract houses, but deeper and lower in one of the world's hottest deserts, fifty feet beneath the sea, are the huge squat buildings where thousands of crates of dates are left to dry. They attract all manner of the creepiest creatures that the planet has on offer — black widows, recluse, a finer variety of scorpions (over a hundred species in the Low Desert alone), and a close relative of the scorpion, the vinegaroon. The vinegaroon grows to four inches, is as fast as a mouse, and incredibly aggressive. The tail is like that of a scorpion except smooth, and although his bite is not as powerful as his cousin's, he is, in Dan's opinion, "a creature from hell and the ugliest thing you have ever seen". They are named after the taste of vinegar they leave on the palate after inflicting a bite.

Although the same species can be found in the High Desert, those around and possibly in Boulder House are scorned by Dan Dan for being not nearly as big or aggressive. Likewise, the scorpions are bigger than ours — the largest growing to seven inches. "They make you real sick," says Dan Dan. "But I'd rather be bitten by a scorpion than a black widow," he adds, before going on to recount working under a sixty-year-old store, feeling in the dark, and placing his hand in a nest of rattlers.

The scene in the date warehouses would send James Cameron off to church. The date crates are stacked five feet from the warehouse walls, which for hundreds of feet are completely lined by the webs of the black widows. In each warehouse there are thousands of these horrifying nests, and again they compete with the even more treacherous and deadly recluse spider's quarters. In the ceilings live the date beetles — monstrous, vile things the size of a large hand, and given to dropping onto Dan's neck as he climbs a ladder to the roof to attach an electronic device.

"They land with a thud on my neck," says Dan with a gruesome grin. "It's all you can do to stay on the ladder."

Dan involuntarily slaps at his neck, remembering the horrible moments when he swayed on a ladder, tearing at the beetle and hoping he didn't fall into the nest of black widows below him.

Boo gave a terrible shriek recently when she found, in the rock room, a scorpion that had strayed into a black widow's nest. For a while we watched the spider slowly and determinedly consuming the scorpion, in a scene made for *National Geographic*. And that was six feet from where she stood.

What a cocktail man and nature have created down below. To the blistering sand, man has added water for crops and golf courses (over one hundred of the latter, with more being built continuously), and to this has been added decades of pesticides and herbicides. From LA rolls a river of smog. In the morning, a green haze lifts from the desert floor as the morning watering of gardens and golf courses evaporates. No wonder that, in this mix of man, mammon, and merciless heat, with a new rich menu for creatures that have spent millions of years adjusting to survival in a wasteland, the creepiest of creatures now flourish. But the desert cities cannot grow further to the south, for there lies the Salton Sea. Cut off from the Sea of Cortez some five hundred years ago, it is now a repository of the chemical run-off from hundreds of square miles of dense agriculture. It stinks so high that Ed Gibson grew sick just driving by. And Ed's about as tough as they get.

Here at Boulder House, perched above it all, we see clear blue skies through the day, and bright stars through the night. It's a half-hour drive away, but a light year from man's waste-bins of the desert.

Exploring the dusty back roads off Highway 66 in Southern California, we were used to happening upon some fairly unexpected sights. However, the area around Helendale — a nothing kind of town — had little to recommend it. After some hours of scrubby, depressing desert that even the cactus looked miserable in, we were considering turning around when we saw the sign: "EXOTIC WORLD BURLESQUE MUSEUM".

It was mounted on a chain-link fence that surrounded forty acres of desert scrub. Inside was a typical nondescript California ranch house. Beside it sat a navy-blue Rolls Royce. The gate was ajar, and we drove in.

The door of the house opened, and Marilyn Monroe appeared. She was dressed in black stretch pants, kitten heels, and a fluffy pink sweater with a tight, plunging neckline. It was about 10.00 a.m.

The extraordinary apparition gave a little wave and sashayed towards us. Up close, Dixie Evans — then in her sixties — bore more than a passing resemblance to the woman she had spent her career impersonating. Beneath the full make-up and perfectly coiffed platinum hair, she was a tantalizing hint of what Ms. Monroe might now look like had she lived — and had a full life.

Dixie was delighted that she had Australian visitors — she was delighted she had *any* visitors — but Aussies were an added bonus, because she had spent her early childhood in Roma, Queensland. Her father, she explained, as she led us towards the museum housed in another building, had worked for an oil-drilling company up there in the tropical north, and her childhood had been very happy. In fact, it had been the happiest time of her life.

The museum itself was fascinating, but not nearly as fascinating as its custodian and guide. In a perfect Marilyn-like whispery voice, and using Fred Astaire's silver cane as a pointer, Dixie showed us lovingly displayed gowns and G-strings of the goddesses of striptease — Lili St. Cyr, Gypsy Rose Lee, Tempest Storm, and all the others. Jayne Mansfield's bathtub was there. Feathers, bling, and pasties of every color each had a story to tell from an earlier, more innocent, age of erotica.

Whether it was the fact that I was a journalist, or that she was simply starved for company, Dixie began recounting story after story of her life during the golden age of American striptease when she had reigned as the "Marilyn Monroe of Burlesque".

She insisted we stay for lunch, and ushered us inside the main house she shared with the widower of another legend of the stage. Jennie Lee, the famous "Bazoom Girl", had died some years earlier after buying the old ex-goat farm out here near Barstow.

Her plan was to provide a retirement home for the former girls of burlesque — and to open a museum honoring them.

Her old friend Dixie was now bringing that dream to life.

Jennie's ashes rested in a lovely urn on the mantelpiece. Her husband came in and welcomed us, and then left his wife's friend to tell her stories. No doubt he had heard them before, but we hadn't. In that strange, dark house, Dixie hauled out box after box of photos and rare memorabilia she was still sorting for the museum. With each photo came a story about the girl smiling or pouting for the camera — the girls who thrilled men for a generation before this art form gradually lost its appeal.

Dixie was lamenting the end of America's interest in the great tradition of burlesque when an extraordinary figure flashed past the window. She peered at us through a blanket draped over her head as she scuttled by. It was hard to tell how old the woman was, but her missing teeth and sun-toughened skin suggested a sad U-turn in her life. Dixie told us she was an ex-dancer, down on her luck, whom they had taken in. Because she couldn't stand being indoors, she was currently living under a hedge.

As if things couldn't get any more bizarre, the door opened and a dog entered. It was lacking a snout. The silly boy, Dixie, informed us, had got it bitten off while sticking his nose down a gopher hole. What with the toothless cloaked woman and the no-nose dog — and with Jennie Lee's ashes presiding on the mantelpiece — I started to feel as if I was hallucinating.

Dixie herself almost seemed unreal — a phantom out there in the middle of nowhere, surrounded by the glitz of another time. She told us she used to strip at one of Jack Ruby's clubs in Dallas, and had her own theory about JFK's assassin. Ruby was evidently obsessed with Jackie — so obsessed that he was prepared to shoot the man who killed her husband. That's love for you! Dixie had absolutely no doubt about this.

The desert gets dark early in winter. Suddenly it was night. Our hostess insisted we stay over. She wouldn't hear of us leaving. We were visitors from her favorite country, and simply had to stay in the "Honeymoon Suite". As alluring as the red heart-shaped bed was, we had to hit the road.

Before the light went, Dixie offered to pose — à la Marilyn — draped across the Rolls Royce. The photo later appeared in an Australian newspaper with my article. We sent her a copy, and she was delighted. Other journalists followed the story up. A friend from British TV came and made a program about the museum and Dixie for a travel show. Maybe, she told us, the world was finally waking up to a chapter of its heritage that it had stuffed away in a drawer for too long.

Maybe Marilyn was finally going to come back from the dead.

30

Sean, who had got lost in a drugged wilderness from which he was emerging, wanted to make a mark on the citizenry for his thirty-eighth birthday. A few weeks before, we had gone together to take some cactus from a former friend of Sean's, an amphetamine dealer who lived in a dilapidated trailer at the base of Goat Hill. It was twenty miles from Boulder House and an entirely different moonscape. Only goats and cactus and speed dealers could possibly live in such a place. Goat Hill is a jumble of broken volcanic brown rock surrounded by barren washes. The dealer had a generator—we were far from electricity—and the thing chugged away as we approached the caravan to inform Sean's acquaintance of our intentions. The dealer wasn't unfriendly, as Sean had once been a major customer.

I looked into the tiny ramshackle dive and saw a girl. She had once been very pretty, but speed had taken care of that. The spots on her face were identical to those I had seen on the coke whores of Venice. Her body was in good shape and most of it was in evidence, but she showed no modesty before my brief glance. The guy had the dope, and she was his chattel. He didn't care who looked at her, and neither did she.

Sean explained our intentions, and the guy said it was cool—which it definitely wasn't. Sweat was running from the leather band of my Stetson. We picked our way through the rubbish, old tires, and equipment that lay baking in the sun as we returned to Sean's truck. By the path stood a wooden box some ten feet long and a few feet high and wide. The remnants of a mattress spewed from a hole in the box, and Sean stopped and appraised this forlorn sight.

"I lived here for six months," he remarked at the box. "In the summer," he added. "I was sick most of the time."

Nothing else needed to be said. Sean was once a top gun in the coast guard. He had a letter signed personally by president Reagan, complimenting him on his role in the detection of a boatload of marijuana some years before. He lost the letter—and everything else—in the course of his speed addiction. He had come a long way from such distinguished service, but was fighting his way back.

The birthday party was partly his way of showing just how far back—and it had to be done right. Sean had been respected by the community for his strength and his mechanical skills, and before sinking into the slops had been well liked in Pioneertown. The party was his chance to let the town know he had returned to the land of the living. But this I was just learning.

We knew we were living in methamphetamine country. All around us were bits of blown-up houses that used to house meth labs, and we had wondered about them. Sean explained the dynamics of the drug.

"You start taking speed, and you are up all night. You might fuck for three hours. And you are drinking and smoking all the time. You can drink a lot of whiskey and smoke a lot of cigarettes on speed. And of course you have to have dope [marijuana].

"And you have to pay for all this, so you work for the speed. You need more speed to work. So you are working for speed. But the work you do is no good. You think you are working hard, but you are just making more work. And you never get the adrenaline naturally, because you are snorting or shooting adrenaline.

"I'd clean a room, but really would have just taken a mess and put it somewhere else. So you lose your job, and you sell your tools for more speed. I once sold my welding equipment for three days of speed. One hundred dollars. It was worth five hundred. Then you start stealing stuff. I never did — I got too sick."

Sean developed pneumonia in the course of a binge. Things got ugly, and his woman took his guns. Things got even uglier, and Sean ended up in the box in the desert, where he lay in delirium while a local Christian brought him food. The payoff for the food was Sean's promise to attend church, so he found himself hiding out on Sundays until things got so bad he decided on religion before speed. His face was full of sores from the impurities in the speed, and his body was about lost.

"I would have died, had I kept going," says Sean, who is now as fit as a trout and as strong as a brace of oxen.

Boo and I went along with the idea of a massive celebration, partly on the grounds that we felt one was due as well. We had successfully moved from the city to the desert, and had made peace with the locals.

Sean went to great lengths to ensure that none of the speed fraternity heard about the party. He wanted to be painted with a new brush in the collective consciousness. I feared that if the speed freaks discovered Boulder House, they would return and steal all but the boulders.

Sean, who was given to waxing Biblical far too often (the Bible had played a major role in his rehabilitation), decided that the party had to include the killing and eating of a fattened calf. I argued that we needed Buzz Gamble and the Daily Blues.

We reached a compromise and agreed on the music, but in the place of the calf settled for a fattened pig.

A few years before, when Sean was amidst his battle with speed, those given to alarm had convinced themselves of the coming of the end of the world due to the year 2000 bug. Sean had taken responsibility for a number of piglets to be raised so they could be eaten when "the system" collapsed.

The year 2000 came and went, and the piglets continued to do what they do best — eat. Knowing about these animals, I had inspected them in their sties, where they had been nurtured on the overflow from Harriet's kitchen, and they all looked delicious. But one had struck me as particularly tasty, and I'd pointed the revolver that we had been playing with at the best-looking pig, and suggested that we — and everyone else — eat the thing.

Sean had agreed. There is something about eating an animal you actually know compared with the "faceless" animals that arrive on most people's tables. We once knew a farmer in Australia called Sam who claimed he bred the best veal in the world. He was always talking with wide-eyed enthusiasm about putting one sort of bull over one of his various breeds of cows, and went to the end of the world to find the perfect combination — ultimately a Sindhi Brahman over, I think, a Hereford Black Angus. Sam was exceptionally strong, and ate steaks, sausages, bacon and eggs, and half a loaf of bread for breakfast. His refrigerator dripped with rich red blood. He butchered his own meat, and this perhaps led to his downfall. Sam couldn't keep his hands off his vealers, and would drive around his property relishing coming meals.

"I can't wait to eat that beast," he would yell as his truck bounced over the fields. He would lick his chops and grin obscenely at the animals, and then at Boo and me. It was as if breeding the animal, delivering it, and then watching it grow to just the right moment for butchering, hanging, and then eating it made for a tastier banquet than a trip to the market for a cut of steak.

Unfortunately for Sam, his appetite got in the way of his wallet. The prize beasts could be sold for far more than the average beeve, but Sam's massive, promiscuous appetite had him eating the profits. A whole animal — worth perhaps $4,000 — would be consumed in a matter of weeks.

Sam started losing money at the rate he gained muscles, and he took to supplementing his income through the production of a notorious cash crop.

Sam ate his way into jail.

I didn't know Sean's pig that well, and have to confess I have forgotten its name. But the experience of selecting, preparing, and eating taught me much about how Sam got into the condition — over a period of six years — he ended up in.

Sean arrived a few days before the big day aboard his tractor, to which he had attached a backhoe, and proceeded to dig an exceedingly deep pit in the granite. It took him the best part of a day — the ground being solid rock — but when he exited the backhoe and accepted a bottle of tequila, he could proudly exhibit a hole deep and large enough for a prize pig and a couple of its friends.

While Sean had been tearing up the granite I had visited Buzz, proposing that his band play at our collective bash. Considering the prospects of the speed fiends turning up and having to be turned away, I hired Mike Bristow to enforce whatever laws he thought should be enforced—and hoped for the best. Harriet warned me that the police would raid Boulder House and that druggies would take off with the silverware, and at one stage Sean suggested that maybe the party should be moved to The Palace.

"Dude," he said (Sean has an irritating habit of calling all and sundry "dude"), "do you really want to go ahead with this?"

"A man doth not put his hand to the plough and turn back," I replied.

The neighbors were duly informed and invited, as the night promised to be long and loud. Though the nearest neighbor was half a mile away, we expected the sound to travel many miles in the thin mountain air.

Buzz readily agreed and promised the attendance of the band, but did mention the matter of money. Four hundred dollars. It seemed a fair deal, given that they would have to drag their equipment all the way to Boulder House, set up and play from six till midnight, and Buzz had a strict policy of "no pay—no play".

A few days later, the butcher arrived with the pig. The porker I had admired in Sean's pens was now both headless and hideless. It was also—I was relieved to see—gutted.

It was dumped on a huge piece of cardboard on the floor of the poolroom some fifty yards from the pit. Having inspected the pig, we lit a fire six feet down at the pit's base, and piled a cord or so of wood onto the flames. We went early to our respective beds the night before the party.

At 3.00 a.m., almost twenty hours from party time, Sean woke me with a bottle of his prized tequila and announced it was time to prepare the animal.

He had bought six pineapples and gallons of plain yogurt after consulting all and sundry on the basics of cooking a pig in a pit, and concluding that this was the appropriate way to go. We stuffed the pineapples into the pig's gutted cavity, and then smeared the yogurt on the flesh. Then we wrapped it in sacking and chicken wire. Finally, we drove an eight-foot pick bar through the thing's throat and the pineapples, and finally out via the back passage. We hoisted the bar, and carried the pig to the fire pit, lowered it onto the white-hot ashes, and, like thieves in the night, repaired to our beds.

If anyone had observed our behavior, an impossible task unless conducted from the air by Edwards Air Force Base F18s and F14s or by satellite, they might have thought they were witnessing a fiendish, satanic ritual. And we both admitted to feeling guilty — not over the fate of the pig, but our nocturnal activities, the burying and cooking of an animal we had come to know.

Sometime before, Tony and I had been chatting up two LA girls in The Club. I was doing my best to make Tony agreeable to at least one of the young filmmakers, and for a while it looked like he was in with a chance. I suggested the girls come back to Boulder House. They were nervous, but Tony gave the place a grand description, and they were almost persuaded.

I thought to put their minds at rest by saying they should not worry.

"It's not like we're going to sodomise you and put you in the lime-pit with the other girls," I remarked jovially.

I heard Tony's face drop. Immediately, I realized that my lighthearted banter had miscued. The girl next to me turned another color, and her acquaintance started fussing and talking about "Getting back on the road" — always a bad sign.

Suddenly, they had both disappeared, and Tony was as close as he could get to a rage. I told him I regretted my comment, but thought it just a frivolous aside.

Tony was boiling.

"A frivolous aside," he almost screamed. "Out here in the desert, where even they would know that bodies are dumped every day!"

Tony gaped, and stared at me in silence.

"I think they overreacted," was the best I could manage.

Clearly, I had said something that had cost Tony a decent chance to get to know a young lass from Hollywood better than he otherwise might, and I felt poorly about the outcome.

But here we were, at dawn's early light, lowering a beast into a burning pit. I had butchered, burnt, and eaten animals in the past, but these activities had not been conducted in the presence of a man who, having lowered steel doors over the pig, returned to his Bible and tequila.

Upon the day that Sean reached his thirty-eighth year, and as the sun slipped behind the mountains, Buzz Gamble, his microphone covered by one of my socks to deny the wind, opened the party proper with "Sympathy for the Devil". From then on, the rocks rocked. A hundred or so people gathered in the amphitheater or danced on the cement dog runs. Elderly ladies from the church adjusted their bifocals and jitterbugged with gay young men in caftans. Bill Lavender perched on a boulder with his girlfriend, Phyllis, watched as the band played, and people danced on the cement that had once been the runs for his famous Rotts. Others sat up high on the rocks that surround Boulder House as the kids of the upper desert thrashed about in the pool under the floodlights. Horseshoes were thrown, and volleyballs were tossed across nets by bikini-clad girls. And so went the night.

Finally, it was time to retrieve the pig. At nine o'clock, when it had cooked for the day, the great steel doors that Sean had placed above the pit were lifted, and the pig was brought forth. Everyone, starving by now, gathered around, salivating. Unhappily, the pig was seared but not actually cooked, Sean having used pine for the fire rather than a hardwood. The starving masses took the disaster stoically — things always went wrong in the desert. But Sean was mortified. His pig was a failure. It reflected poorly on him at a time when he was trying desperately to prove he had made a successful return to the land of the living.

"There's only one thing to do," he muttered, pulling me aside. "Chinese takeout. I'll leave now."

Sean was trying to remember where his car was, so he could embark on the twenty-mile trip to Yucca and back, when a Hawaiian gentlemen whom no one seemed to know materialized and called for more wood and coal. The man happened to be an authority on the cooking of pigs in pits, and, almost at midnight — after the good folks of the High Desert had demolished mountains of beer — the Hawaiian brought forth a perfectly cooked pig.

To me fell the task of carving the animal. Much of the outer layer was fat, but the people of Pioneertown, Pipes Canyon, and Rimrock could no longer be restrained. They tore, like beasts, at the huge slabs of pork that I slashed from the carcass. Knives, forks, and plates were forgotten by the multitude, as people grabbed cuts of hot dripping pork from my hands and stuffed themselves. The temperature was still high at midnight, and I had stripped down to an undershirt. The fat gushed from the pig, and soon my butchering had rendered me slick from the waist up, my arms and shoulders and even my head dripping with fat as I took part in a fantastic, bloodthirsty orgy of delicious, unforgettable food.

In the early morning hours the guests began leaving, only to find police cars parked at the end of Coyote Road. The cops could have locked up half of the citizens of the High Desert, but instead determined who was drunk at the wheel and had them replaced by more sober passengers. They had been alerted by the noise and had come up from Yucca, but for once their concern was not to fill the jail but to see the residents safely home. People marvel at that to this day.

31

The most hazardous activity in the High Desert is undoubtedly driving. Last year, no fewer than sixteen people went to be with Jesus within ten miles of my front door. This, in an area with a total population of twenty-six thousand. If translated to, say, Los Angeles, that would result in an annual death toll of sixteen thousand. Nationally, it would mean a road toll of millions, a figure that would equal and maybe eclipse the murder rate inflicted by the tobacco industry. Locals, taking a cue from the nations to our south, have begun erecting crosses and shrines, and Pioneertown Road has developed an Andean look.

The cause of this carnage in the area is the chronic alcoholism, the ageing population, a considerable adolescent population, the chronic consumption of speed, inadequate roads, and the endless stream of concrete trucks that roll down Old Woman Springs Road. Driving out to 29 Palms to pay a fine at the DMV, I witnessed an extremely old and frail woman have her license renewed. She had shrunk, apparently, and was about the size of Lenin after eighty years in his tomb — and in equally poor shape. So blind was the old duck that she couldn't locate the place to sign her form, so some helpful locals lifted her high enough to be able to reach the counter, and the DMV official guided her hand to the correct spot. Then she was held up so her photo could be taken and — presto! — the right to drive was confirmed. At times like this, the expression "defensive driving" assumes a new perspective. Usually, such person's lives are terminated when they wander before a cement truck while driving white Cadillacs.

Another cause of the carnage was exemplified of late when a woman lost her Harley on Pioneertown Road when she got into trouble and decided to use the front brakes to slow down while negotiating a bend. Thousands of would-be outlaw bikers visit the area every year, and, though they have spent a fortune trying to get the look right, they have not learned to ride big motorcycles. This lady who was AirEvac'd to civilization and lived—we know that because the coroner, for once, was not sent to the scene—did what poorly trained riders and drivers inevitably do when confronted: she hit the brakes. It's the last thing most people who are killed in accidents do.

A fundamental reason for this "massive road crisis" is the assumption, one of many, that there are no other cars out there to worry about. Because the roads—and there are only three tarred ones—appear to be bereft of vehicles, a driver used to the intense concentration required for negotiating a freeway is blinded by the absence of fellow travelers and assumes none exist. But they do, and they appear when the unwary are unwary. And no one likes to be surprised by a cement truck.

Though the dead are many, the escapees are also plenty-fold. Corners are actually named after amazing saves. The best known is Barrymore Bend on Pioneertown Road—named after the actor John Barrymore JR., who spent, until lately, much of his retirement at Ernie and Carole's motel, and had regularly crashed on a difficult bend halfway down the road.

A few nights after Sean's party, Crinkly Jim and Lil Debbie rolled their car on a particularly nasty stretch of Pioneertown Road. Neither was injured, but a tire had blown, and the car, having landed in the long-suffering yucca forest, sank into the soft soil that follows the rains. Both were too drunk to negotiate the replacement of the tire — their jack having sunk deeper into the soil. Figuring the same would happen to my dinky jack, I repaired to The Club to arrange for a few locals to get Jim and Lil Debbie from harm's way before the authorities at Yucca got to hear there was money to be made up the hill. The hour was not late, but it was the Sabbath, and few were prepared to take the chance of driving to a wreck and having the cops inquire into their sobriety.

Only Dan Dan would come to the succor of Crinckly Jim and Lil Deb, and we set off to right the situation. Much of the beer in Crinkly Jim's car had exploded under impact of the roll, and the trunk was dripping with a telltale smell. Worse, Jim had found a bottle of cheap vodka, a polyester cup, and some orange juice, and he and Lil Debbie were mixing a fresh drink as I crawled under the wheel to help place the industrial-size jack that Dan carried in his truck. I wasn't nervous about the police because I had managed only two beers. Not for long. Jim set the vodka bottle up on the truck, and with the first movement of the jack it fell on its side, delivering a stream of vodka across the truck's surface and down onto my head.

I stank like Boris Yeltsin visiting Ireland. But we righted the car, and somehow Crinkley Jim and Lil Debbie were soon careening home while necking the remnants of the vodka.

I pulled out as soon as I was sure they could move and get home safely. The next day, I ran into Dan Dan, who informed me that Debbie or Jim had rolled the car again about half a mile further down the road.

I had noticed some alarming skid marks on the road at that point, but it had not occurred to me that these idiots could manage to roll a car, successfully, twice in the space of a thousand yards. How could they have even got up the speed?

A few days later, I called to see if all was well. Dan Dan's version of the story was, as all stories told locally, wrong. They had not rolled the car again. The skid marks were from when Jim had rolled the car the day before. A completely different incident, Jim informed me indignantly.

Following the party, Sean's life got better with each passing day, and soon he was lost to us in favor of Debbie, a high school friend whom he had re-met at their twenty-year high school reunion up at Big Bear. They married, and Sean got a steady job — leaving me with a few tools and little expertise to finish the renovation of Boulder House. This was a task akin to the work carried out by the Egyptians at the time when all but the higher reaches of the High Desert were still part of the Sea of Cortez.

The next day, I heard that Buzz was sick. For a time, Buzz was increasingly, alarmingly, sick. His liver, according to the VA, had almost ceased to function, and his survival was a source of wonder to all. But the same was said of Crinkly Jim's liver, and he had, for the moment, kept the undertakers at bay.

"The people at Loma Linda told me they don't do new livers for alcoholics," Buzz said, with half a smile and half a grimace.

Buzz served his nation, but it wasn't a two-way deal. I told him, "You can't die. You're Buzz Gamble," and he seemed to think that might be true. But he was truly sick.

I discussed the matter with Dan Dan, one of Pioneertown's success stories, a man sought out far and wide for his skills with music and lighting systems. We agreed that if Buzz was to eat—and he hadn't in a week—he'd have a better chance. His only nutrition in six days had come from the Sprite that he'd been adding to his bourbon. I wondered if the drinks they give people with AIDS and other diseases that attack the appetite—little cans that contain, in fact, meals—might help. Dan Dan said they were expensive, and threw twenty bucks on the bar.

It's not exactly health care, but Buzz is amongst the most uninsurable people in America. The only doctors he can afford to see are those at the Loma Linda Veterans hospital—a two-hour drive that has always ended in him being told to take counseling. Buzz needs more than counseling. He needs a new liver. But the position of the state is that alcoholics are to be denied livers until they give up drink, and can prove so. Buzz used booze to get off a twenty-three-year-old heroin habit, and he thought that was something of an achievement. But those who have sworn to give their life to healing the sick must think that alcoholism is not a sickness. Certainly not one that should be encouraged by handing out fresh livers.

The fact that Buzz might just be the best white blues man in the US, that he gives joy to all who know him as a singer and as an all-round guy, that the blues are his blues due to the pain of being him, a pain that he treats with booze 'cause heroin just means jail—does not make him worthy of a fresh start with a fresh liver.

According to the medical dictionaries, which are all we are able to consult in the absence of a health system, stopping drinking, followed by rest, is essential for the liver to have a chance.

But Buzz needs to work, and his job is as day barman at the Joshua Tree Saloon, a bar at the foot of the Joshua Tree National Park. It's not the place to give up drinking. It's a desert bar, a bar where people come to drink, and drink a lot. It's an old-fashioned bar—a drinker's and a smoker's bar. Probably the worst place on earth to give up drinking. But it's his job, and, apart from singing, is pretty much the only thing he can do.

Dan Dan and I discussed this situation at some length. Buzz should have been on sick leave, but as with many jobs in the desert, Buzz and everyone else are paid under the table. He gets $3.50 an hour—more than a dollar under the legal hourly wage. Buzz lives off the tips. Being a showman and something of a local hero, he does better than most men. But he can work twelve hours, and leave with only fifty dollars. The question of sick leave was not even raised by his employers.

But it was by Dan Dan, whose business had been flourishing, improbably enough because of the resurgence in religious activity. The local churches, flush with money, were lining up to put in the sort of sound systems that The Rolling Stones would be proud of.

Dan asked me to watch his beer. As it was a Bud Lite, I said I'd rather not, but he headed out to his truck, returning with a check for two hundred dollars.

"Take that around with the health drinks, and tell him there is more when that runs out," Dan proclaimed.

I drove the few hundred yards to the home of Buzz and Laura, his girlfriend. Buzz waved me in, too sick to get up. He was in his cell, the tiny TV room about the exact size of a jail cell, and the room he feels most comfortable in.

He was naked except for a blanket, and was running hot and cold, shivering all over. After an hour or so, Laura came home and I headed out. The sun was a few inches above the San Bernardino range, and the light was at its best.

Old Jack, the honorary mayor of Pioneertown and long-time resident of the motel, had just made it through to his going-away party. He was as yellow as a submarine, but the party was a happy affair. Jack's days were numbered in hours—about fifty of them, as it transpired. Most of the town was in attendance, and the young girls flocked to old Jack, who smiled and gleamed like a fifteen-year-old. He was presented with a gray top hat—the last having been stolen—and a fine gray cane. Jack's face never lost its toothy grin. Two days later, he was dead.

Bob Dix wanders the world with a concoction that he calls coffee but which is, in fact, homemade Black Russian. It saves him money at the bar. His constant companion, Adam, will drink nothing but Budweiser unless he's run out of it, which doesn't seem to happen often. In the absence of Bud, Adam will drink pretty much everything except the excellent water from his well. Debbie used to drink only Kessler—a sign of her loyalty to Buzz, as Buzz would drink nothing else. But as Buzz had shown no intention of leaving Laura, Lil Debbie recently kicked the stuff completely and now just as religiously drinks vodka with orange.

Crinkle Jim did not cheat The Reaper. Having exquisitely renovated the house by the pool, he repaired to Lil Debbie's, weakened by the daily assault on his liver and a bout with Hepatitis C. Boo visited, and, alarmed by his color, took him to the emergency section of High Desert Memorial Hospital in Palm Springs. The doctors rushed him in, one remarking, "Sir, you are glowing!"

Jim was in high spirits, and expected to be discharged quickly. But when Lil Debbie went to see him a few days later, she found a virtual corpse. His skin had gone dark, he was snoring loudly, and was dead to the world. She tried to wake him, but he snored on. Finally, a nurse coldly informed her that her man would never wake up again. He was effectively dead.

32

Jim passed away in Palm Springs — not his favorite town, but one he must get used to, as the local hospital refuses to release his mortal remains to the likes of us, and now, six months later, he is still on the slab awaiting pickup by a relative. As Jim had no known living relatives, and the hospital was reluctant to pass him into the possession of his fiancée, Lil Debbie, he may remain there for some time to come.

The dead of Palm Springs are indeed many. Gene Autry is credited, along with Roy Rogers, with creating Pioneertown in 1946, but found himself drawn to the bottle and to Palm Springs when the cowboy period had passed.

Bob Dix, the son of Richard Dix, a man in his time more famous than Autry or Rogers, has retired to Pioneertown. He knew Autry, and testified to the massive drinking habits of "the singing cowboy".

"He was a mean drunk," recalls Bob. Autry himself conceded, "No one can live in a bottle and build, or maintain, a multi-million-dollar enterprise."

But he did all right, and died worth $600 million. It was not a lot by local standards, leaving him a pauper compared with neighbors such as Walter Annenberg, Marvin Davis, and the rest of the big big-money crowd, but enough for a few more bottles.

When Boo first dragged me down to Palm Springs — she was dying for some traffic lights, and green grass and flowers, and movies that showed stuff other than the first-run Hollywood crap they played in Yucca Valley — I hated it. While she went happily gallivanting off through museums and thrift shops, the only type of store she can stand, I propped myself up in a corner of a bar on the main drag with *The New York Times*. Every so often I would glance up to watch the world go by, and found myself staring at a life-sized sculpture of Lucy Ricardo sitting on a park bench opposite. Lucy's ties with Palm Springs go way back. She and Ricky started one of the first gay hotels back when the word 'gay' still meant 'happy'.

Palms Springs was then — and, some say, remains — the closest center of civilization to our version of the Wild West.

Civilization or hedonism. And money — waves of money that have washed down from the San Jacinto Mountains and found root in the "downstairs desert" since Hollywood started hiding out there in the late 1920s to sin. Where women could have other women and men take boys, and everybody knew and nobody cared. As long as nobody talked. Until recently, no one did — for this is a place where some hotels, like the old Silver Sands, which adjoined Errol Flynn's Casa del Sol, provided "blue movies", lubricants, and much more for guests who, like Errol, enjoyed it both ways.

Every president since Ike Eisenhower has partied there. For decades, the Reagans thought it unthinkable not to spend New Year's Eve at Walter and Leonore Annenberg's palace,

Sunnylands. The Reagans took time out from Ronnie's 1976 presidential campaign to attend the wedding party of Frank Sinatra and Barbara Marx at Frank's sprawling desert pad, which then housed an art collection worth a cool hundred million. When JFK came to stay in Palm Springs, he incensed Sinatra by keeping clear of him and staying with Bing Crosby, driving Frank into the Republican camp. He had been bragging for months that the president was coming, and had spent millions on securing and improving the compound for his guest. But Bobby Kennedy, horrified by the prospect of his brother being tarred with the mob brush, banned the visit, and Frank took a sledgehammer to the newly installed presidential heliport.

Nixon hid out from the media at Sunnylands when he was on the run from the media hounds during the last days of Watergate. George Bush senior, never an insider amongst the Hollywood crowd, incurred the wrath of the Annenbergs when he allowed the release to Agence France-Presse of a photo of himself and Japanese prime minister, Toshiki Kaifu, relaxing by their pool. No one invaded the privacy of Walter's 32,000-square-foot home and its 6,400-square-foot living room.

Pioneertown fears and hopes that the super-rich will discover their idyllic world, which is a little more than an hour away. The people from the gated communities do venture up, and what they see and smell scares them. They stagger in, weighted down by age and jewelry, and are horrified to see our wild bunch and to smell not only tobacco but marijuana in the air. When the police arrive, the long-suffering Harriet calls in the DILLIGAF high command, who put the word out that the smoking must stop. And for a time it does. No one wants Harriet to lose her license, and all try their best not to inhale. But it's hard to have to walk twenty yards or so from one's drinks to have a furtive smoke. So the habit remains.

The irony is that the old rich enjoyed hedonism and criminality on a scale that would make the Edwards family blush collectively. But in a town that tolerated the drunkenness, promiscuity, and homosexuality of Jim Bakker while he called on the world to repent its ways, the irony seems lost.

The one thing we have in common with the filthy rich is a fondness for drink. Of debauchery we have very little, and few can match the drinking excess of the now-departed Sinatra and Dino Martin, the leaders of a whole town running on booze for fifty years.

Of the great debauched families of Palm Springs, the Daryl F. Zanucks stand out. Zanuck, at the height of his power at Twentieth Century Fox, had a seventy-foot swimming pool, known as the "Palm Springs Yacht Club", and his pick of the stars at the studio. A wonderful life indeed, and one that was to soon dissipate the fortunes of the studio. But the family did not prosper, and son Richard was tossed out of Fox after attempting a palace coup in 1970. Daughters Susan and Darrylin fared worse. Susan was beaten to the grave by her father by only six months—she died of "massive alcohol consumption" in 1980 at the age of forty-six. Her son followed suit, choking on his vomit after a goodly dose of heroin and cocaine a year later. He was buried with his needles, headphones, and favorite cassette tapes. He believed, apparently, in life after death.

Salvation, of a kind, came to the lower valley when Betty Ford opened the world's most famous drug- and booze-treatment center in Rancho Mirage. A more appropriate place, on the outskirts of Palm Springs, could not be envisioned, but its cost for a three-week stay is out of the price range of just about every member of Pioneertown.

Palm Springs is known as the "gay nineties", a reflection on the town's sexual bent as well as the folks' age.

This is a little unfair. Although the small resort town has always enjoyed a gay bent, the age of the sexually active population is being lowered somewhat by the influx of the retiring gay population from cities such as San Francisco, LA, and San Diego. Every Easter, twenty thousand gay men descend on the little enclave for the famous White Party, one of the West Coast's largest gay festivals.

They are not the only ones dancing. Since the late nineties, local realtors have watched the desert's new chic reputation send property prices soaring right up there with the mighty San Jacinto mountain that looms above the good life below. Sparked by the revival of the late-modernist architecture known as "Palm Springs Modern," homes have been snapped up at prices of up to $5 million — for cash. These are fabulous, sleek houses of glass, rock, corrugated metal, and cement, with walls that vanish to usher in desert views and breezes. Designed by visionary, futuristic architects such as Richard Neutra, Albert Frey, and John Lautner, they are perfectly suited to the desert environment, which has been described as "Nature's version of modern art". Lautner's extraordinary hilltop home for Bob Hope resembles a giant mushroom, and presumably that is what Hope was on when he okayed the design.

Although one consciously knows that summer is ending when September comes around, the month itself seems unaware that it's time to move from the stage and let fall fall. In fact, as if possessed by a desperate need to establish its dominance, summer unleashes a final fury.

Those with something approaching a brain try for cooler pastures. With the heat, September brings upon us a monsoonal mugginess that defies the swamp cooler's best endeavors. Boo finds it necessary to visit LA more often, and some of the local men consider the necessity of fishing.

The nearest decent trout stream is many hours away, up in the upper reaches of the Owens River, way along the 395. It's a place where Desmond has contacts. That part of the Sierra Nevada is some four thousand feet higher than the High Desert, and is commensurately cooler. Snow on the peaks is in evidence well into summer.

So it was that Sean, Rodney, Ed Gibson, Buzz, Desmond, and I took it upon ourselves to provide the womenfolk with sufficient trout to last much of the winter to come — by taking ourselves many miles into the mountains.

It was deemed that a week was needed to supply sufficient trout to feed the multitude, and one day in September we headed to the supermarket to buy supplies. Vast quantities of foodstuffs were purchased, and the carts groaned as we steered them towards that part of the store given to the provision of liquor.

Ed Gibson headed for the selections that involved bourbon, and packed a few bottles of Gentleman Jack — a form of Jack Daniels considered to be, after Knob Creek, the best drop that money could buy. Rodney had already ordered a goodly supply of that substance, so it was left for Buzz to hook up a half-dozen bottles of Kessler, Sean to snap up the Mexican agave crop in the form of tequila purchases, and me to buy beer.

Desmond mulled over his requirements, and settled for a few bottles of Jack and quite a few boxes of beer.

In all, I figured, we set out on the fishing trip with some twenty bottles of hard liquor and maybe five hundred cans of beer. It was not much for a week's fishing, but a start.

We settled into our hut by the Owens River, and the fishing soon got confused with the drinking. Not that we didn't fish. Buzz attacked the river with an alacrity that shamed Sean and me into doing likewise. Desmond, the truly wild specimen of these wild men, disappeared into the stream's higher reaches to find wilder trout. Rodney wandered far across the valley, and by the evening of the first day we had caught more fish than we had destroyed bottles of hard liquor.

The men of the High Desert keep unusual hours, and all bar I would be up and working on breakfast — the most serious meal of the day — before the sun had made its appearance, and while I steadfastly slept.

Rodney took charge of most of the cooking. He is a superb bush chef, hearty in every sense of the word. Rodney advocates removing the horns from a steak before cooking it, and his concept of bacon and eggs required whole pigs and more eggs than one could point a stick at. When not sleeping, drinking, fishing, or playing cards, his robust person could be found in the kitchen with great iron skillets sizzling, bowls of chili boiling, trout in various stages of preparation, whole loaves of bread being put to work, and biscuits being baked.

Desmond had found a suitable log for practising his axe-throwing on, which he did successfully, though he was rather taken aback to discover I could throw an axe equally well. Desmond is long, lean, wiry, and wild. His hair and beard untrimmed, his skin etched deep by the sun and wind, and a wide grin almost always present, he is forever delighting in life.

On the morning of the third day, I was woken at about 6.00 a.m. by the men, whose conversation had taken a troubled tone. In that fitful condition between sleep and consciousness, I heard Rodney mutter something to the effect that our supplies of booze were running short.

I had sat up reading the previous evening while the men snored. We were all crammed into a few small bedrooms, Buzz and Sean sleeping (we imagined) in the same small bed. The only place to read without the light keeping the early risers awake was the bathroom, where I had spent some hours struggling with *Finnegan's Wake*, having cast aside the only other book available, *The Coming War with China*, as being far more fictitious than anything Joyce could contrive. Before tiptoeing to my cot beside Rodney, I noticed that a hole had appeared in our liquor stocks.

A few hours later, in the gray of morn, I was awakened by conversation, and from the tone of that conversation the situation regarding the alcohol was becoming grave.

"I think we might have to drive into Mammoth," I heard Rodney remark.

"Either that, or reduce our drinking," Sean reflected.

By the time I stumbled from the cot, my companions had headed into the town some twenty miles away, and I had time to reconnoiter the remaining supplies. We had been reduced to one and a half bottles of Kessler, one bottle of Knob's Creek, a quart of Jack, and fewer than three hundred cans of beer. A desperate situation indeed.

I took out the rod and squelched through the grassy, watery valley to the stream. After not seeing grass, flowing water, and mud, and after not being cool for months, the sensation was sensuous, especially around my toes. As I pulled in my second trout (twenty-four inches) — Buzz won fifty dollars for coaxing a twenty-eight-inch brown trout onto the bank — the men returned with supplies.

The liquor store at Mammoth had been closed, so they had driven on to Lee Vining, that apple of a town that invites one to enter Yosemite. Here they had found sufficient supplies of bourbon and beer to make the next few days livable, and we all sat in the cool shade and engaged in a few days of serious poker.

We returned to Pioneertown with six hundred pounds of trout and many a feast. It was time well spent.

We also returned to discover that Buzz's mother had come home, a matter that had occupied Buzz's mind for a good part of the fishing, drinking, and gambling (not necessarily in that order) expedition. Buzz's attitude to Alice, who had moved east six months ago, was not that of the average loving son. He figured she'd be back, and had informed us over a bottle that he'd pay good money to have her "popped".

"Two hundred dollars, and the contents of her purse", was there to be taken by any soul willing to take the old lady out of the game.

"Popping" Alice, Buzz assured us, would not be difficult, as her only form of transport was a golf buggy that took her the three hundred or so yards from Ernie and Carole's motel to The Palace at a slow pace.

"I heard you were trying to kill me," Alice hissed over the phone line.

"So, what's your point?" Buzz replied.

Death is never far away in the desert. The inherent dangers of an outdoor life are multiplied by the fact that we are all getting older fast, yet disregarding nature's plea to slow down.

Probably no one has seen more than Frances, a once dazzling beauty now touching eighty, yet holding on hard to her almost girlish good looks. Before she took over Pioneertown and created The Cantina, which would grow to become The Palace, she had lived more lives than most get to read about. She had been kidnapped down in Baja fifty years back by a Mexican smitten by her looks, but managed to escape by diving off the yacht she was being held captive on and swimming to shore.

She lived and loved as she chose, and no one tamed her. She was quick with her fists, and as the old hierarchy of the Hells Angels doted on her, she could punch a lug off a barstool with impunity. If there was any fighting to do in The Cantina, she would do it, and if people cared to play with guns and knives, they did so outside. Petite all the while but with the eyes of a fox, she was the mother of Pioneertown and the queen of San Felipe.

One warm summery day, I wandered into Chuck's Wagon at the back of The Palace where Chuck Heis serves his delicacies—hot dogs and beers—to the DILLIGAF fraternity. A whole heap of the locals shook hands as though they hadn't seen me the day before and the day before that, but Desmond took me aside. Wild as he is, Desmond is given to tears if the situation demands such, and Desmond was choked up. He had just heard that Frances's fearless heart had burst. Frances had died and been revived, and few thought she had a chance. It had happened on a trip to Oregon to visit relatives.

Boo and I had just spent a week with Frances and John in San Felipe, where being their friends meant being treated as deities even by the Federales, who man their absurd checkpoints all over a part of Mexico that the US didn't even bother to grab in 1848.

Now she was on full life-support, being attacked by paddles as her heart floundered, and it was as though the spirit of life itself was in jeopardy.

My tears mingled with Desmond's on his bare broad shoulders. Others, including Ed, soon joined us in a huddle. Fortunately, Harriet and Rodney were with Frances and John, but they were kept mostly away from the hospital as the doctors battled to rebuild the entire top of Frances's great heart.

But hope was a stranger to all.

Mary, Frances's other daughter, had, perhaps prematurely, begun funeral proceedings. The wake was to be held at The Palace, and then a procession of mourners led by the Hells Angels (as many as five hundred) was to lead us to San Felipe — scattering her ashes on the way.

The Hells Angels, great lovers of ceremony, like all military and quasi-military organizations, were ready to ride, but Frances had not given up the ghost. All her organs had begun shutting down, and she had lost 80 per cent of her blood in one minute when the surgeon opened her up and the aneurysm ruptured. But she was not dead.

She was, in fact, in a hospital just out of Portland, and the hospital happened to have the premier heart unit of the US — and therefore the world. The doctors, who had met Frances for half an hour as they prepared for the surgery, had warmed to this delightful battleaxe of a lass and were not sending her off easily. For days, then weeks, they fought death while the citizens of Pioneertown mulled over her chances. To me fell the task of making the almost daily calls north. Each time I visited The Palace, all would ask for news, and as the days passed, skepticism turned to hope, and after fourteen days a glimmering of confidence. That day, I learnt Frances would live. She would have to learn to talk again — at eighty-one — and to walk again, also at eighty-one. But she would live to hear her coyotes cry their plaintive tune of the desert.

33

Being able to see the stars wasn't something that affected property values until people around America began noticing that the stars had gone out. They are actually still there, but only 10 per cent of US citizens can look to the firmament and see same. Pollution and reflected light from the cities now deprive most of our fellow citizens of a right that might have found its way into the Bill of Rights had anyone imagined that much of the population might one day be deprived of such a right. Children growing up in inner and not so inner cities may spend their lives as ignorant of the heavens as they are the waves of the sea. When we lived in Venice, Boo and I would often entertain kids from South Central LA, and I would take them to the beach.

It was a harrowing experience as the kids, as old as thirteen, had mostly never seen the sea, even though they lived a mere fifteen miles from it. Their knowledge of waves was limited to watching sporting events, and at first they were all terrified of the things, even though the waves at Venice are mostly just large laps. Had they been introduced to the ten-footers common at Sydney beaches I would have lost the lot. But soon, kid by kid, fear by fear, they would be frolicking in this wondrous new world as I stood in their midst counting, always counting. In numerous trips I never lost a child, and it is possible these excursions did some good.

The stars are another matter. Throughout history, people have lived and died without seeing the sea or even a large lake, but the stars have been in evidence for all humanity for the best part of eternity. No longer.

In the High Desert, the stars shine so brightly that after many months I still would stare in wonder at their brilliance. The Milky Way in the southern hemisphere, the canopy that Boo and I had grown up under, is a mite thin compared with that of the north, and as a kid I sort of resented being deprived of its glories. I guess kids like stars more than adults do, but it's hard to tell if they can't see them. One of the main causes of this deprivation is street lighting, which is supposed to give us a sense of security, and help us find our way about. But as John Edwards, who lives in Yucca Valley, where there is some street lighting, points out, he and his neighbors are never robbed, while the section that is lit constantly suffers from theft on such a scale that he fears members of the Bush cabinet may have moved in. So much for safety. As for guiding folk home, surely it has been the stars that have achieved that purpose since men and women had the sense to look up. An Indian and a coyote are never lost.

Why there is no mass political movement to "bring back the stars" is surprising, given that people will spend their lives fighting for the right to have a larger handgun or a more automatic rifle. Perhaps my fellow DILLIGAF members, who can spend an entire afternoon discussing the attributes of the most obscure of armaments, can be excused from not fighting for the right of kids to see the heavens. They can see all the stars they like if they remain sober until dark. In fact, we are in one of those special parts of the world where the stars can be seen more brightly than in those less special areas where they can't. This is due partly to elevation; partly to the existence of the San Bernardino Mountain Range, which blocks all light from LA; and partly to air movements that sweep pollution off to less fortunate places.

So much is this the case that photographers from the *Los Angeles Times* and even *The New York Times* trek out here for the regular meteorite showers that turn the night sky into something more like a racetrack. Boo was, inevitably, away for the first night of the Triffids, but Ed and Candace had come to stay, and though the night was as cold as a nun's bosom, out we went, armed only with a bottle of Jack to brave the waves of falling stars.

The land around is pockmarked by meteorites that made it to earth, so the act took some courage. But the greatest problem was in the watching. Candace would cry, "Look at that one," but by the time one swung one's head around, it was fading or gone, and Ed was yelling, "Look, there goes two."

The trick, we soon learned, was to identify that part of the sky where most of the shooting stars seemed to shoot, and ignore the distractions. The show went on for hours. We huddled together with blankets and more Jack until the early hours, when the squeals of delight began to mix with yawns, and sleep called.

We staggered into the house. Below us were the lights of half-a-dozen other homes dotting the flats far below.

If they get water up here, the developers will come and put in street lighting and thousands of houses, and take out the stars. When, I wondered, is it appropriate to take up arms or dynamite against such a sea of troubles?

An alert reader might recall that we made this momentous move away from the world of coffee houses and outlets for such exotica as *The New York Times*, in part, because we were threatened by a neighbor — The Man with No Brain.

It was not until we had said goodbye to our little piece of Dodge City and settled at Boulder House that we discovered the prison system would soon disgorge one of its millions of minions almost onto our front doorstep — Danny, the man who had shot Adam, who, with his father, John, his uncle Jerry, his brother Brandon, and the countless wives, cousins, sons, and daughters made up the tribal alliance I came to call The Adams Family.

News that Danny would soon be getting out began to spread until it became, after the preparations for the DILLIGAF Christmas party, the most talked-about coming event on the social calendar. Being the closest neighbor, in fact the only neighbor, I was constantly asked whether he had been sighted — and what plans I had in mind. Except to play things by ear, I had no plans.

But a would-be killer coming home was a matter that could not be ignored, and it played on my mind more than I would admit.

The Blade Runner took Boo aside, and told her what to expect from Danny.

"I am warning you," he said. "I am serious."

The Blade Runner was nothing if not serious.

"He is dangerous, and I am not joking. Be very careful, and don't ever be alone with him."

These and many other threats fell upon our ears.

The DILLIGAF consortium suggested we collectively write to the authorities informing them that Danny was not welcome in the community. It was widely believed that such a letter would have him released but banned from San Bernardino County, and prevent him from returning to our tiny part of that immense domain. Naturally, given the nature of an organization that concentrates its activities on preparations for the Christmas party, the discussion of the attributes of firearms, and the need for greater enforcement of the death penalty (I once suggested it be retrospective), nothing was done.

One sunny morning, I noticed Ed Edge, a fine fellow who had given me some help with the well, working on some pipes at Danny's little cabin. I went over for a chat and maybe an update on what was on everybody's mind — Danny's homecoming. There had been considerable activity around the cabin, and Danny's father had replaced the chimney the previous week.

There was then the unmistakable sound of a motor car and the equally unmistakable evidence of a small white truck moving up the almost sheer incline to what had been, until this moment, our secluded world.

I recognized immediately old man Salazar, and knew that the figure beside him was Danny. Adam's would-be killer.

It was a tricky moment. Danny jumped from the truck and was formally — by local standards — introduced by his father.

We shook hands in a pregnant pause. Danny stood a full foot below me and had an innocent, almost childlike, look. I grasped his hand and welcomed him home. Another pregnant pause.

"I believe you are a poor shot," I suggested, hoping to cut the ice about Adam from the very start.

He grinned nervously, and seemed to agree, being in a friendly mood. I did my best to be friendly, but I wasn't over the moon, and saying I had work to get on with, left. Danny, who represented something of a potential date with destiny for the occupants of Boulder House, moved into his cabin.

At first, the small Mexican-Indian was on his best behavior, and we were convinced that the warring parties would no longer seek to do battle. I even arranged a peace conference where Danny and John Edwards agreed to a formula that, in retrospect, might have been drawn up by Neville Chamberlain.

The tiny hamlets of Pioneertown, Pipes Canyon, and Rimrock responded to the return of a man who had, for no apparent reason, shot a well-known member of the community, as one would hope they might. With detached consideration.

Boo met Danny, a few days after his return, while walking the dogs. He approached her warily, no doubt knowing that a strategic alliance would be helpful to his cause, which seemed to be, in principle, not returning to prison.

"I guess you have heard some bad things about me," he remarked.

"Well, I heard you shot Adam," she replied.

Danny admitted he had.

He told Boo he was sorry for what he had done, that he had done his time, and done it hard.

"I did it like a man," he added.

Soledad has earned its reputation as being one of California's hardest prisons, and Danny was treated in the spirit of redemption by what passes as a community. As usual, Ernie and Carole led the way, putting him to work at the motel, and were delighted with the results. Cathy, his former girlfriend, and the regular cleaner at the motel, moved into his cabin, and Danny, when not doing the yard work at the motel, began improvements on his own yard, and began lining the cabin with cedar.

Soon he had saved enough to buy a nice motorcycle, a road bike, but one suited to the desert. We had him over for a few beers, and in return he helped me with the pool.

I soon discovered there was something childlike about Danny, and had to remind myself that the thirty-three-year-old was definitely no child.

My attempts to befriend Danny were at first moderately successful. He came over again to help me with the pool. Having more knowledge of plumbing than Gordon Liddy, he was of some use. As we did battle with the filtration system, he told me he had spent his childhood on the Hopi Indian reservation in northern Arizona, not far from the Grand Canyon and even closer to Monument Valley. Perhaps they are the most filmed and photographed places on earth. But the film crews rarely make it to the dusty Hopi reservation.

As we struggled in the sun, I tried to remember our brief visit to the tiny reservation ten years before, hoping to better place the man by knowing the world of his childhood. I remembered its barrenness. The red hues of Monument Valley were evident in the clay-like earth and, at least when Boo, I, and Harry the dog made our brief inspection, red earth and ramshackle housing were about all there was. A few stalls sold hand-crafted goods — jewelry, turquoise inlaid in silver, rugs, and pottery — some of the best that will ever be made. A few hungry dogs wandered the baked streets of a settlement not unlike those found in Australia's "red center". The reservation, which is about forty miles square, does not have rivers but washes. Nevertheless, it is home to one of North America's oldest cultures, and the pueblos atop the mesas date to the ninth century — making them the oldest continuous human communities in North America.

Danny had lived there twenty years before our visit, when the reservation was even more isolated and primitive.

The Hopi Indians call themselves Hopitu, meaning "peaceful" or "the peaceful little ones". But while Danny is indeed little, one had to question his peaceful nature.

Danny informed me he was eight years of age when his parents went to LA. Danny's father hailed from Yuma, a forlorn town a few hundred miles south of the Hopi lands.

Again, I tried to reconstruct Yuma from a brief visit years before. The town existed mostly because it was the site of the West's first federal prison. The federal authorities built a jail with walls so thick (three meters) that Saddam himself might have felt safe in one. Yuma Prison was also the first in the West to employ steel reinforcing.

I recalled that only one man ever escaped from Yuma, and he was thought to have drowned in the Colorado River, which in those days flowed wide and strong past the prison and into Mexico.

Prisons are a recurring theme in Danny's life, I thought, as we finally got the pool's water level right.

He had stripped off his top, revealing the mandatory prison tattoos. Some mystified me, but he explained, in his high singsong voice, that inside he had joined a Native American gang. Imprisoned African-Americans have usually been members of gangs before graduating to prisons, as have most Latinos. Whites often join the Aryan Nation soon after incarceration, even though they might have no affinity with its racist creed.

Danny told me of the sweat lodges that he and his Indian brothers enjoyed in Soledad. It seemed incongruous, yet uplifting, that such a freedom could still exist.

Moving to the metropolis of Los Angeles from an isolated reservation, with his father, from a town that only existed because it provided the last chance to steal Mexico's water and was a suitable place for a prison, might have unsettled Danny. It led, he said, to his desire to return to the desert, and somehow to the end of Coyote Road.

The pool had iced over. The swamp cooler had been shut down. Wood had been delivered in great quantities, and the fire blazed constantly. Tony, the word was going around, would be heading back any day now—as soon as the ground back in Wisconsin froze.

Christmas would soon be upon us. People were making each other gifts. Lil Debbie was busily creating her little "desert Christmas trees", made from the tops of dead yuccas and decorated with exquisite tiny ornaments.

Pioneertown was aglow with lights. Cactus and wagon wheels sparkled with what we grew up calling fairy lights. Even Danny's cabin was lit up, and twinkled in the dark, cold night.

As the days and weeks passed peacefully, I saw more of Danny. His skin, where not covered in tattoos, had turned a coppery color. He had taken to blackening the area around his eyes, and invariably wore a headscarf. The effect was handsome. But Danny had used the gun and the knife before, and as the weeks passed it seemed increasingly apparent that an unwillingness to bury the hatchet—as it could not more appropriately be described—existed in his heart. Of the one hundred and twenty thousand persons paroled in California each year, seventy thousand return to prison, and it was reasonable to expect that Danny would find his way home if relations with Adam went south.

Danny's parole officer, I soon learnt, was a Mr. Smith, reputedly a hard man. He seemed to visit Danny sporadically for the spot checks and whatever else parole officers do as they make their rounds. And being in the desert, Mr. Smith's rounds were extensive. I was working in the yard adjacent to Danny's cabin with Art, a local who professes some knowledge of trees and gardening. I like to work with Art, because if I don't, things can go wrong fast. Art is not given to contemplating the consequences of his actions—a fact that had brought him to the attention of the same Mr. Smith.

According to Art, the cause of his incarceration had been a misunderstanding over the dumping of peculiarly noxious poisons, and Art had been grievously wronged and jailed. This had rather impressed me, as I had never heard of an American being jailed for dumping toxins. Had Art been skippering a supertanker while drunk, and lost a few million barrels of crude, he would have walked free. But the amount was small, and Art did sixteen months.

When Mr. Smith bounced up Coyote Road, we were applying Henry's—a tar supposed to seal roofs—to the garage. Art, who is probably the least criminal of all Mr. Smith's parolees, was delighted to see his officer in charge, and hollered loudly—no doubt to draw Mr. Smith's attention to the fact that though he was disposing of a noxious tar, he was doing it atop my garage. That is, not only was he working, but working legally.

Mr. Smith waved back and disappeared into Danny's cabin as Art beamed at me. At their next meeting, the coming Tuesday (Art, not being a drug offender, was not subject to random tests), he would be able to tell his parole officer of his new position as foreman at Boulder House. A reputable position indeed, if it existed.

About this time, Danny's girlfriend, Cathy, brought home a small pup, a pit bull that had been mixed, it seemed from its growth, with an elephant. The creature had been left in one of Ernie and Carole's motel rooms, and was dubbed LD — short for Little Dog. It grew, and within months was twice the size of Sailor — and still a pup.

Sailor, convinced he was top dog, decided to bring this usurper down to his own size. But his efforts were forlorn at best. LD was friendly to all, as pups invariably are, but Sailor took a dim view of this challenge to his mastery of the hill, and soon tempers flared. We repeatedly appealed to our neighbors to have LD's private parts removed, knowing that one day it would finish the issue of who was top dog, and Sailor would inevitably lose badly, suffering an inevitable mauling and possibly death. We even offered to pay for the surgery.

But Danny seemed to consider any attempt to reduce the conflict an assault on the few rights he possessed as a parolee. Bitter words were exchanged, with me informing Danny that he was a "fucking imbecile".

People, noting that Danny's disposition had grown increasingly aggressive since his release, suggested he was — like a goodly proportion of the denizens of the desert — on speed. But I argued that this was unlikely, given the random urine tests. Speed hangs around in the system for days, and Danny was in reality still in jail, parole being jail without the bars. Any such infringement would put him back in complete confinement, and the job of the penal system was to get as many back as possible. Institutions exist to perpetuate their existence, and the prison system was coming close to perfecting its purpose. If Danny was on speed, he'd likely be behind bars already, I argued.

But I began to find Danny's soft, sing-song tone sinister. As I stood more than a foot above him, I doubted he would attack me with his fists. But as his record was for the use of that great equalizer—the handgun—this was small comfort.

We found ourselves in the midst of hostilities far more deadly in potential than the one that had us flee to the mountains in the first place.

Danny, being on parole for the shooting of Adam, was, under law, prevented from being in Adam's company. The conception of such ideas—that warring parties be separated—was admirable enough, but it became apparent far too quickly that in such a tiny rustic world only UN peacekeepers could ensure that the demarcation lines would be respected.

Trouble began at the home of Vietnam Bob, a man not averse to gunfire after enduring a long and unpleasant sojourn in the rice fields and jungles of Vietnam. Bob may not be the best-armed man in the High Desert, but he has definitely made every effort to protect himself and his loved ones. He is not trigger unhappy, and has a personality that can range from mild-mannered to seriously ferocious.

Bob and Adam are friends and neighbors of many years' standing, and Adam would frequently drop by for a visit. On one such day, ensconced in the living room and enjoying a cold beer with them sat Danny. Adam offered his hand in friendship some five times, and each time it was slapped away. Hugs were not exchanged, and Danny told Adam he had been thinking of him—for five years—every day.

Adam took this as something of a declaration of intent. Presumably, Danny had not lain awake in Soledad prison wishing him well. In fact, Danny was of the opinion that Adam had let down the side by going to the police over the matter of the bullet that had bounced around his head and found its way into his spine. Adam found it difficult to explain to his old adversary that once one is admitted to a hospital in California, even with such a minor infliction as a bullet to the head, the arrival of the police is a formality. The hospitals are required by law to inform their servants of such matters.

Danny was of the opinion that Adam had betrayed him, and was further incensed by the fact that the police, on arrival at his cottage next to Boulder House, had also uncovered what they believed, and the courts agreed, was the basis of a methamphetamine laboratory — something common to these parts.

Rumor had it that Danny's time in jail was rendered less pleasant because the expensive ingredients of the speed lab were confiscated by the authorities, causing chagrin to the criminal fraternity that had invested in the materials.

That Danny's time in Soledad and other such places had been difficult was attested to by the absence of his top and bottom front teeth. Locals recalled that those teeth had been firmly attached to his gums before his incarceration.

Teeth are not regarded as a necessity in the High Desert. Buzz is of the opinion that teeth are best replaced, and a standing joke in these parts runs along the lines of "What have you got when you line up thirty-two Pioneertown women?"

"A full set of teeth."

Such a joke might be lost on Danny.

His response to Adam's outstretched hand was the sort of diplomatic gesture one might expect from a refugee from the prison system, or, for that matter, from the current incumbents of the White House. A unilateral act from a man with an increasingly small power base.

Then, late one Saturday night, Adam rang.

"Have you seen a white Chevy low rider at Danny's?" he asked, alarm in his voice. We hadn't.

"Cholos, three of them, drove around my house this afternoon, in a white low rider. They are connected to Danny. They were real threatening. I could tell they were packing."

Boo did recall hearing a vehicle, but in the middle of the night she could only see the lights.

I thought that Adam, sometimes Pioneertown's *prima donna assoluta*, might be using a product other than his faithful companion, Budweiser, and promised to drop around the next day. Cholos were from the gangster world of East LA, and though Yucca might have a few would-be gangsters of the Chicano variety, it was hard to imagine them driving all the way out here, and hardly believable they would threaten an Edwards.

But when I arrived at Adam's tiny cottage on Sunday morning, the clans had gathered. The living room was full of automatic rifles and beards, and it seemed there was cause for alarm. From a babble of excited rushes of conversation, I pieced together the events that had led to this drama.

A criminal who had been released from jail at the same time as Danny, and who had since managed to get himself 86'd from the bars of Yucca — no easy task — had arrived at Adam's in the aforementioned white Chevy Suburban and driven around his house five times. Then the criminal had entered, and as Adam knew him vaguely, he had welcomed him. But the ex-con was not polite, and instead told Adam he had brought some friends from East LA to "party with hillbillies". He added that he expected

Adam to be wearing overalls, an item not in Adam's wardrobe. As there were two women in the house and the gangsters had clearly "scoped" the place, Adam could not find recourse to his guns. As soon as they left he called his dad, John, who had by now arrived with Uncle Jerry.

Jerry and John are both mountain men, and fools might think them hillbillies. Jerry had spent some time with the LAPD, and both were competent trackers.

The boys in the low rider might not have figured that driving on dirt roads left tire tracks. The roads of East LA might be bad but are not dirt, and they hadn't reckoned that unique low rider tires would stand out, especially after five passes. But Jerry and John had already tracked the tires, and had done so to Coyote Road.

If anything was guaranteed to bring fury to the clan, not to mention the general community, the arrival of outside gangsters was it. Word was spreading, and people who had long dreamed of defending their town were arriving. More could be summoned, but as I went out to inspect the still-fresh tire prints, I imagined we had enough facilities to handle a few city gangsters driving a vehicle not exactly designed for the ruts that pass for roads in these parts. I detected three submachine guns in the back of one of the trucks, and my confidence grew. The Cholos might have similar weaponry, but they were self-taught, and usually ended up killing the wrong target. These rednecks had mostly been trained by the US army. Some had used guns, year in and out, against the people of Vietnam. Adam himself had been put in charge of twenty-eight men when he was a young ranger.

In these enlightened days, killing is done by either depraved individuals or the state. But community killing, vigilante killing, is something that has passed into history. In California and the West, death without trial at the hands of a mob or a posse has a rich history. A few generations ago, men were hanged from the nearest tree — if there was a nearest tree — partly on the grounds that the jails were so poorly constructed that a stick of dynamite could free a comrade who might have stolen a horse. Better to hang him on the spot. Mob murder was first introduced in San Francisco, and reputedly its first victims were Australians. These were the Sydney Ducks: a gang of ex-cons who found their way to the town with plunder rather than work in the goldfields on their minds. Such were the crimes of these men that, given the absence of law, the vigilante killings were understandable, even though it irks me to say so of fellow countrymen.

Perhaps you could say I was privileged to be in a room where the fevered excitement that comes with the lust for blood was evident. But evident it was. Even Boo, who had seen her fair share of human folly since we'd met twenty years before, was worried. I found myself reminded of Pat Buchanan, who, in the 1996 presidential campaign, cried, "When you hear the sound of the guns, ride, boys, ride."

Had Danny or someone in a white low rider appeared that Sunday morning, they could have expected a hail of bullets. Fortunately for Danny, they did not. By the time we left, it was agreed no action be taken. The passion for killing had, for the moment, passed. Instead, as we lived opposite, it was agreed we would keep an eye on things.

I saw Danny, and he asked me if his life was in danger.

We were in The Palace, and a few hours had passed. He seemed a mite nervous, as befitted a man who had a lot of gunmen keen on finding him in their sights. He himself, on the other hand, would return to prison for a long time if found in possession of a single gun.

The question was rather a "curate's egg" one, in that, while telling the truth was unpleasant and might make matters even more dangerous, lying was also unacceptable. I told him I was doing my best, and tried to put a decent spin on the fact that I had just left some of the hardest men in the hardest country in a hard nation, and they were all oiled up and looking for bear.

Danny didn't thank me for my efforts, and I moved to other, friendlier drinkers, reflecting that, while he had a lot on his mind, he was doing a poor job of saving his own neck by not even appreciating that I was constantly trying to construct a peace.

A rough barricade was erected next door. A heavy chain was slung across the driveway. Windows were boarded up.

In this cauldron, the problems with the Man with No Brain seemed like days of innocence and hope. Whereas in that other life I had brushed aside the .45 that my Venice neighbor John had offered, I now embraced a pump-action shotgun and some other deadly items. Whereas once I had told the cops it was their job to kill the Man with No Brain, I now found myself and my loved ones in a world where the cops scarcely existed.

Today, we endure tense times at Coyote Road. Sure, Danny had lived here before us and had every right to return home. But the things that might threaten our safety had been, up until now, the rare mountain lion and the not-so-rare rattlesnake. A human with a violent record was a great invasion, and Danny's presence was an ever-present cloud over our sunny home. If not paradise lost, it was definitely paradise flawed.

But there are other equally pressing matters at hand. Soon I must off to the Friday meeting of DILLIGAF, and with another

Christmas only six months away, some other vital decisions must be made. Who, for instance, will play Santa? Last year's Santa was hired in, and didn't quite fit the bill. Some are suggesting Mike Bristow—the hardest of all the hard men—the man who for seven years kept a mountain lion as a pet. Not exactly a reindeer, but it's a mite hot for reindeers in these parts.

AFTERWORD

by Valerie Morton

We didn't see Danny for a long time. He stopped sleeping in his house, and began camping out in the vast network of caves that crisscrossed our backyard wilderness. Hiking through the rocks, David and I would come across rough camps and the remains of a warming fire and a recent dinner. It was winter, so snow, a gleaming decoration on the surrounding mountains, was always threatening to fall. Despite deteriorating relations, we felt bad for our neighbor. Sometimes at dawn we would hear his motorbike hitting the dirt back roads where no one was likely to be waiting for him, and would see his small frame bent over some task in Pioneertown, fulfilling his parole work requirements.

Walking the dogs alone along Coyote Road one day, I bent down to collect the ball and smashed my head against a metal-hard desert oak tree. Blood flowed down my face, and as I stood there with the world spinning around me, an old car pulled up alongside, and Danny got out. He asked if anyone was at home to help me, and reluctantly I admitted there was not. He insisted I come up to his house for some first aid. The Blade Runner's warnings to never be alone with this dangerous felon rattled around my now aching head, but only briefly.

Minutes later, I found myself inside the murderer's house. Through the blood and the wooziness, I could see that a lot of care had gone into Danny's cabin. Hannibal Lecter's lair, it was not. My host made me a cup of tea and sat me down to examine my head. He gently washed it and assured me it was only a superficial wound. Would I like him to put in some stitches? Calmly for someone being treated by a notorious "killer" in a remote cabin at the end of a remote road, I asked him what he would use. He produced a packet of dental floss, and I declined, settling instead for a butterfly clip, which was tenderly applied.

I commented on some fine Native American art on the walls, and Danny told me it was his own work. Some of it had been done in the penitentiary, and I asked him what it had been like in there. It was okay, he said. Being Native American, he had been allowed to join a sweat lodge, the right to religious congregation guaranteed under the Constitution, and had had the protection of his brethren. He had made jewelry inside, too, and brought out a box with beautiful beaded earrings. I admired a pair with an eagle depicted in the design, and Danny insisted I have them. The eagle was his totem. They reside with me, today, along with other mementoes from Danny: letters written from prison when he was sent back, inevitably, for breaking the conditions of his parole. Once the system has you, you are had. We remained pen pals for a long time, and I regret losing touch.

By then, David, too, had departed Coyote Road, his departure even more dramatic, for this is a land of high drama, and the West is merciless. Late one summer night, after a card game at a local property, he had, as he put it, "parked the car upside down".

Over the coming weeks, the Palm Springs Memorial Hospital experienced some unusual visitors in Intensive Care. On one occasion, three large men in their best Western outfits and outsized Stetsons, looking like they'd stepped out of the 1860s, blocked the doorway, tears in their eyes. Community support for "Aussie Dave" was overwhelming, but the US medical system's limitations eventually meant we had to return to Australia. There, David's injuries ultimately claimed his life.

Neither of us was sorry to leave the High Desert. The area was beginning to change fast, and the Old West that we had come out to live amidst was vanishing. Money was moving in. This little enclave of the Eastern Mojave was being discovered by Los Angeles, and a mini land boom would soon explode. Speculators rolled in. Ramshackle homes were snapped up and renovated with Western themes. The old crowd was dying or moving away, leaving Pioneertown and the surrounding desert in the hands of a new wave of immigrants — weekend refugees from city life. Today, they are flooding in even faster, the artists and entrepreneurs from further afield, Silicon Valley and New York City. The Hollywood producers and agents have arrived in their cowboy boots.

These days, you have to book weeks in advance to get a table at Pappy and Harriet's. The food, I am told, is still sensational, especially the ribs, and the bands never fail to attract. The town is now a happening music scene. When Paul McCartney played there recently, three thousand people turned up in the hope of scoring one of the three hundred tickets available to see him. Boulder House, now transformed into a hip Airbnb, was featured in the *LA Weekly*'s "Best in LA", extolled as a fixture amongst young weekend warriors "in need of serious relaxing and otherworldly exploration". *The New York Times* recently ran an article about Pioneertown wanting to be the new Wild West.

But they aren't making any more Old Wests. Not authentic ones. The Old West is dead and buried. The ghosts of Buzz and Ed Gibson, David, John Edwards, Pappy, Horseshoe Freddy, Frances and John, Fleet, and too many others to mention, walk the land, marking the changes. These were easygoing people who didn't object to progress. They just didn't want it in their backyard. The Blade Runner, gone now, too, to meet his maker, is no doubt disgusted by a bunch of wild men carousing out there amongst the coyotes in a most ungodlike fashion.

The desert looks on and watches. It has all the time in the world. Earthquakes, alien landings, one-thousand-year droughts, fires, human mayhem, and crazy military activity — it has seen it all. Nothing surprises it anymore. Nothing ever did.